Studies in Economic Ethics and Philosophy

Springer
Berlin
Heidelberg
New York
Barcelona
Budapest
Hong Kong
London
Milan
Paris
Santa Clara
Singapore
Tokyo

Studies in Economic Ethics and Philosophy

P. Koslowski (Ed.)
Ethics in Economics, Business, and Economic Policy
(out of print)
192 pages. 1992

P. Koslowski and Y. Shionoya (Eds.)
The Good and the Economical
Ethical Choices in Economics and Management
(out of print)
212 pages. 1993

H. De Geer (Ed.)
Business Ethics in Progress?
124 pages. 1994

P. Koslowski (Ed.)
The Theory of Ethical Economy in the Historical School
345 pages. 1995

A. Argandoña (Ed.)
The Ethical Dimension of Financial Institutions
and Markets
264 pages. 1995

G.K. Becker (Ed.)
Ethics in Business and Society.
Chinese and Western Perspectives
232 pages. 1996

P. Koslowski
Ethics of Capitalism and Critique of Sociobiology.
Two Essays with a Comment by James M. Buchanan
153 pages. 1996

F. Neil Brady (Ed.)
Ethical Universals in International Business
255 pages. 1996

P. Koslowski and A. Føllesdal (Eds.)
Restructuring the Welfare State
Theory and Reform of Social Policy
410 pages. 1997

Guido Erreygers
Toon Vandevelde (Eds.)

Is Inheritance Legitimate?

Ethical and Economic Aspects of Wealth Transfers

With 2 Figures
and 8 Tables

Springer

Prof. Dr. Guido Erreygers
Universiteit Antwerpen
SESO-UFSIA
Prinsstraat 13
B-2000 Antwerpen 1
Belgium

Prof. Dr. Toon Vandevelde
Katholieke Universiteit Leuven
Centrum voor Economie en Ethiek
Naamsestraat 69
B-3000 Leuven
Belgium

Cataloging-in-Publication Data applied for

Die Deutsche Bibliothek - CIP-Einheitsaufnahme

Is inheritance legitimate? : ethical and economic aspects of wealth transfers ; with 8 tables / Guido Erreygers ; Toon Vandevelde (ed.). - Berlin ; Heidelberg ; New York ; Barcelona ; Budapest ; Hong Kong ; London ; Milan ; Paris ; Santa Clara ; Singapore ; Tokyo : Springer, 1997
(Studies in economic ethics and philosophy)
ISBN 3-540-62725-1

ISBN 3-540-62725-1 Springer-Verlag Berlin Heidelberg New York

Printed in Germany

Hardcover Design: Erich Kirchner, Heidelberg

SPIN 10569755 42/2202-5 4 3 2 1 0 – Printed on acid-free paper

PREFACE

On 8 November 1995 we organized the conference *Is Inheritance Legitimate? Ethical and Economic Aspects of Wealth Transfers* at the University of Antwerp (UFSIA). The conference brought together economists, philosophers and other social scientists to discuss the issues of bequest and inheritance. The conference programme featured five invited contributions; the revised versions of these five papers consitute the core of this book (Chapters 2, 3, 4, 6, and 7). Also included in this book are the written versions of the comments presented by the two discussants (Chapters 5 and 8). We also gave the opportunity to the authors who defended two radically different opinions on bequest and inheritance to comment upon one another's position (Chapters 9 and 10). Chapter 1 serves as an introduction; it situates the debate on inheritance in a broader ethical and economic framework, and summarizes the main points of the book.

The conference was organized as part of a research project funded by the Flemish *Fonds voor Wetenschappelijk Onderzoek* (project number G.0032.95). Within UFSIA the conference was hosted by the 'Vakgroep Arbeidseconomie' of the *Studiecentrum voor Economisch en Sociaal Onderzoek* (SESO) and the *Centrum voor Ethiek*. The secretarial staff of SESO, in particular Annemarie Bunneghem and Linda Teunkens, did an excellent job in organizing the conference. Patricia De Bruyn and Tom Schatteman were extremely helpful in preparing the manuscript for the publisher.

Antwerp, January 1997.

Guido Erreygers and Toon Vandevelde, Editors

CONTENTS

CONTENTS

LIST OF FIGURES

LIST OF TABLES

Chapter 1

Inheritance Taxation, Equal Opportunities and the Desire of Immortality

TOON VANDEVELDE

The question of the legitimacy of inheritance and inheritance taxation disturbs the familiar oppositions in economic and ethical thought and in political philosophy and practice. Some libertarians, who otherwise advocate an absolute respect for property rights, are nevertheless in favour of limitations to the freedom to bequeath. Socialists who proposed to abolish inheritance encountered strong resistance in their own organisations. Even in the First International the abolition of inheritance failed to obtain a majority.[1] Communitarians who mostly take side with socialist reformists tend to disagree with them on this issue. Liberal economists using efficiency arguments clash with liberal political philosophers defending equity and equality of opportunity. The disruption of the fixed ideological and philosophical landscape is, however, not necessarily a bad thing. Ultimately the discussion about a topic like inheritance taxation shows better than any abstract controversy between schools of thought the limits of communitarian, liberal, libertarian, egalitarian or socialist theory. By

1 See ERREYGERS (1996), pp. 27-31.

pointing to some examples of ambivalence towards inheritance (taxation) we try to highlight the implicit value debate at stake here.

I. Communitarianism

Communitarian authors reject individualistic atomism and stress the social nature of human beings: morality is less the result of abstract rational deliberation than the expression of the adherence to community-standards of good and evil. People adhere to norms and virtues transmitted by tradition and shared within the family or group to which they belong. Also equity and justice are primarily rooted in the concrete loyalty towards particular persons and not in rationalistic or universalistic schemes of thought. Communitarianism displays a hermeneutic or interpretive style of analysis: it tries to discover inchoate norms in our actual practices.[2] It states explicitly the spontaneous ethos of (groups of) people in order to reinforce moral norms which are already implicitly present in their actual practices. Instead of criticizing ideological distortions and faulty conceptions of ordinary people, it takes seriously their actual commitments and moral intuitions.

From this perspective it is easy to understand why communitarianism is bound to defend the right of bequest.[3] Taxes are seldom popular, but estate taxation is even less popular than other forms of taxation. The fact that nowhere in the world inheritance taxation yields a substantial revenue to the government reveals the extent of popular resistance against it. For communitarianism this is not so much a reprehensible expression of free-rider preferences as the result of the spontaneous conviction that considerations of equity and justice cannot be opposed to the solidarity with friends and family, but have to be in line with it. We are, however, not just members of small networks in our immediate neighbourhood. We also

---

2 For a defence of the 'interpretive' method without any reference to communitarianism, see McCaffery (1994).

3 As far as we know no one among the most famous communitarian authors wrote about inheritance taxation. That is the reason why we discuss here the logic of the communitarian argument and not the points of view of particular communitarians.

belong to larger communities and most communitarians do not want to undermine national social security systems, more or less based on patriotic feelings. Hence communitarianism cannot avoid a certain ambivalence towards estate taxation. On the one hand, by way of gifts and bequests a fine-grained kind of distributive justice, taking into account all the relevant differences between family members, can be achieved within the family. On the other hand, communitarians cannot be wholly insensitive to the issue of distributive justice among families, even when this objective can only be achieved in a very crude way. Neither can they totally dismiss the rawlsian argument that too much concentration of wealth and economic power is detrimental to political liberty. The coherence of national or political communities around a more or less unified conception of the general interest requires that the tendency towards the dualization of the opportunities in life offered to individuals should be stopped. The concern for equality of opportunity, however, is typically a liberal theme.

II. Liberalism

Partisans of inheritance or estate taxation invariably refer to the value of equality of opportunity. Not only socialists but also liberal political theorists from Bentham and Mill to Rawls and Dworkin are more or less inspired by egalitarianism. Critics have often argued against equality of outcome or against equality of money - or of resources, more generally - but this criticism seldom applies to equality of opportunity. For instance the well-known philosopher Harry Frankfurt has rejected economic equality as a moral ideal on the grounds that money is a mere means to get other things that morally matter in life and not an end in itself.[4] Egalitarianism induces people to concentrate on things of minor importance: instead of trying to realise one's own plans, of reflecting upon one's own goals in life, one concentrates on the quantity of economic resources that are at the disposal of others. However it is possible to reply to this that some means - for instance Rawls's primary goods - are absolutely necessary to fulfill one's life plan whatever its content may be. So our interest in equality of opportunity may

4 See FRANKFURT (1987). See also the reply by GOODIN (1987).

be derivative from our interest in a way of life that truly matters to us, but that does not make our interest in this means any less strong or any less legitimate.

It may also be the case that the individual desire for more equality is sometimes motivated by envy or by 'other-directed' preferences which are considered to be less high-principled, but even this does not discredit equality, especially equality of opportunity, as an important social and political ideal. Equality of opportunity can be seen as an essential means to achieve equality of respect or even as an expression of our concern for equality of respect. Undoubtedly the kantian idea that equal respect is owed to each man as a rational moral agent capable of a purposeful life is morally relevant.[5] Of course complete equality of opportunity would require a totalitarian state or absurd forms of coercion. However the aim is not to achieve complete equality of opportunity, but rather to eliminate major sources of inequality.

But is an income-maximizing estate tax a good means to enhance equality of opportunity? Economists like Becker and Kotlikoff [6], and in this volume Bracewell-Milnes, emphasize that inheritance taxation makes spending relatively cheaper for the rich. Rational agents will by all means try to avoid a form of taxation which most of them consider to be illegitimate. Moreover they have plenty of ways at their disposal to do so. This means that altruistic rich people who find themselves confronted with huge estate taxes will be inclined to spend much more on the education of their children. This need not always be entirely positive. Maybe somewhat more children of rich people will be spoilt so that they eventually will squander their chances in life. But surely some of them will seize the opportunity and will, for instance, study for a second universitary degree. Others who have wasted some years of their life will get the chance to take a new start. Now it is fairly reasonable to assume that education is more important for success in life than an inheritance received at the age of 45.

So the immediate consequence of a more or less confiscatory inheritance tax may be that the inequality of opportunity will increase rather than diminish. Only in the long run will inheritance taxation lead to a more even distribution of wealth and hence to more equality of opportunity. But as the inequality in wealth built up in one generation can already be considerable,

---

5 See WILLIAMS (1973).

6 See BECKER (1991); KOTLIKOFF (1992).

the problem of unequal opportunities will remain acute. This leads to the conclusion that estate taxation may not be the best means to achieve more equality of opportunity. A progressive income tax or the provision of accessible public goods of sufficiently good quality may be more important in this respect.

III. Libertarianism

One could expect that at least the libertarian view on inheritance taxation would be unequivocal. In *Anarchy, State and Utopia* Nozick does not directly address this topic, but it is clear that his entitlement theory of justice is based on a very extended conception of the right to property excluding any restriction of the freedom to exchange or to give away. Nozick rejects all 'patterned distributions' resulting from so-called 'end-state principles of justice'. Once one starts to correct a distribution which is the result of spontaneous gifts and exchanges, one engages on a slippery slope and one ends up continuously interfering with people's lives. So the search for individual freedom as non-interference in another's private domain urges us to reject estate taxation.

Hillel Steiner, however, has shown that even when starting from libertarian premisses it is possible to contest the legitimacy of inheritance taxation.[7] Steiner refuses to equate bequests and gifts. Rather a bequest is a form of insurance for the bequeather, "a lever by which the bequeather can, during his/her lifetime, strongly influence the behaviour of aspiring heirs".[8] The bequeather lies under no obligation whatsoever to the potential heir. He can change his will until the very last moment. In fact he gives nothing at all. The heir can get the bequest only after the death of the bequeather, but then the donor is not there anymore. Referring to Hohfeld's classification of rights, Steiner concludes that the precise juridical status of bequests is unclear: the bequeather endorses no obligations and the heir has no right of inheritance. Inheritance is based upon a legal fiction, i.e. the fiction of uninterrupted ownership, which involves the denial of death. In fact when a

7 See STEINER (1992) and also STEINER (1994).

8 See STEINER (1992), p. 84.

person dies his property becomes unowned. As such bequests have the same statute as natural resources; their private appropriation is admissible but subject to a tax liability. This is entirely in accordance with libertarianism because it forbids taxation of the fruits of labour, but considers the only just tax to be a tax on nature.

IV. The Quest for Immortality

This quick survey of communitarian, liberal and libertarian arguments shows that within neither of these schools of thought agreement about the legitimacy of inheritance and inheritance taxation can be reached. Now one of the most puzzling elements of this problem is the strength of popular resistance against inheritance taxation. In most schemes of taxation only (relatively) big bequests are taxed heavily. So most people will hardly suffer from inheritance taxation, either because they do not inherit or bequeath anything valuable, or because their bequests fall below or only slightly above taxation thresholds. Maybe people want to keep open the possibility that they will ever be the beneficiary of an important gift, however improbable this may be. Maybe also the perception of inheritance taxation as unfair reveals the importance of one of the most fundamental but also one of the most secret human motivations, namely *the quest for immortality*.

We know that we will die, but we have the feeling that we are able to survive in the heart and soul, and - why not? - in the hands of friends, relatives, children or grandchildren by the things we bequeath to them. Our bequest materializes somehow the care, attention and love we dedicated to them when we were still alive, or the care, attention and love we regret not to have dedicated to them when we had the opportunity to do so. As Burkard Sievers has shown in an inspiring book, all social conflicts in hierarchical settings, ranging from the class struggle to the struggle between the sexes, can ultimately be understood as a quarrel about immortality. We admire and envy rich and wealthy people because they seem to have the key to immortality. Viewed from this perspective partisans of inheritance taxation are rationalist children of Enlightenment. They want to dissipate the illusion of immortality: it may be an illusion that makes people happy - even people that won't be able to bequeath anything - but still it is an illusion, the object of an irrational desire. Sievers explains in his book that equality in its most fundamental dimension, i.e. equality of respect, can only be achieved when all members of society accept their common fate, that is to say when people at the top as well as people at the bottom of society accept the reality of their mortality.[9] Now we could add that apparently people are unable to live within such a disenchanted reality. Hence their attachment to inheritance. Hence also the lack of success of life annuities.

V. Economic Arguments

Is inheritance legitimate? Let us take a brief survey of the answers offered in this volume.

Guido Erreygers retains from the history of economic thought some proposals to limit the rights of bequest and inheritance. Jeremy Bentham thought that the only legitimate bequests are in favour of near relatives of the deceased, i.e. in favour of the surviving spouse and descendants, parents and descendants of parents. In the absence of legal heirs or of near relatives, government is allowed to confiscate partly or even totally the bequest. Bentham surmised that this kind of inheritance law would raise little resistance, especially so when the law would have changed people's motivations. The Saint-Simonians were much more radical. They presented an efficiency argument in favour of the abolition of the right of bequest. They thought the means of production should - after the death of their owner - go to the persons who can make the best use of them. An unlimited right of bequest offers no guarantee for that. John Stuart Mill proposed to set a maximum to the sum one should be permitted to receive by gift or inheritance. Yet Erreygers attaches most attention to a proposal which was almost simultaneously but independently formulated by Eugenio Rignano and Ernest Solvay. Both of these authors suggest that inheritance taxes should be progressive in time. For instance the wealth a person has gathered during his lifetime by his own work and efforts can be passed on without any taxation, but the wealth he has received from others should be taxed. At

9 See SIEVERS (1994).

each transfer by gift or bequest the tax rate should increase, until after some generations the original bequest is totally confiscated.

Robert Nozick, who in his recent work criticizes part of his earlier libertarian theses, defends a simplified version of the Rignano-Solvay proposal in *The Examined Life*. Nozick is still in favour of a deregulation of inheritance law. People should be allowed to make many bequests, not only to their partner and children, but also to their grandchildren and friends. Nozick does not talk about gifts to organizations or foundations and maybe this is not totally accidental. In his opinion a bequest expresses the importance of a personal bond to the receiver: a bond of caring, affection and identification, which is intensified by the gift. But this also means that the bequest has to be limited to one passing that cannot be repeated. So the right to bequeath an item is not transferable by bequest but adheres only to the original earner or creator. What people have not earned themselves, cannot be passed on by inheritance.[10]

Luc Arrondel, André Masson and Pierre Pestieau present an economic view on the question of the legitimacy of inheritance and inheritance taxation. Masson and Pestieau give a survey of different bequest motives and models of inheritance. They distinguish accidental, capitalist, altruistic, retrospective, paternalistic, exchange and strategic bequests. Not all of these types have received the same attention in theoretical literature and there exist several versions of them. Especially the opposition between accidental and altruistic bequests has often been discussed in the literature. When people accumulate wealth out of precaution, i.e. make provisions for themselves for when they will be old, without the intention of leaving anything to their children, relatives and friends, we talk about accidental bequests. Estate taxation does not alter their size, but an increase in retirement pensions does. Parents who care about the future needs of their children as much as they do about their own welfare, leave altruistic bequests. They try to reduce intergenerational disparities of wealth between themselves and their children and sometimes even intra-generational

10 "To determine what amount is first to be subtracted in tax, the monetary value of what one has received in inheritance would be calculated in contemporaneous dollars, corrected for inflation or deflation but not including actual or imputed interest earned. Placing an inheritance in a position to earn interest does count, I think, as an earning that may be passed on, after the amount of the original bequest is subtracted from the total." (Nozick, 1989, p. 31n).

disparities between their children. An increase in estate taxation will cause parents to save less, to increase their investment in education and to invent strategies to evade taxes. Whether an increase in estate taxation will yield more revenue to the government thus roughly depends on the proportion of different types of bequest motives in the population. Generally one can assume that poor people leave mostly accidental bequests, that rich people leave more altruistic bequests and that middle class people have mixed or intermediate motivations.

Yet in a second paper, Arrondel, Masson and Pestieau show that it is very difficult to gather reliable empirical information about bequest motives. The authors come to the amazing conclusion that the preference of the researchers for one or another bequest model strongly influences their empirical findings and their theoretical conclusions. For a long time most American economists were convinced that altruism was the dominant bequest motive and empirical evidence seemed to confirm that hypothesis. Recently this quasi-unanimity was broken up and attention shifted towards exchange-motivated bequests.

Pestieau and his colleagues think that the main problem raised by estate taxation is not that the rate of savings and capital accumulation would decline, but rather that it would cause distortions in the spending behaviour of living generations. Inspired by the theory of optimal taxation these authors state that there is no intrinsic reason to tax consumption and labour income more than savings, gifts and inheritances. Considerations of (intragenerational) justice imply that estate taxation should be progressive. However uncertain the empirical evidence may be, the comparison of bequest behaviour in the U.S. and France suggests that estate taxation could be somewhat more efficient in the latter case and also that it could be more efficient in equalizing wealth and income.[11]

In his comment on the paper of Arrondel, Masson and Pestieau, Erik Schokkaert highlights the peculiarity of the analysis of the authors. Normally economists assume that preferences are simple, stable and uniform and that economic choices are determined by situational constraints. In order to explain existing bequest practices, however, one has to appeal to complex and mixed motivations and to uncertain expectations concerning the future earnings power of children, the evolution of fiscal policy, etc. These motivations and expectations are important for the assessment of the

11 See MASSON and PESTIEAU (1994).

effectiveness of redistributive fiscal policy, but they cannot be reliably deduced from observed behaviour. Hence Schokkaert argues that in this case the revealed preference method should be supplemented with survey research in order to get more information about the motivation of bequeathers. Moreover it is reasonable to suppose that motives are strongly influenced by social norms which are in their turn influenced by public policy. Especially the change in the preferences of bequeathers caused by a radical change of inheritance regulation and taxation is difficult to predict. In these circumstances a welfarist approach, which deduces the desirability of policy measures from people's preferences, loses its normative content.

VI. The Ethical Discussion

Starting from an elaborated version of the productivity ideal of distributive justice, David Haslett strongly attacks the legitimacy of inheritance. When everybody has to be rewarded according to his productivity, there is no room left for unearned wealth. Nowadays we all agree that slavery is inhuman and that the heredity of political power is inconsistent with political democracy. Analogously Haslett argues that the heredity of wealth or economic power is inconsistent with economic democracy and with the implicit values of contemporary capitalism. More than any alternative economic system capitalism is able to boost productivity and efficiency and to maximize people's well-being, provided that one condition is fulfilled, namely that equal opportunities are created for all members of society. For Haslett equality of opportunity is both intrinsically valuable and instrumentally useful as a norm conducive to overall well-being. However, equality of opportunity is not an absolute value, but only a prima facie value. This means that it can be overruled to a certain extent by other values. A complete equalization of chances of life would require the abolition of the family and absurd forms of genetic engineering. This is clearly unacceptable to whomever is attached to the value of freedom. Nevertheless the fact that one cannot achieve complete equality of opportunity does not detract from its value.

Existing inheritance practices lead to enormous concentrations of economic power which should be broken up. This could be a reason to plead for the abolition of inheritance, as done by Haslett in an older article [12], but actually, in this volume, he advocates the institution of a lifetime inheritance quota. An upper limit should be set to what a person is allowed to receive by gift or inheritance from others. The amount of the quota could be determined by the average value of the estates of the adults who deceased in the last year. Small gifts, gifts and bequests between spouses, gifts that are necessary to support minor children and other dependants, and gifts to charitable organizations should be excluded from the quota. The institution of such an accessions quota would oblige wealthy people to spread their fortune among many beneficiaries. Haslett hopes this will induce a radical turn towards a much more equal distribution of wealth, income and opportunities in life.

Barry Bracewell-Milnes defends a stance exactly opposite to Haslett's. In former publications he has raised many economic arguments against inheritance taxation [13], but in the article published in this volume, he focuses on the destruction of immaterial wealth caused by estate taxation. He repeats and develops Adam Smith's argument which states that "All taxes upon the transference of property (...) are more or less unthrifty taxes that increase the revenue of the sovereign, which seldom maintains any but unproductive labourers; at the expence of the capital of the people, which maintains none but productive".[14] Inheritance taxation curtails the time horizon of economic agents. It makes spending relatively cheaper for the rich than for the poor and it discourages saving and investment. From an ethical point of view inheritance taxation can certainly reduce the inequality of wealth, but in the long run it will increase the inequality in spending, which Bracewell-Milnes considers to be the most important form of inequality. The author agrees with Haslett that a society with heavy inheritance taxes will be highly competitive, but he predicts that competition will manifest itself rather in the sphere of consumption than in the sphere of production. People will rival in sumptuous life styles but the gains in productivity and efficiency to be expected are limited due to the lack of saving.

For Bracewell-Milnes wealth does not only consist of material goods and services. Ultimately wealth is created in the mind. The author extends the

---

12 See HASLETT (1986).

13 See BRACEWELL-MILNES (1994).

14 See SMITH (1976), p. 862.

well-known economic analysis of consumer's surplus to the saver's surplus, the owner's surplus and the donor's surplus. Giving is not just a transfer of goods or money, where the donor loses what the donee receives. In a voluntary transaction a donor reveals his preference for giving compared to alternative uses of a good. This means that the worth of the gift to him is at least as large as its market value. Adding the value the recipient gets to the worth the donor derives from his gift, Bracewell-Milnes concludes that the act of giving at least doubles the value of the gift. This form of wealth creation is very fragile: even a small tax on gifts and bequests can make it disappear. Hence, for the funding of public services voluntary giving is preferable to compulsory taxation. Inheritance taxation threatens not only the moral (and utilitarian) value of giving, but also perpetual saving. The latter activity, which could be linked to the retrospective bequest motive distinguished by Pestieau et al., is extremely useful to society: it provides services to others and it is enjoyed for its own sake by the owner. Moreover it changes the attitude of the owner. Instead of taking a purely consumptive stance towards his property he will behave as a steward and devote himself to the conservation and maintenance of his heirloom. Bracewell-Milnes argues that generally all kinds of assets are best and most efficiently looked after by long term family owners. Taxation should not discourage this.

In his reply to Bracewell-Milnes, Haslett defends less the imposition of inheritance taxes than the institution of an inheritance quota. With such a quota the ethical and spiritual value of giving will be entirely respected. Also in Haslett's proposal charitable gifts and bequests are exempted from the quota. So they will be greatly encouraged. However, Haslett contests Bracewell-Milnes's claim that the value of the gift is at least doubled by the act of giving. Very often gifts imply a sacrifice on behalf of the donor. Using a famous distinction made by Amartya Sen one could say that the motivation for many gifts is *commitment* rather than *sympathy*. In the latter case the concern for others directly affects one's own welfare, whereas in the former case the choice is counterpreferential: you help another person although you believe that this act will yield you less personal welfare than an alternative which is also available to you.[15] Of course the value that family estates have for family members will often exceed their market value, but family members can be protected against the loss of these items by a suitable regulation granting them lenient credit terms or offering them priority to

15 See SEN (1982).

purchase family heirlooms, family farms or family businesses. Moreover, in our time wealth and people are much more mobile than before. So the importance of heirlooms in the total amount of bequests has diminished greatly. Finally, Haslett thinks that it is almost impossible to predict the effect of inheritance taxation and inheritance quota on saving and accumulation. If ever it becomes evident that savings and investment will be curtailed, then government has many measures at hand to boost capital accumulation.

In his comment Philippe Van Parijs disagrees with Bracewell-Milnes's suggestion that all taxes are unthrifty. Whether the welfare loss caused by inheritance taxation exceeds the welfare gain brought about by the public services financed by it, is a priori not sure. Van Parijs also dismisses Bracewell-Milnes's criticism of the principle of equality of opportunity, but at the same time he disagrees with Haslett on the importance of inheritance taxes to ensure equal starts in life for everybody. There are many more important kinds of gifts than just bequests and gifts of material wealth. Education, training, differences in talent or sheer luck are all factors conducive to unequal opportunities and especially to unequal access to jobs. Hence Van Parijs's plea for an appropriate income tax as the best means to ensure equal opportunities. This conclusion rejoins a warning dressed by Masson and Pestieau.[16] Although nominal rates of taxation on gifts and bequests are often quite high, due to various loopholes the effective rate of taxation is in most countries quite low: 6% in France, less than 10% in most other countries. Actually the yearly stream of gifts and bequests represents approximately 1% of national wealth. This means that each year only 0,1% of total national wealth is collected by inheritance taxation. Knowing the strong resistance of the public against this form of taxation, it is obvious that one should not nourish great hopes concerning the ability of inheritance taxation to bring about more equality of opportunity.

16 See MASSON and PESTIEAU (1994).

References

BECKER, G.S. (1991): *A Treatise on the Family*, Cambridge (Harvard University Press).

BRACEWELL-MILNES, B. (1994): *Will to Succeed. Inheritance without Taxation*, London (Adam Smith Institute).

ERREYGERS, G. (1996): *Early Socialist Thought on Bequest and Inheritance* (Paper presented at the 23rd Annual Conference of the History of Economics Society Conference, University of British Columbia, Vancouver), University of Antwerp (UFSIA-SESO), mimeo.

FRANKFURT, H. (1987): "Equality as a moral ideal", *Ethics*, 98, pp. 21-43.

GOODIN, R.E. (1987), "Egalitarianism, fetishistic and otherwise", *Ethics*, 98, pp. 44-9.

HASLETT, D.W. (1986): "Is inheritance justified?", *Philosophy and Public Affairs*, 15, pp. 122-55.

KOTLIKOFF, L.J. (1992): *Generational Accounting. Knowing Who Pays, and When, For What We Spend*, New York (Free Press), 1992.

MASSON, A. and PESTIEAU, P. (1994): "L'héritage et l'Etat", in: P. PESTIEAU (Ed.): *Héritage et Transferts Entre Générations*, Bruxelles (De Boeck), pp. 15-44.

McCAFFERY, E.J. (1994): "The political liberal case against the estate tax", *Philosophy and Public Affairs*, 23, pp. 281-312.

NOZICK, R. (1974): *Anarchy, State and Utopia*, Oxford (Blackwell).

NOZICK, R. (1989): *The Examined Life: Philosophical Meditations*, New York (Simon & Schuster).

SEN, A. (1982): "Rational fools: A critique of the behavioural foundations of economic theory", in: A. SEN, *Choice, Welfare and Measurement*, Oxford (Blackwell), pp. 91-9.

SIEVERS, B. (1994): *Work, Death and Life Itself. Essays on Management and Organisation*, Berlin (de Gruyter).

SMITH, A. (1976), *An Inquiry into the Nature and Causes of the Wealth of Nations*, ed. by R.H. Campbell, A.S. Skinner and W.B. Todd, Oxford (Oxford University Press) (= The Glasgow Edition of the Works and Correspondence of Adam Smith, Vol. II).

STEINER, H. (1992): "Three just taxes", in: P. VAN PARIJS (Ed.): *Arguing for Basic Income. Ethical Foundations for a Radical Reform*, London, New York (Verso), pp. 81-92.

STEINER, H. (1994): *An Essay on Rights*, Oxford (Blackwell).

WILLIAMS, B. (1973): "The idea of equality" in: B. WILLIAMS, *Problems of the Self. Philosophical Papers 1956-1972*, Cambridge (Cambridge University Press), pp. 230-49.

Chapter 2

Views on Inheritance in the History of Economic Thought

GUIDO ERREYGERS

I. Introduction

It would probably be exaggerated to say that economists, in general, have considered the issues of succession, bequest and inheritance to be of the utmost importance; it would, however, certainly be false to speak of a complete neglect. Many economists have dealt with the question of the transference of property rights when a person dies[1]; in this paper I review some interesting contributions which have been made over the years. I have not aimed at being in any sense complete; the paper is more a personal *tour d'horizon* than a systematic inquiry. I will not say anything about recent developments in the field; the paper ends somewhere in the 1940s.

1 Economists have often treated substantial *inter vivos* gifts as equivalent to bequests at death; in what follows, the notions of bequest and inheritance must always be understood to include these gifts.

Moreover, it is biased towards approaches which try to combine liberalism and socialism, coming from authors who, as Cannan (1926, p. 236) once put it, argued that a reform of inheritance would lead to situations in which "the individualist lamb would lie down with the socialist lion". It is indeed striking that many authors thought that a reform of the laws of inheritance would allow society to move towards more equality, especially equality of starting conditions in life, without disrupting the delicate framework of incentives which regulate the economic activities of individuals, in particular decisions to work and save. Typical for these approaches is that they take a middle course between two extreme positions towards inheritance. One is the 'maximal' individual liberty position: every person has the right to decide what should happen with his or her property after his or her death; in this view, the right of bequest is a 'natural' right. The opposite position is that of 'minimal' individual liberty: a person has no right at all to decide what should happen with his or her property after his or her death; in this view, property rights do not include such a thing as a natural right of bequest. These two positions are motivated by different attitudes towards liberty and equality; I contend that the most interesting writings about inheritance are from authors taking a 'middle' position, i.e. from authors who try to reconcile liberty and equality.

In the paper I concentrate upon the proposals of Jeremy Bentham, the Saint-Simonians, John Stuart Mill, and Eugenio Rignano, and I consider some of the contributions to the debate on the Rignano-proposal. For a more detailed and more complete study of inheritance in the history of economic thought, I refer the reader to Hugh Dalton's extremely valuable book *Some Aspects of the Inequality of Incomes in Modern Communities* (Dalton, 1920); this can be supplemented by Josiah Wedgwood's *The Economics of Inheritance*, originally published in 1929 (Wedgwood, 1939).

II. Jeremy Bentham (1748-1832)

It is not surprising that Bentham, who devoted his life to reform the science of law (Halévy, 1901, p. 55), elaborated a reform proposal on the subject of inheritance. Two publications are important in this regard: the pamphlet *Supply without Burthen, or Escheat vice Taxation*[2], published in 1795, and the treatise *Theory of Legislation*, the bulk of which was written in the last two decades of the 18th century[3]. It seems that especially in the years 1794-1795 the question of inheritance held his attention. Apparently he was so confident in the merits of his proposal that he decided to bring it under the attention of the men in power. He sent a copy of the pamphlet to Charles Long, at that time Pitt's co-secretary to the Treasury; but Long's cool reaction to the reforms advocated by Bentham soon tempered his enthusiasm. This explains why he never wrote the comprehensive treatment of the subject he originally planned to write (Stark, 1952, pp. 61-2). What Bentham wrote in this period is undoubtedly deeply influenced by the French Revolution and the events which followed it. More than once his disapproval of the ideas proclaimed by the French Revolutionaries comes to the surface. He made it quite clear that he did not appreciate what they tried to accomplish in the name of liberty and equality; he saw it as his duty to propose social reforms which would prevent outbursts of this type.

The reform which Bentham had in mind with respect to inheritance must be seen in the light of his theory of the principles which the law ought to incorporate. The two most important principles are 'equality' and 'security'[4]. Bentham realized that these cannot always be reconciled; in cases where a choice has to be made, his preferences were clear:

"When security and equality are in conflict, it will not do to hesitate a moment. Equality must yield. The first is the foundation of life;

2 I will cite from the version published in 1952 in *Bentham's Economic Writings*, edited by W. Stark; this version contains more material than the one originally published.

3 The treatise was published for the first time in 1802, edited and translated into French by Etienne Dumont, under the title *Traités de Législation Civile et Pénale*; the later English editions are translated from this 'original' French edition. The matter is examined in detail in Appendix I of HALÉVY (1901, pp. 369-97). I will cite from the translation by R. Hildreth (1882, 4th ed.).

4 For BENTHAM 'security' includes 'liberty': "Some persons may be astonished to find that *Liberty* is not ranked among the principal objects of law. But a clear idea of liberty will lead us to regard it as a branch of security. Personal liberty is security against a certain kind of injuries which affect the person. As to what is called *political liberty*, it is another branch of security, - security against injustice from the ministers of government." (BENTHAM, 1882, p. 97)

subsistence, abundance, happiness, everything depends upon it. Equality produces only a certain portion of good. Besides, whatever we may do, it will never be perfect; it may exist a day; but the revolutions of the morrow will overturn it. The establishment of perfect equality is a chimera; all we can do is to diminish inequality." (Bentham, 1882, p. 120)

The pre-eminence given to the principle of security implied, according to Bentham, that the legislator should first of all protect the *status quo* of the existing property relations:

"He ought to maintain the distribution as it is actually established. It is this which, under the name of *justice*, is regarded as his first duty. This is a general and simple rule, which applies itself to all states; and which adapts itself to all places, even those of the most opposite character." (*ibid.*, p. 119)

The first duty of the law is to provide security; yet at some occasions the law has the chance of giving more weight to the principle of equality. In other words, by seizing the right opportunities, it *is* possible to diminish inequality without endangering the principle of security:

"Is it necessary that between these two rivals, *Security* and *Equality*, there should be an opposition, an eternal war? To a certain point they are incompatible; but with a little patience and address they may, in a great measure, be reconciled.

The only mediator between these contrary interests is time. Do you wish to follow the counsels of equality without contravening those of security? - await the natural epoch which puts an end to hopes and fears, the epoch of death." (*ibid.*, p. 122)

Hence it is clear that Bentham's inheritance proposal must be understood as an attempt to reconcile security (liberty) and equality, as Stark (1941, pp. 77-9) has stressed.

Bentham did not believe that in matters of succession and inheritance one could speak of natural rights. First of all he denied in very explicit terms that there was something like a natural right[5]; the metaphors he used in this connection all express the idea that for him a natural right is a contradiction in terms:

---

5 For more details on Bentham's vision on natural rights, see HART (1982, pp. 79-104).

> "Of a natural right who has any idea? I, for my part, I have none: a natural right is a round square [or] an incorporeal body. (...) A natural right is a son that never had a father. By natural right is meant, a sort of a thing which is to have the effect of law, which is to have an effect paramount to that of law, but which subsists not only without law, but against law: and its characteristic property, as well as sole and constant use, is the being the everlasting and irreconciliable enemy of law. (...) A natural right is a species of cold heat, a sort of dry moisture, a kind of resplendent darkness." (Bentham, 1952, pp. 334-5).

When one looks at bequest and inheritance, Bentham continued, the wide diversity of existing regulations and the peculiarity of some of them testify that also in this case the notion of natural right is an absurdity:

> "Succession a natural, an universal right? How can that be? - when in no two nations it is the same! If natural right had any place in the subject, if the doctrine of natural right had any truth in it at all, or were to the purpose in respect of any branch of the matter of succession, it should surely be in that which respects the the succession of children to parents. Yet what becomes of natural right even here? In one and the same nation - no to speak of various nations - in one and the same nation - in our own nation - among men of landed property in most instances the eldest son gets every thing - in a few instances it is the youngest son [who] gets every thing, and here the eldest nothing - and in both cases what becomes of the daughters?" (*ibid.*, p. 332)

By this critique of natural rights Bentham created an opening which his proposal to change the existing legal framework regulating inheritance could fill. The alternative for a system justified by an appeal to natural rights had to be a system based upon the utilitarian calculus.

There are some differences in the way the reform proposal is presented in the treatise *Theory of Legislation* and in the pamphlet *Supply without Burthen*. In the treatise the emphasis is on the legal aspects; one of the chapters contains a model for a law of succession comprising 15 articles, derived from the following general principles: "1st, Provision for the subsistence of the rising generation; 2nd, Prevention of disappointment; 3rd, The equalization of fortunes" (Bentham, 1882, p. 177). In the pamphlet, on the other hand, the emphasis is more upon aspects of public finance; my exposition will mainly be based upon the pamphlet.

Let me begin with a brief explanation of the title *Supply without Burthen, or Escheat vice Taxation*. The term 'supply' refers to *financial supply*, meaning the revenue of the government. The term 'escheat' refers to the *law of escheat*, a law of feudal origin, which stipulated that in the absence of legal heirs an estate becomes public property. Bentham proposed to widen the scope of the law of escheat, in combination with a limitation of the power to bequest. The main advantage of the proposal would be its 'unburthensomeness': paradoxically, the new system would allow the government to collect a greater revenue from inheritance, but individuals would not feel it as a greater burden.

The essential feature of the proposal is an extension of the scope of the law of escheat, by changing the criterion which must be fulfilled to set the law in operation. Bentham proposed to replace the condition of the absence of legal heirs (which could only arise in cases of intestacy) by the condition of the absence of *near relatives* of the deceased:

> "Of the extended Law of Escheat, according to the degree of extension here proposed, the effect would be, the appropriating to the use of the public all vacant successions, property of every denomination included, on the failure of *near relations*; will or no will, subject only to the power of bequest as hereinafter limited." (Bentham, 1952, p. 283)

As near relatives Bentham considered surviving spouse and descendants, parents, and descendants of parents (Bentham, 1882, pp. 178-81). He did not go as far as to propose that the whole estate of persons dying without near relatives would automatically become public property, which would mean that they have no right of bequest at all. All persons would have a right to bequest, but for those without near relatives this right would be considerably reduced:

> "As to the latitude to be left to the power of *bequest*, I should propose it to be continued in respect of *half* of whatever property would be at present subject to that power: the wills of persons in whose successions no interest is hereby given to the public, to be observed in all points as at present; as, likewise, those in whose succession an interest *is* given to the public, saving as to the amount of that interest: the plan consequently not trenching in any degree upon the rights of parents." (*ibid.*, p. 284)[6]

The proposed system rests upon a neat distinction between the rights of those who are 'single' and those who are not, with the latter "in a situation

---

6 In the *Theory of Legislation* he proposed to give proprietors without near relatives the right to dispose of *at least half* their property by will (BENTHAM, 1882, p. 186).

of privilege and pre-eminence" (*ibid.*, p. 295). Bentham even noted: "Whatever restriction it imposes, is all at the expense of the celibatary and unmarried. If with propriety it could be stiled a *tax*, it would be a *tax on celibacy.*" (*ibid.*). Interestingly, Bentham suggested that the way his proposal would work is comparable with the way the law deals with cases of bankruptcy, as if dying without near relatives is similar to going bankrupt. This is clear from the role ascribed to the public office dealing with estates falling under the new law of escheat:

> "What will also be seen to be necessary is, that, wherever the public has any interest at all in any succession under the proposed law, the officer of the public, that is, the officer of the Crown, shall enter into the possession and management of the whole in the first instance, in the same manner as assignees of bankrupts do in respect of the whole property, *real* and *personal*, together, or administrators or executors do in respect of the personalty: not to mention the *real* in some cases, as where, by a clause in the will, it is ordered to be sold." (*ibid.*, p. 285)

It remains to be seen how Bentham thought this system could be introduced 'without burden', as a "victory without blood", to repeat the expression he used in a letter to Charles Long (Stark, 1952, p. 61).

Bentham's reasoning is based upon the notion of expectation, and upon the power of the law to change people's expectations. According to Bentham, the existing regulations make heirs believe that they have a right to inherit the *whole* estate of the deceased. Any inheritance tax is then felt as a sacrifice and a burden:

> "Under a tax on successions, a man is led in the first place to look upon the whole in a general view as his own: he is then called upon to give up a part. His share amounts to so much: this share he is to *have*; only out of it, he is to *pay* so much *per cent.* His imagination thus begins with embracing the *whole*: his expectation fastens upon the whole: then comes the law putting in for its *part*, and forcing him to quit his hold. This he cannot do without pain: if he could, no tax at all, not even a tax on property, would be a burthen: neither land-tax nor poor's rate could be too high." (*ibid.*, p. 292)

In other words, an inheritance tax is seen as a burden because it *takes away* something people regard as belonging to them. Yet the law can change people's expectations:

> "In the case of acquiring or not acquiring, of retaining or not retaining, no hardship without previous expectation. *Disappointment* is expectation

> thwarted: in the distribution of property no sense of hardship but in proportion to disappointment. But expectation, as far as the law can be kept present to men's minds, follows with undeviating obsequiousness the finger of the law. (...) In matters of property in general, and succession in particular, thus then stands the case: *hardship* depends upon *disappointment*; *disappointment* upon *expectation*; *expectation* upon the dispensations, meaning the *known* dispensations of the law." (*ibid.*, pp. 290-1)

Bentham argued that under the new law there would be no hardship because people would be *kept from* the property which they considered as their own in the old system. The new law would be a 'tender' law:

> "The utility of that part of the proposal which gives to the public officer possession of the whole, whether the public in conclusion is admitted to the whole, or only to a part, may now be seen in full force. It is a provision not more of *prudence* with a view to the public, than of *tenderness* with a view to the individual. Had he been suffered to *lay his hands* upon the *whole*, being afterwards, or even at the time, called upon to *give* up a *part*, his attention would unavoidably have grasped the whole, the giving up the part would have produced a sensation, fainter perhaps, but similar to that produced by an unexepected *loss*: on the other hand, as according to the proposal, he *takes* nothing that he does not *keep*, no such unpleasant sensation is produced." (*ibid.*, p. 292)

As additional advantages of the proposal Bentham listed an expected reduction of the number of cases of litigation, the encouragement given to marriages, especially prolific marriages, and the 'natural' popularity of the proposed measure.

Summing up, we can say that Bentham was in favour of a legal framework in which the surviving spouse and children were somehow protected against total disinheritance (he judged the French *légitime* institution to be "a convenient medium between domestic anarchy and paternal tyranny" (Bentham, 1882, p. 185)), but such that the power of bequest gave proprietors the means "to correct the imperfections of the law in all those cases which it cannot foresee" (*ibid.*, p. 183). He saw the power of bequest therefore as an instrument "to prevent private calamities" and "for the encouragement of virtue in their families and the repression of vice" (*ibid.*). An individual with near relatives will normally ensure that they receive a substantial part of his estate when he dies; according to Bentham, this is something in which the state should not interfere. An individual without near relatives, on the other hand, does not have to make provisions for his close family; Bentham's position is that in this case the state may as it were 'substitute for' the missing family and reserve half of the property for itself.

III. The Saint-Simonians

The second view on inheritance which I would like to present comes from the followers of Saint-Simon. Saint-Simon himself wrote almost nothing about inheritance; everything the Saint-Simonians expounded in this regard was a development of their own. Nevertheless, we will see that the question of inheritance was a very important one for the Saint-Simonians.

After the death of Saint-Simon (1760-1825) his followers tried to keep his memory alive and sought ways to spread the Saint-Simonian 'faith'. One of their activities was the organization of a series of lectures in which the leaders of the movement explained, in a more or less systematic way, the basic elements of the doctrine of Saint-Simon. These lectures were held in Paris in the period 1828-1830, i.e. before the movement split apart and began to degenerate into a kind of religious sect[7]. The lectures were mainly the joint work of the 'deux Pères' of the Saint-Simonian movement at that time, Saint Amand Bazard (1791-1832) and Barthélemy Prosper Enfantin (1796-1864)[8]. They treated the issue of inheritance at length, especially in the sixth, seventh and eight lectures, held in February and March 1829.

The Saint-Simonians had read Bentham's proposal with regard to inheritance. Although they sympathized with his attempt to reformulate

---

7 For more details, cf. WEILL (1896) and BOUGLÉ and HALÉVY (1924); BOUGLÉ and HALÉVY stress that at the time of the lectures, the Saint-Simonians were trying to rationalize their beliefs, "ils se forcent pour un temps à parler le langage de la science" (1924, p. 29).

8 The text of the lectures was originally published in two volumes in the years 1830-1831. I will cite from the 1924 edition of the first volume by BOUGLÉ and HALÉVY, *Doctrine de Saint-Simon, Exposition, Première Année, 1829*, which I will refer to as *Doctrine*.

property and inheritance rights on the basis of a utilitarian calculus, they criticized him for not going far enough in this direction. Bentham, they argued, should have thought deeper about the *social utility* of an institution:

> "Nous sommes trop admirateurs de BENTHAM pour passer ses travaux sous silence. Il a bien vu que c'était seulement par leur *utilité* qu'on pouvait légitimer les institutions, et ce premier pas est fort grand, sans doute, mais il ne suffit pas, il recule simplement la difficulté, puisqu'il faut encore définir ce qu'on doit entendre par l'*utilité sociale*." (*Doctrine*, p. 310)

In what sense did Bentham lose sight of social utility when dealing with inheritance? The key argument of the Saint-Simonians is that the means of production should belong to those who have the capacity to work with them. Under the existing system of succession, and also under Bentham's proposed modification of it, there is no guarantee that the means of production will, after the death of the person who owned them, fall into the hands of persons who are capable of using them:

> "(...) BENTHAM lui-même, en cherchant à établir un des principes généraux de législation, n'a pas su se défendre de l'influence des mots. En prononçant celui de *succession*, il n'a pas pu le séparer du fait que ce mot représente dans nos sociétés modernes.
>
> *Succéder*, ce n'est cependant que *remplacer*; or pour remplacer un homme occupé d'un travail quelconque, il est *utile* que le remplaçant satisfasse à certaines conditions de *capacité*; pour succéder à un propriétaire, il suffit d'être son plus proche parent. Si le grand *partisan du principe de l'utilité* s'était aperçu de cette différence, s'il avait examiné d'où elle provient, il aurait vu qu'elle résulte de ce que, pour être propriétaire, il n'est pas indispensable que l'on soit *capable de faire quelque chose*; alors, sans doute, il aurait bravé l'erreur générale, et déchirant cette page du *catalogue banal* des choses *utiles*, il aurait déclaré *vicieux* nos préjugés sur l'héritage; car un homme que l'on nourrit dans l'abondance, *quoiqu'il ne sache rien faire*, doit être aux yeux d'un *utiliste* une *nuisible* superfluïté." (*ibid.*, p. 314)

The 'capability' issue was, of course, fundamental to the 'industrial' vision of the Saint-Simonians, as witnessed by their slogan "à chacun suivant sa capacité, à chaque capacité suivant ses œuvres" (*Doctrine*, p. 94). It was clearly a kind of efficiency argument which made them believe that each should have a place in society according to his or her capacities, with the reward in proportion to the work delivered. The existing inheritance regulations are an obstacle to the efficient organization of society, is the message which runs through their critique of property rights. Inheritance is a 'blind' way of distributing the means of production among the members of society, and even when the means of production are put at the disposal of workers who know how to use them, the rewards will be appropriated by the wrong persons:

> "*Le hasard de la naissance* distribue en aveugle les *instrumens de travail* quels qu'ils soient, et si l'héritier, le propriétaire oisif les confient aux mains d'un travailleur habile, il est bien entendu que le plus pur produit, le premier gain est pour le propriétaire incapable ou paresseux." (*ibid.*, p. 142)

One could perhaps say that the Saint-Simonians, instead of believing in an invisible hand working in the interest of society (cf. Smith, 1976, p. 456), were convinced of the existence of a blind mechanism working against the interest of society. The critique of inheritance is in fact not a critique of the individual capitalists, but a critique of the way in which a particular *function* is organized in society. According to the Saint-Simonians, the function of capitalists is to allocate the means of production; the problem is that the service delivered by the capitalists is of poor quality and highly expensive:

> "Cette fonction, la seule qu'ils remplissent, en tant que propriétaires ou capitalistes, la remplissent-ils avec intelligence, à peu de frais, d'une manière favorable à l'accroissement des produits industriels? En voyant l'abondance relative dans laquelle vivent ces hommes, dont le nombre est considérable, en pesant la large part qui leur est attribuée dans la production annuelle, on est obligé de convenir qu'ils ne rendent pas leurs services à bon marché. D'un autre côté, si l'on considère les crises violentes, les catastrophes funestes qui désolent si souvent l'industrie, il est évident que les *distributeurs des instrumens de travail* apportent peu de lumières dans l'exercice de leur fonction, et il serait injuste de leur en faire une reproche; car si l'on réfléchit que cette distribution, pour qu'elle fût bien faite, exigerait une connaissance profonde des rapports qui existent entre la production et la consommation, une longue habitude du mécanisme qui fait mouvoir les rouages de l'industrie, on reconnaîtra l'impossibilité que ces conditions soient jamais remplies par des hommes qui reçoivent leur mission du *hasard de la naissance*, et qui restent étrangers aux travaux dont ils fournissent les instrumens." (*ibid.*, pp. 257-8)

Moreover, the existing system is responsible for "l'hérédité de la misère" (*ibid.*, p. 239) and for the prolongation of the exploitation of man by man since it gives some people by birth "le privilège de vivre sans rien faire" (*ibid.*, p. 244). The only legitimate property right, they concluded, is the right based upon the capacity to use the property:

> "Le seul droit à la richesse, c'est-à-dire à la disposition des instrumens de travail, sera la *capacité* de les mettre en œuvre.(...)
>
> Nous disons que dans l'avenir le seul titre à la propriété sera la *capacité* de travail pacifique; le seul titre à la considération, les *œuvres*; nous ajouterons, pour préciser notre pensée, que ce titre doit être direct pour chaque propriétaire, ce qui comprend implicitement cette autre idée que le seul droit conféré par le titre de propriétaire est la direction, l'emploi, l'exploitation de la propriété." (*ibid.*, pp. 254-5)

The existing property rights, including the rights of bequest and inheritance, therefore had to be modified. With Bentham the Saint-Simonians observed that legal modifications, especially with respect to inheritance, had occurred frequently and, more importantly, had always been followed by a corresponding change in moral approval by the people. A last change is required, they argued; it consists simply of the abolition of the right of citizens to inherit property:

> "Aujourd'hui un dernier changement est devenu nécessaire; c'est au moraliste à le préparer; plus tard, ce sera au législateur à le prescrire. La loi de progression que nous avons observée, tend à établir un ordre de choses dans lequel l'Etat, et non plus la famille, héritera des richesses accumulées, en tant qu'elles forment ce que les économistes appellent le *fonds de production*." (*ibid.*, p. 248)

The alternative which the Saint-Simonians proposed was that the State, or rather the "association des travailleurs", should inherit all property of the deceased. Despite their criticism of of the functioning of the 'liberal' economy, the Saint-Simonians did not display much critical sense when it came to describe the functioning of their ideal economy in the *Doctrine*. The following long quotation illustrates that they had a somewhat naïve vision of the 'new world' they wanted to create:

> "Transportons-nous dans un monde nouveau. Là ce ne sont plus des propriétaires, des capitalistes isolés, étrangers par leurs habitudes aux travaux industriels, qui règlent le choix des entreprises, et la destinée des travailleurs. - Une institution *sociale* est investie de ces fonctions, si mal remplies aujourd'hui; elle est *dépositaire* de tous les instrumens de la

production; elle préside à toute l'exploitation matérielle; par là, elle se trouve placée au point de vue d'ensemble, qui permet d'apercevoir à la fois toutes les parties de l'*atelier* industriel; par ses ramifications elle est en contact avec toutes les localités, avec toutes les genres d'industrie, avec tous les travailleurs; elle peut donc se rendre compte des besoins généraux et des besoins individuels, porter les bras et les instrumens là où leur nécessité se fait sentir, en un mot, diriger la production, la mettre en harmonie avec la consommation, et confier les instrumens de travail aux industriels les plus dignes, car elle s'efforce sans cesse de reconnaître leurs capacités, et elle est dans la meilleure position pour les développer." (*ibid.*, p. 261)

The Saint-Simonians were keen to stress that the system they proposed would be different from a system of perfect equality. They were clearly not in favour of an egalitarian society:

"Nous devons prévoir que quelques personnes confondront ce système avec celui que l'on connaît sous le nom de *communauté des biens*. Il n'existe cependant aucun rapport entre eux. Dans l'organisation sociale de l'avenir, chacun, avons-nous dit, devra se trouver *classé* selon sa capacité, *retribué* suivant ses œuvres; c'est indiquer suffisamment l'INÉGALITÉ de partage. Dans le système de la communauté, au contraire, toutes les parts sont égales; et contre un pareil mode de répartition, les objections nécessairement se présentent en foule." (*ibid.*, p. 248)

It deserves to be noticed that the Saint-Simonians were well aware of the fact that they were attacking deeply rooted principles. They realized that many seemed to consider inheritance as something sacred, as one of the last remaining principles of order in society; any proposal to abolish inheritance would therefore be likely to meet with much resistance.[9] There was indeed resistance to their proposal, also from those who were highly critical of the existing economic system. Charles Fourier, for instance, was full of contempt for the Saint-Simonian proposition to abolish inheritance; in a letter of 28 January 1831 he declared:

"J'ai assisté au prône des Simoniens dimanche passé. On ne conçoit pas comment ces historiens sacerdotaux peuvent se former une si nombreuse clientèle. Leurs dogmes ne sont pas recevables; ce sont des monstruosités

9 In a heated passage they compared inheritance to a 'skeleton of the middle ages', to a privilege which even 'the most violent adversaries of the past' defend 'like the ashes of a beloved' (*Doctrine*, p. 287).

> à faire hausser les épaules; prêcher, au dix-neuvième siècle, l'abolition de la propriété et de l'hérédité!" (Fourier, 1890, p. xxiv, n. 1)

A similar attitude can be found in Pierre-Joseph Proudhon's writings. In *Théorie de l'Impôt* he characterized the principle of hereditary transmission as "une des meilleures lois de l'économie, de l'administration et de la police des sociétés" (Proudhon, 1861, p. 128). Inheritance taxes were only acceptable if carefully framed; the abolishment of inheritance in favour of the State was certainly to be condemned:

> "La suppression de l'héritage au profit de l'Etat, ce serait le communisme gouvernemental, la pire des tyrannies, une sorte de panthéisme où les individus seraient régentés, nourris, entretenus, exploités par une volonté impersonelle, pour la gloire d'une idée abstraite, mais où il n'y aurait pas plus de société que de familles, pas plus de familles que d'individus." (*ibid.*, p. 136)

In *Système des Contradictions Economiques ou Philosophie de la Misère* he argued that not inheritance, but economic conflicts were the cause of inequality; if you want to have a more equal society, there is no need to reform inheritance: "L'hérédité prend les choses comme elle les trouve: créez l'égalité, et l'hérédité vous rendra l'égalité." (Proudhon, 1923, T. II, p. 200). He remarked that poverty and inequality have nothing to do with the principle of hereditary transmission as such ('l'hérédité'), but with the fact that there are large inequalities in the amounts that people receive by inheritance ('l'héritage' vs. 'la déshérence'):

> "L'*hérédité* existe dans la famille du pauvre comme dans celle du riche: ce droit sacré et inaliénable, le prolétaire l'a définitivement conquis dans notre grande révolution, et l'a opposé comme une barrière infranchissable aux déprédations de la noblesse. (...) Ce qui manque aux pauvres, ce n'est plus l'hérédité, c'est l'*héritage*. Au lieu d'abolir l'hérédité, songez plutôt à faire cesser la *déshérence*." (*ibid.*, p. 203)

To end this presentation of the Saint-Simonian thought on inheritance, I have to add that Enfantin in 1831 formulated views which are substantially more moderate than the ones exposed in the *Doctrine*.[10] Instead of

10 These can be found in the articles "Les oisifs et les travailleurs. Abolition des successions collatérales" and "Institution des Banques" which were published in the Saint-Simonian journal *Globe*, in the issues of 28 March and 4 April 1831; they are part of ENFANTIN's book *Economie Politique et Politique*, which has been reprinted in 1970.

confiscating all inheritances, he proposed in fact to abolish only collateral inheritances and to instore a progressive tax on inheritances in the direct line (he thought of an average tax rate of 20%). The money and property gathered in this way would then be transferred to a newly created 'Banque Commanditaire de l'Industrie', which would have the task of allocating the funds and goods to the persons most capable of using them. Ideally, this would be a 'good' policy with respect to the distribution of wealth.[11] In reality, however, errors would be inevitable; Enfantin clearly perceived that a centrally-led allocation of goods would present difficulties, but he estimated that under the new allocation mechanism the chances of arriving at a 'just' distribution would be higher than under the blind mechanism of birth:

> "Or nous voulons uniquement montrer qu'il serait possible de les distribuer, au moins en partie, et *malgré toutes les erreurs inséparables de l'imperfection humaine*, avec plus de discernement que par le *hasard de la naissance*; nous prétendons que, lorsqu'on se *proposera* de les répartir selon la CAPACITÉ, il y aura infiniment plus de chances que la répartition sera équitable et fructueuse pour la société entière et pour les individus que lorsqu'on se résout à la distribution aveugle, fortuite, imprévoyante, de l'ordre selon la *naissance*; et nous ajoutons surtout que, quand bien même les premiers essais présenteraient beaucoup d'erreurs et d'imperfections (qui seraient d'ailleurs encore moins choquantes que celle de la loterie de l'hérédité actuelle), on ne tarderait pas à introduire un perfectionnement sans cesse croissant dans l'appréciation des *crédits* à ouvrir, c'est-à-dire des CAPACITÉS À COMMANDITER." (Enfantin, 1970, p. 114)

---

11 ENFANTIN distinguished between good, bad, and blind policies: "Lorsque la richesse, qui est toujours ou un *instrument de travail* ou un *aliment d'oisiveté*, parvient à des mains LABORIEUSES, la mesure qui l'y conduit est bonne; elle est mauvaise si elle dirige l'instrument de travail vers des mains OISIVES; enfin cette mesure est aveugle, si elle laisse au *hasard* le soin de cette distribution." (ENFANTIN, 1970, p. 85).

IV. John Stuart Mill (1806-1873)

It is well-known that both Bentham and the Saint-Simonians had a great impact on John Stuart Mill's thinking; this is certainly the case for his thinking on property and inheritance. Mill knew Bentham from the beginning of his life, and in his youth he was a disciple of Bentham (cf. Stark, 1946). In his *Autobiography* he wrote that he was introduced to the leaders of the Saint-Simonian movement, Bazard and Enfantin, in 1830, and that one of their followers, Gustave d'Eichtal, regularly informed him of the activities of the movement. He described their influence as follows:

> "Their criticisms of the common doctrines of Liberalism seemed to me full of important truth; and it was partly by their writings that my eyes were opened to the very limited and temporary value of the old political economy, which assumes private property and inheritance as indefeasible facts, and freedom of production and exchange as the *dernier mot* of social improvement." (Mill, 1981, pp. 173-5)

This interest in the Saint-Simonian movement is also reflected in numerous letters (cf. Mill, 1963). The main source for Mill's views on inheritance is his *magnum opus* originally published in 1848, *Principles of Political Economy, with Some of Their Applications to Social Philosophy*[12]. The subject of inheritance is dealt with in Book II 'Distribution', especially Chapter ii, and in Book V 'On the influence of government', especially Chapters ii and ix.

In a letter of 1830, Mill had written that he agreed with Bentham's proposal to exclude some collaterals as heirs in cases of intestacy (Mill, 1963, p. 63). In the *Principles of Political Economy*, however, he indicated that he wanted to go further than Bentham in the limitation of the number of legal heirs in cases of intestacy. Mill proposed to exclude *all* collateral relatives of the deceased; those who do want collateral relatives to receive part of their estate, should make a will to this effect:

> "Mr. Bentham long ago proposed, and other high authorities have agreed in the opinion, that if there are no heirs either in the descending or in the ascending line, the property, in case of intestacy, should escheat to the State. With respect to the more remote degrees of collateral relationship,

12 The seventh and last edition was published in 1871. I will refer to the edition as published in the *Collected Works of John Stuart Mill*, Vols. II-III, 1965.

> the point is not very likely to be disputed. Few will maintain that there is any good reason why the accumulations of some childless miser should on his death (as every now and then happens) go to enrich a distant relative who never saw him, who perhaps never knew himself to be related to him until there was something to be gained by it, and who had no moral claim upon him of any kind, more than the most entire stranger. But the reason of the case applies alike to all collaterals, even in the nearest degree. Collaterals have no real claims, but such as may be equally strong in the case of non-relatives; and in the one case as in the other, where valid claims exist, the proper mode of paying regard to them is by bequest." (Mill, 1965, p. 220)

According to Mill only the surviving spouse and the descendants of the deceased would be entitled to inherit in the absence of a will. The expectations of more distant relatives are "created by the provisions of the law", and Mill saw "no reason why collateral inheritance should exist at all" (*ibid.*). In this his position is quite similar to the one taken by Enfantin in the *Globe*.

The reason why Mill strengthened Bentham's proposal in cases of intestacy is connected with his conception of property. Mill started from the following general principle:

> "Nothing is implied in property but the right of each to his (or her) own faculties, to what he can produce by them, and to whatever he can get for them in a fair market; together with his right to give this to any other person if he chooses, and the right of that other to receive and enjoy it." (*ibid.*, p. 218)

The right of bequest was, in Mill's eyes, an essential part of the property right; in contrast to Bentham, Mill therefore absolutely avoided to put limits to the right of bequest. On the other hand, the general principle remains silent on the right of inheritance; when a person dies who did not make a will, there is *a priori* no reason why there *should always* be another person with a right to inherit:

> "It follows, therefore, that although the right of bequest, or gift after death, forms part of the idea of private property, the right of inheritance, as distinguished from bequest, does not. That the property of persons who have made no disposition of it during their lifetime, should pass first to their children, and failing them, to the nearest relations, may be a proper arrangement or not, but is no consequence of the principle of private property." (*ibid.*)

In Mill's reasoning the right of inheritance should exist for those persons only who have 'legitimate' claims to the property of the deceased. Mill explicitly stated that he regarded the claims of children to the property of their parents as "real and indefeasible", and hence these claims should be rewarded even in cases of intestacy. These claims are based upon the fact that parents have a special responsibility towards their children:

> "The duties of parents to their children are those which are indissolubly attached to the fact of causing the existence of a human being. The parent owes to society to endeavour to make the child a good and valuable member of it, and owes to the children to provide, so far as depends on him, such education, and such appliances and means, as will enable them to start with a fair chance of achieving by their own exertions a successful life. To this every child has a claim; and I cannot admit, that as a child, he has a claim to more." (*ibid.*, p. 221)

This last sentence is not without importance; Mill in fact affirmed that there is no reason why the children of the deceased should always inherit the *whole* estate. In other words, children should have a right of inheritance, but a limited right:

> "I hold that to no child, merely as such, anything more is due, than what is admitted to be due to an illegitimate child: and that no child for whom thus much has been done, has, unless on the score of previously raised expectations, any grievance, if the remainder of the parent's fortune is devoted to public uses, or to the benefit of individuals on whom in the parent's opinion it is better bestowed." (*ibid.*, pp. 221-2)[13]

In the case of intestacy, therefore, the State ought to intervene to ensure that the children of the deceased have a fair chance in life; if the estate turns out to be greater than required for this purpose, the remainder should fall into the hands of the public:

> "A provision, then, such as is admitted to be reasonable in the case of illegitimate children, for younger children, wherever in short the justice of the case, and the real interests of the individuals and of society, are the only things considered, is, I conceive, all that parents owe to their

---

13 In a later chapter MILL specified in the following way the part which descendants would be entitled to receive by bequest: "(...) if there are descendants, who, being unable to provide for themselves, would become burthensome to the state, the equivalent of whatever the state would accord to them should be reserved from the property for their benefit (...)" (*ibid.*, p. 887).

> children, and all, therefore, which the State owes to the children of those who die intestate. The surplus, if any, I hold that it may rightfully appropriate to the general purposes of the community." (*ibid.*, pp. 222-3)

Are similar rules to be introduced in the case in which a will has been made? I have already pointed out that Mill regarded the right of bequest as part of the right of property. Mill argued that you cannot have private property without the right to bequest:

> "Unlike inheritance *ab intestato*, bequest is one of the attributes of property: the ownership of a thing cannot be looked upon as complete without the power of bestowing it, at death or during life, at the owner's pleasure: and all the reasons, which recommend that private property should exist, recommend *pro tanto* this extension of it." (*ibid.*, p. 223)

The only limitations to the right of bequest which Mill was willing to accept are the "obvious" ones which prevent the right of bequest to be exercised so "as to conflict with the permanent interests of the human race" (*ibid.*). These restrictions would for instance make it impossible to prescribe the use of property in perpetuity.[14]

Substantial restrictions to the right of bequest, such as those specified in the French system of the *légitime*, Mill regarded as unappropriate. This does not imply, however, that Mill simply defended the then existing English system of inheritance laws, of which the freedom of bequest was one of the cornerstones. Mill's objections were chiefly directed to the predominant role of the custom of primogeniture in the English system. According to Mill, the main motive behind the introduction and maintenance of this system was political, viz. "to keep up large hereditary fortunes, and a landed aristocracy" (*ibid.*, p. 888). The motivation behind the French system was exactly the opposite; although Mill quite agreed with the reasons behind the restrictions to the right of bequest introduced by the system of the *légitime*, he thought there were more appropriate means available to reach the intended aim. Here we come to the core of Mill's proposal, which consists of a limitation of the right of inheritance:

> "Were I framing a code of laws according to what seems to me best in itself, without regard to existing opinions and sentiments, I should prefer

14 For instance, the following rule could be introduced: "In conclusion; all owners of property should, I conceive, have power to dispose by will of every part of it, but not to determine the person who should succeed to it after the death of all who were living when the will was made." (*ibid.*, p. 895).

> to restrict, not what any one might bequeath, but what any one should be permitted to acquire, by bequest or inheritance. Each person should have the power to dispose by will of his or her whole property; but not to lavish it in enriching some one indiviual, beyond a certain maximum, which should be fixed sufficiently high to afford the means of comfortable independence. The inequalities of property which arise from unequal industry, frugality, perseverance, talents, and to a certain extent even opportunities, are inseparable from the principle of private property, and if we accept the principle, we must bear with these consequences of it: but I see nothing objectionable in fixing a limit to what any one may acquire by the mere favour of others, without any exercise of his faculties, and in requiring that if he desires any further accession of fortune, he shall work for it." (*ibid.*, p. 225)

Mill did never specify very precisely how high the maximum amount of property should be that a person would be entitled to acquire by inheritance. As far as the more practical aspects of his proposal are concerned, he advocated high and progressive inheritance taxation:

> "(...) I conceive that inheritances and legacies, exceeding a certain amount, are highly proper subjects for taxation: and that the revenue from them should be as great as it can be made without giving rise to evasions, by donations *inter vivos* or concealment of property, such as it would be impossible adequately to check. The principle of graduation (as it is called), that is, of levying a larger percentage on a larger sum, though its application to general taxation would be in my opinion objectionable, seems to me both just and expedient as applied to legacy and inheritance duties." (*ibid.*, pp. 811-2).

On the benefit side of his proposal, Mill reckoned that a greater part of the estates would be earmarked for public uses, and that the distribution of wealth would become less unequal:

> "If the restriction could be made practically effectual, the benefit would be great. Wealth which could no longer be employed in over-enriching a few, would either be devoted to objects of public usefulness, or if bestowed on individuals, would be distributed among a larger number." (*ibid.*, p. 226)

Mill was aware of the fact that the public might not be prepared to accept all aspects of his reform proposal at once. As an 'intermediate course' he therefore thought it reasonable to postpone the introduction of the restriction to the right of inheritance.

V. Eugenio Rignano (1870-1930)[15]

The influence of the Saint-Simonians and Mill is clear in some less known reform proposals presented in the second-half of the 19th century. Let me mention here briefly the contributions of Huet and Ely. In his book *Le Règne Social du Christianisme* (1853) the Frenchman François Huet (1814-1869)[16] tried to give form to the idea of 'christian socialism'. One of his proposals consisted of limiting the right of bequest to property which has been accumulated during the life of its owner. Huet argued that one should make a distinction between property which an owner has accumulated as a result of his or her own efforts and property which he or she has inherited from others. He proposed to change property rights in accordance with the following distinction: 'self-created' property may be bequeathed freely, but 'inherited' property will be confiscated by the State when the owner of it dies. Everything which is confiscated by the State in a given year must then be equally distributed among all the young people of a given age, so that all dispose of a certain amount of 'basic wealth', so to speak (for more details, cf. Huet, 1853, pp. 263-303, and Ferrero, 1990, pp. 3-5).

Another interesting figure of this period is the American Richard T. Ely (1854-1943). This is how he described the problem he tried to solve: "What is wanted is widely-diffused property, and it is deserved to bring about this

15 Most of the material presented in this and the next Section is treated with more detail in ERREYGERS (1994).

16 From 1835 to 1850 Huet was professor of philosophy at the University of Ghent (Belgium), where he was the leader of a group of disciples known as 'La Société Huet', of which the economist Emile De Laveleye is probably the most famous (see DUJARDIN, 1983). They gathered informally to discuss philosophical and social questions; COPPENS (1972, p. 138) mentions that they discussed the work of the utopian socialists Fourier, Proudhon and Saint-Simon, and that one of the subjects they treated was the "injustice of the inheritance right". In 1850 the Belgian Minister of Internal Affairs more or less forced Huet to abandon his professorship in Ghent (HOFFMANN, 1913). Huet's contribution to economics is mentioned by SCHUMPETER (1954, p. 461n).

wide diffusion without injustice, and without injury to the springs of economic activity." (Ely, 1891, p. 54). He found that three major policies were required to this end: (1) more education, (2) the abolition of private monopolies, and (3) a reform of the laws of inheritance. His reform proposals comprised legal provisions to protect the wife and children of the deceased, and increased inheritance taxes: "All inheritances of every sort should be taxed, provided the share of an heir exceeds a certain amount. The state or the local political unit - as town or city - must be recognized as a co-heir entitled to a share in all inheritances." (*ibid.*, p. 61). Ely wanted the inheritance tax to be progressive, graduated according to the degree of relationship and to the amount inherited, with a tax rate of 20% as the maximum rate. The proceeds of the tax should be used for various forms of investment, "to effect improvements which cost too much to be defrayed out of the ordinary taxation" (*ibid.*, p. 64).

In the same period the question of inherited wealth also received special attention from a few extremely rich 'captains of industry' who by their publications showed that they had reflected about the pressing social and economic problems of their time. Curiously, perhaps, they were rather critical of the existing inheritance regulations. I mention here the names of the American Andrew Carnegie (1835-1919), who was in favour of high inheritance taxes (Carnegie, 1903, pp. 1-44)[17], and the Belgian Ernest Solvay (1838-1922), to whose contribution, now almost forgotten, I will return later in the paper.

In the first half of the 20th century, the debate on inheritance within economic science was dominated by the propositions of the Italian author Eugenio Rignano.[18] This prolific author and editor of the journal *Scientia*, published books and articles in the fields of economics, sociology, philosophy, and psychology. His first book was on economics: *Di un Socialismo in Accordo colla Dottrina Economica Liberale*, published in 1901.[19] In this book Rignano tackled the following question: does there exist

17 The text was originally published in the *North American Review* in 1889.

18 Details on Rignano's life and work can be found in ERREYGERS (1994).

19 The book was translated in French in 1904 (*Un Socialisme en Harmonie avec la Doctrine Economique Libérale*). One year later Adolphe Landry 'composed' a shorter version of it by extracting and rearranging some parts of it, and by adding a little bit of new material (*La Question de l'Héritage*). This shorter version was translated in German and together with a preface by Eduard

a way to socialize the means of production without destroying the incentives that make individuals work and save? Rignano's answer was that a change of the existing inheritance taxation regime could do the job; inheritance taxes had to be made 'progressive in time'.

The discussion on Rignano's proposals gained new impetus after the First World War. In a number of articles in Italian and international journals, Rignano and others presented modified versions of his original scheme. The element which seems to have triggered the renewed interest was that Rignano's reform proposals were seen as a means to come to grips with the enormous public debts created during the war[20].

Rignano's sources of inspiration were many and diverse. He often referred to the works of Karl Marx and Achille Loria, but also to those of John Stuart Mill, François Huet, the Saint-Simonians, Emile De Laveleye, Henry George, Herbert Spencer, and many others. It is clear that he had a solid knowledge of the scientific literature on inheritance, not only in the field of economics, but also in the fields of sociology and law. It is also interesting to note that in 1921 Rignano wrote a review article of Hugh Dalton's *Some Aspects of the Inequality of Incomes in Modern Communities* in which he related his work on inherited wealth to that of Ely and Cannan (Rignano, 1921b).

Bernstein published in 1906 under the title *Los von der Erbschaft!*. Although at that time no English translation seems to have been available, Rignano's work was also known in English-speaking countries, as is testified by the (sympathetic) reference to Rignano's 1901-book in PIGOU's *Wealth and Welfare* (PIGOU, 1912, pp. 376-7).

20 Immediately after the war RIGNANO publicized his ideas in articles in leading international economic journals such as the *Economic Journal* (1919) and the *Revue d'Economie Politique* (1921a); moreover he assembled some of his articles in Italian journals, with replies to his critics, in the book *Per una Riforma Socialista del Diritto Successorio* (1920). A selection of this book was translated in French by Georges Bourgin and published as *Pour une Réforme Socialiste du Droit Successoral* (1923). An English translation and adaptation was made by William J. Shultz; it was published in the USA with an introduction by Edwin Seligman under the title *The Social Significance of the Inheritance Tax* (1924), and in a modified form in England with an introduction by Josiah Stamp under the title *The Social Significance of Death Duties* (1925).

The background of the Rignano proposal as originally formulated in the 1901-book is a critique of the capitalist system loosely based upon the works of Karl Marx and Achille Loria. Rignano seemed to endorse Marx's theory of surplus value, according to which labourers are exploited and capitalists are constantly trying to find ways to keep wages as low as possible. He stressed that the existing inheritance systems tend to *perpetuate* the alienation of the working class and to confer an *immortal* character to private capitals. After a thorough examination of the arguments *pro* and *contra* the existing inheritance systems Rignano concluded that a change was required. The main step in Rignano's reasoning, which also suggests the direction of the required change, is, I believe, the following. Rignano took for granted both the necessity and the desirablity of the accumulation of capital, and he acknowledged the superiority of private saving over collective saving when it comes to ensure the formation of capital. He also accepted that the existing inheritance régimes provided people with powerful incentives to work and save. At first sight, then, a strong case could be made in favour of maintaining the existing régimes. Yet this was not Rignano's conclusion; instead Rignano drew two other conclusions, one negative and one positive. The negative conclusion was that from the premisse that private saving is the best way to ensure the *formation* of capital it does not follow that the *conservation* of capital, once it is formed, should be taken care of by letting it remain forever in private hands. The positive conclusion was that it might perhaps be possible to reform the existing inheritance régimes in such a way that the stimuli which incite individuals to work and save were increased.

Rignano looked for a modification which would bring about ameliorations from three points of view, viz. the utilitarian principle, the interest of the proletariat, and fairness. (Rignano believed these principles were perfectly coincident.) He translated these principles into a set of more precise conditions, the most important of which seem to be the following:

1) the new system should lead to a vast nationalization of the means of production and capital in general;
2) the new system should de-cumulate private capitals fairly rapidly, so as to prevent the creation of large inequalities in the distribution of private capital;
3) the new system should give powerful stimuli to work, saving and new capital formation.

The first of these conditions requires that all private capitals eventually come to be confiscated by the state. The third implies that the right of bequest cannot be abolished completely; if individuals were not allowed to bequeath at least part of the goods they have accumulated by their own work and saving, then they would not have much of an incentive to work and save. The second principle, finally, suggests that the moment at which the final confiscation will take place should not be pushed too far away in the future.

Taking into account these three considerations Rignano came up with the proposal to differentiate the right of bequest according to the 'origin' or 'age' of the property to be bequeathed. The Rignano scheme would work as follows. When a man dies, the monetary value of his possessions will be split up into different parts according to the number of times his possessions have been transferred by means of inheritance or gift. This means that a distinction is made between the property which constitutes the own savings of the defunct (0 transfers), the property which he has inherited from other persons and which came from their own savings (1 transfer), the property which he has inherited from other persons who in their turn had inherited it from others (2 transfers), etc. The Rignano principle stipulates that the higher the number of transfers a piece of property has been subject to, the smaller the power of the owner to dispose of it by will. In other words, the rate of inheritance taxation levied at each transfer of property will increase with the number of transfers, and after a given number of transfers reach the level of 100%.

To illustrate things, let the inheritance tax rate of property which has already been transferred i-1 times be equal to t_i, i.e. t_i is the tax rate applicable at the i-th transfer of a property ($i = 1,2,...$). Any proposal of the Rignano type can then be described by a vector $T = [t_1, t_2, ..., t_k]$, such that $0 < t_1 < t_2 < ... < t_k = 1$, where k is the number of transfers it takes for private property to pass completely into the hands of the State. After j transfers ($1 \leq j \leq k$), the part of the original property still in private hands would be equal to $(1\text{-}t_1)\times(1\text{-}t_2)\times...\times(1\text{-}t_j)$, whereas the rest would have been transformed into public property. The taxation part of Huet's proposal is of course a special case of Rignano's proposal, as Rignano (1901, pp. 61-3) himself recognized: in Huet's case we have $T = [0, 1]$. What happens with the proceeds of the tax is, however, completely different in both cases.

Rignano suggested two interesting characterizations of his proposal. The first is that a modification of the inheritance system along the suggested lines comes down to the introduction of a new principle of progressiveness in inheritance taxation, viz. the principle of an inheritance tax *progressive in time*[21]. The new principle can supplement other principles of progressiveness which are eventually already in use, such as graduation of the tax according to the amount of bequest or inheritance, and graduation according to the relationship between the testator and the inheritor. The second characterization is that the limitations to property transfers brought about by the scheme have the effect of giving to private property owners a *temporary patent right in accumulations of capital*[22]. The purpose of ordinary patents is to encourage inventions, by awarding the inventors the privilege of the exclusive use of their inventions during a limited period of time. The Rignano proposal is meant to encourage individuals to work and save; to do this individuals have the right to own and bequeath private property, but only insofar as it is necessary and sufficient to make people work and save.

Rignano termed his approach 'socialist' but not without stressing that it differed both from the orthodox Marxist, or 'collectivist', and from the utopian socialist approaches. Rignano rejected Marx's mechanistic theory of evolution which is supposed to culminate in a violant revolution, with the proletarians expropriating the capitalists and instoring a collectivist régime. Such a revolution would ruin the whole delicate mechanism of economic production, wrote Rignano (1921a, p. 3) a few years after the bolchevik revolution, thereby repeating the critique of collectivism which he formulated in his first book. Instead of a brutal expropriation Rignano advocated a gradual nationalization of private property, brought about by a change of the laws which regulate property rights. This is why Rignano (*ibid.*) characterized his approach as one of *legal socialism* ("socialisme juridique").

To end the presentation of the Rignano proposal, I feel obliged to say a few words about its originality. As we will see in the next Section, there was a serious debate among economists about the 'Rignano-principle'. But was

---

21 Of course the period of time between two successive transfers can vary widely, but RIGNANO seemed to believe that on average the number of transfers is a good approximation of the period of time elapsed since the 'creation' of the property (RIGNANO, 1901, p. 63).

22 This is how DALTON (1920, p. 132) translated "brevetto di capitalizzazione o d'accumulazione a durata limitata" (RIGNANO, 1901, p. 93).

Rignano really the first to formulate the principle that inheritance taxes should be graduated according to the number of transfers? He was not. As I have shown elsewhere (Erreygers, 1995, pp. 13-6), Ernest Solvay formulated the principle already in 1897, in an article entitled "Etude sur le progrès économique et la morale sociale". The principle was not something Solvay referred to only casually; it was an important part of his social reform program, which he elaborated in numerous publications of the period. Solvay, who made a habit of forging new words and terms, coined the principle the 're-iterated inheritance tax' ("l'impôt successoral réitéré", a term first introduced in "Le productivisme social", published in 1898). A good summary of Solvay's views on inheritance is the one given in his article "Principes de politique sociale", again of 1898; in this "avant-pojet de programme politique de principes", he proposed with respect to the inheritance tax:

> "1. Réforme des impôts en vue d'assurer leur plus juste proportionnalité possible à la fortune réelle et en ayant pour objectif l'impôt unique, l'acquittement de l'impôt quel qu'il soit ne devant finalement s'effectuer qu'à la mort du contribuable.
> 2. Distinction à établir entre la fortune directement acquise par les efforts de celui qui la possède et la fortune reçue par voie de transmission; entre la fortune n'ayant subi qu'une transmission - par exemple celle provenant du père et de la mère - et la fortune ayant subi deux transmissions - par exemple celle provenant de grands-parents - et ainsi de suite, le taux d'impôt devant varier en proportion ou en progression du nombre de transmissions effectuées. Moyens à employer pour arriver par la suite à établir la distinction entre la fortune acquise et la fortune transmise: comptabilisme social." (Solvay, 1927, pp. 201-2)

Clearly, there are huge differences between the approach of Rignano and the one of Solvay (e.g., Solvay advocated a reform of the monetary system as a means to make his inheritance tax work). The similarities between their propositions on inheritance taxation are, however, striking and undeniable. Since there is no evidence available which would indicate that anyone of them was aware of the other's proposal in the period around the turn of the century, I think it would be more appropriate to speak of the Solvay-Rignano-principle than of the Rignano-principle.

VI. The Early 20th Century Debate

The publication of Rignano's book in 1901 and of the translations which appeared shortly thereafter provoked some discussion, but did not lead to any practical results. The Rignano scheme, interesting as it may have been, seemed destined to slowly fade away. World War I changed everything, however, and the Rignano proposal got a second chance. Immediately after the end of the war Rignano as well as others reformulated and modified the original proposal. A debate was started, especially in Great-Britain, during which both the weak and the strong points of the proposal were examined, and which lasted at least until 1929. In this Section I will focus on the highlights of this debate.

In 1923 Rignano published a French translation (and adaptation) of his 1920-book under the title *Pour une Réforme Socialiste du Droit Successoral*; in the book he introduced a distinction between a maximum and a minimum project. The maximum project consisted of the original proposal, characterized by the confiscation of property after two or three transfers; the minimum project, on the other hand, concentrated on the fiscal aspects of the scheme and did not aim at (rapid) confiscation. The distinction was clearly made in order to increase the chances of the proposal ever being realized. Apparently the prospect of a large-scale nationalization of private wealth frightened too many of those who were interested in the practical realization of the scheme.

In the same period a number of economists picked up Rignano's idea and gave it favourable comments. The list includes Hugh Dalton, Josiah Stamp, Corrado Gini and Giovanni De Francisci Gerbino. Dalton did perhaps the most to promote Rignano's ideas. In Dalton's book *Some Aspects of the Inequality of Incomes in Modern Communities* Rignano's work is cited several times, and described as "remarkable" but also as "curiously little known" (Dalton, 1920, p. 316). As far as the principle is concerned, Dalton judgement was very favourable:

> "(...) the proposal itself is exceedingly suggestive and highly original. It points the way to new and unexplored fields of economic analysis, and to possibilities of compromise, hitherto quite unconsidered, between the system of private property, as it exists in modern states, and socialist systems, as commonly conceived." (*ibid.*, p. 133)

There is a detailed discussion of the scheme, especially of its practical applicability, towards the end of the book (*ibid.*, pp. 316-27). Dalton identified the division of the inheritance into different parts according to the number of transfers as the main practical problem. This division can only be made on the basis of monetary values. But then, Dalton remarked, it seems desirable to take into account changes in value for which the proprietor is not responsible:

> "(...) it will be necessary, ideally, to make an allowance for changes in value, which are due, not to the action of the proprietor, but either to changes in the general rate of interest, or to changes in the relative value of different sorts, or particular pieces of property." (*ibid.*, p. 318)

The problem will be less severe, however, if the division only relates to the distinction between a person's own savings, on the one hand, and his or her inheritances and gifts on the other. Two tax rates will then suffice, a low one for own savings and a higher one for inheritances and gifts, i.e. $T = [t_1, t_2]$, with $0 < t_1 < t_2 < 1$. This is what Dalton called the "simplified Rignano principle" in contrast to the original "full Rignano principle" (*ibid.*, p. 320); the distinction coincides more or less with the distinction between the minimum and the maximum project. Another aspect of Dalton's examination is that he compared the effects on inequality and on production of the Rignano principle and other principles of inheritance taxation. With respect to inequality the results are "speculative and uncertain", but with respect to production the Rignano principle definitely appears to be superior. The argument is that with a Rignano tax the will to save may be diminished less than with other inheritance taxes, as Pigou maintained, or that the will to save, and also the will to work, may even increase, as Rignano believed (*ibid.*, pp. 322-5). All in all, Dalton was quite enthusiastic about the Rignano proposal. This is also clear from the fact that in the penultimate chapter of the book, containing his own suggestions for a reform of the law of inheritance, Dalton gave a place to the Rignano principle: one of his propositions was to combine a tax on the simplified Rignano principle with a graduated tax on individual inheritances (*ibid.*, pp. 339-41). In later publications, such as *Principles of Public Finance* (Dalton, 1945), he regularly returned to the Rignano proposal and formulated modified versions of it.

Compared to Dalton, the support of Josiah Stamp for the Rignano proposal has always been more conditional. Around 1925 Stamp wrote a preface for the English translation/adaptation of Rignano's *Per una Riforma*

Socialista del Diritto Successorio, which was also published in Rignano's journal *Scientia* under the title "The influence of death duties on the socialisation of wealth" (Stamp, 1925). According to Stamp, three questions have to be answered to assess the value of the Rignano proposal: 1) is it "unnatural"?; 2) is it against fiscal or economic principles?; and 3) is it administratively practical? The anwers to questions 1 and 2 seem to be a qualified 'no', the qualification being "unless in so doing the State goes to such a length as to commit economic suicide by thwarting individual initiative, and drying up the springs of social action" (*ibid.*, p. 36). The third question, "perhaps the most vital aspect for consideration", is hardly discussed at all; only a list of the most important problems is given:

"a) Changes in the value of money, or rate of interest, where the same real fortune may show a fictitious increase or decrease for taxation purposes.

b) The succession of life interests.

c) Changes in valuations of variables, etc., such as mines depending upon an estimate of length of life.

d) The impossibility of stereotyping the forms of wealth received as inheritance, and of holding to original valuations where the forms into which exchange has been made exhibit changes.

e) Rapid successions horizontally along the same generation, i.e., from brother to brother." (*ibid.*, p. 40)

Mention must also be made of two Italian writers who in this period have favourably written about Rignano's proposal: Corrado Gini (1921), who drew attention to difficulties connected with changing prices, and Giovanni De Francisci Gerbino (1925), who focused on the potential of the Rignano-proposal to extinguish national debts, which had reached peak levels after the First World War.

The mid-twenties were a crucial period for the Rignano proposal, since the situation seemed fertile for the introduction of a kind of Rignano tax. In Great Britain, for instance, a committee was appointed in 1924 "to consider and report on the National Debt and on the incidence of existing taxation, with special reference to their effect on trade, industry, employment and national credit" (*Report of the Committee on National Debt and Taxation*, 1927, p. viii). This *Committee on National Debt and Taxation*, also known as the *Colwyn Committee*, worked from March 1924 to November 1926, and published its report in 1927. In fact two reports were delivered, a majority report and a (much smaller) minority report. Both of these reports discussed the Rignano proposal, and their appreciations of it differed considerably. In the majority report the Rignano proposal was examined in a section entitled 'Schemes of taxation and debt repayment' (*ibid.*, pp. 313-6). The committee submitted the fiscal aspect of the proposal to three tests, viz. (a) practicability, (b) equity, and (c) the effect on savings; it even asked the Board of Inland Revenue to write a memorandum to assess the practicability of the proposal. The overall conclusion was that there was something good in the idea, but that its practical translation left much to be desired:

> "The principle of the Rignano scheme - differentiation between saved and inherited wealth - has not yet been embodied in a form promising reasonably fair treatment to the individual taxpayer, while the administrative problems are very formidable and the risk of evasion is serious. Some of us, however, find the principle in itself attractive, and think it possible, from such consideration as we have been able to give of the idea, that it may in course of time have useful developments and enable some improvement to be effected in the existing death duties system." (*ibid.*, p. 316)

The Minority Report of the Committee (*ibid.*, pp. 418-23) was much more favourable to the Rignano proposal. The administrative problems were considered not to "present any insuperable difficulties" (*ibid.*, p. 423), and the authors agreed "with Professor Rignano that the effect of a duty graduated on this basis would be positively to stimulate entreprise and saving" (*ibid.*, p. 421). Their conclusion was the following:

> "The result of such consideration as we have been able to give to this proposal is certainly to suggest that the principle of graduation according to the 'relative age' of estates might, with great advantage, be introduced into the British system of death duties." (*ibid.*, p. 422)

Another important date was February 16, 1926, when H.C. Scott read before the Royal Statistical Society a communication entitled "Some administrative aspects of the Rignano scheme of inheritance taxation", which together with a summary of the discussion following the presentation was published in the *Journal of the Royal Statistical Society* of the same year. A very original aspect of Scott's paper is that he constructed a model which enabled him to forecast the yield of the Rignano scheme in Britain over a fifty-year period. His calculations showed:

> "(...) that while the annual yield would be considerable after some thirty or forty years, no great increase would result for many years after the commencement of the scheme. This is not, of course, an argument

against the scheme as part of a complete fiscal system operating over a long period, but it does rather militate against its immediate utility and political possibility." (Scott, 1927, p. 270)

Although he admitted "the solid economic sense behind the Rignano idea" (*ibid.*, p. 281), his overall judgment of the scheme appeared to be rather negative[23]:

"The general line of criticism in this paper may seem to be mainly destructive. It is not, however, put forward for that reason, but rather, if anything in it is of value, to drive inquiry more into the line of administrative practicability, which is, after all, the final consideration in connection with any proposal of taxation." (*ibid.*, p. 270)

The fatal blow to the Rignano proposal was delivered by Josiah Wedgwood, whose book *The Economics of Inheritance* was published in 1929[24]. The last chapter of the book, 'Recent proposals for the reform and extension of the death duties', is almost entirely devoted to Rignano's proposal and modified versions of it. Wedgwood's analysis is probably the most complete and thorough analysis that has ever been made of the Rignano proposal. Wedgwood recapitulated and discussed a lot of the critiques made by previous writers; in addition he criticized the Rignano proposal on the basis of the distinction between 'earned' (or 'saved') and 'inherited' property:

"(...) when one comes to try to apply this distinction in practice, it seems anything but clear and definite. 'Inherited' property is clearly intended to cover all property received either by inheritance, bequest or gift during life; and all such property is to be taxed at a higher rate than property acquired in other ways, which is described by Rignano as 'earned' and

---

23 The discussion which followed the presentation of the paper ended with the following enigmatic reply of SCOTT: "Someone asked for my own 'carefully concealed' opinion on the scheme. I feared I had not concealed it enough. But, very briefly, it is that if Rignano's historical thesis is correct, then by the time the property-owning classes are sufficiently concerned to be willing to concede such a solution to their relations with the proletariat, much bigger things are likely to happen than the Rignano scheme." (*ibid.*, p. 282)

24 I will cite from the 1939 Pelican edition; interestingly, in the introduction to this edition WEDGWOOD asked the reader to "pardon the references in the book to now almost forgotten writers like the Italian liberal Rignano, or the German Jew, Walter Rathenau" (WEDGWOOD, 1939, p. 10).

> by others as 'saved'. But to describe all property acquired otherwise than by gift or inheritance as 'earned' or 'saved' is rather misleading, if one accepts the usual interpretation of those terms. For a good deal of property is not the result of the owner's effort or thrift; and not all that is the result of his efforts represents an economic service to the community." (Wedgwood, 1939, p. 260)

One of the effects of the introduction of a Rignano tax might be that speculation is encouraged:

> "There is bound, therefore, to be a large element of luck in the assessments of 'earned' and 'inherited' property. (...) In general, the tax will differentiate in favour of those who are fortunate in their investments and speculations and against those who are unfortunate." (*ibid.*, p. 262)

In the end, Wedgwood appeared to be very sceptical of the Rignano proposal since it could very well produce adverse effects:

> "Hence, in general, one cannot escape the conclusion that, in a pure and undiluted form, Rignano's proposals, though intended to put a premium on industry and thrift, may at the same time encourage speculation and avarice, and, in discouraging the spendthrift, may put a penalty on generosity and altruism." (*ibid.*, pp. 264-5)

These criticisms torpedoed the Rignano project. During the twenties and thirties his ideas inspired a number of modified proposals, none of which were realized, and by the end of the thirties Rignano's name was, indeed, "almost forgotten". One variant of Rignano's scheme was formulated by Hugh Dalton (1925, p. 298; 1945, pp. 117-8); the basic idea of his proposal was to collect the inheritance tax due on the *second* transfer (i.e. the tax on inherited wealth) at the moment of the *first* transfer. The authors of the Majority Report of the Colwyn committee rejected it (*Report of the Committee on National Debt and Taxation*, 1927, pp. 316-8), but Pigou (1928, pp. 166-7) described it as "an ingenious alternative plan". The Dalton variant of the Rignano proposal resurfaced briefly in 1935, when both Colin Clark (cf. Durbin, 1985, p. 221) and James Meade (1988, p. 52) mentioned it in memoranda for the British Labour Party. After that, the project seems to have been abandoned for good, a fact which Carl Shoup commented on as follows:

> "No practical support has developed for the Rignano plan or its variants, which would tax especially heavily and eventually confiscate inheritances that came from inheritances, after two or three generations.

It is instructive to recall that an inventor of one of these variants, Hugh Dalton, made no move to introduce it into British law while he was chancellor of the exchequer in the late 1940s." (Shoup, 1968, p. 558)

VII. Concluding Remarks

What lesson can this brief digression in the history of economic thought teach us? We have seen that a number of authors had high hopes of a reform of inheritance: it would bring society closer to social justice, and this would be accomplished without endangering the incentives for individuals to work and save. Although it is beyond the scope of this paper to assess the influence upon economic policy of all the reform proposals presented, it is safe to say that the hopes have to a great extent been transformed into illusions. The fate of the Solvay-Rignano proposal stands out as an example. Ironically, this project, originally devised as a step towards more social justice, was criticized and rejected because, among other things, many feared that in practice it might create more inequities. I believe this also illustrates that the question of inheritance and inheritance taxation is not a question which can be tackled by purely 'economic' arguments alone. Any serious discussion about the economics of inheritance seems to require that one also takes into account the ethics of inheritance. The relative importance of the values of liberty and equality, the interpretation of the notion of equality, the status of the family, etc., are among the crucial factors that influence the way one looks at inheritance. Perhaps existing inheritance systems have stronger roots than many reformers have imagined; if so, those who would like to drastically change the rules, should be aware that they have to be armed with powerful arguments.

References

BENTHAM, J. (1882): *Theory of Legislation*, London (Trübner & Co).

BENTHAM, J. (1952): "Supply without Burthen, or Escheat vice Taxation", in: W. STARK (Ed.): *Jeremy Bentham's Economic Writings*, New York (Burt Franklin), Vol. I, pp. 281-367.

BOUGLÉ, C. and HALÉVY, E. (1924): "Préface" in: *Doctrine de Saint-Simon. Exposition. Première Année, 1829*, Paris (Marcel Rivière), pp. 5-69.

CANNAN, E. (1926): "Review of 'The social significance of death duties' by Eugenio Rignano", *Economic Journal*, 36, pp. 235-8.

CARNEGIE, A. (1903): *The Gospel of Wealth and Other Timely Essays*, London (Frederick Warne & Co), 3rd edition.

COPPENS, E.C. (1972): "La Société Huet. Tussen revolutie en reaktie", *Handelingen der Maatschappij voor Geschiedenis en Oudheidkunde te Gent*, N.R. 26, pp. 131-51.

DALTON, H. (1920): *Some Aspects of the Inequality of Incomes in Modern Communities*, London (George Routledge and Sons); New York (E.P. Dutton).

DALTON, H. (1925): "Taxation of income and inherited wealth", in: H. TRACEY (Ed.): *The Book of the Labour Party: Its History, Growth, Policy and Leaders*, London (Caxton), Vol. II, pp. 285-301.

DALTON, H. (1945): *Principles of Public Finance*, London (George Routledge and Sons).

DE FRANCISCI GERBINO, G. (1925): "New means for the more rapid extinction of the British national debt", *Economic Journal*, 35, pp. 233-44.

Doctrine de Saint-Simon. Exposition. Première Année, 1829 (1924), ed. by C. Bouglé and E. Halévy, Paris (Marcel Rivière).

DUJARDIN, C. (1983): *De Société Huet (1846-1851). Ideeënstudie van een Progressief-Liberale Kring te Gent*, K.U. Leuven (Faculteit Letteren en Wijsbegeerte, Departement Moderne Geschiedenis), unpublished thesis.

DURBIN, E. (1985): *New Jerusalems. The Labour Party and the Economics of Democratic Socialism*, London (Routledge and Kegan Paul).

ELY, R.T. (1891): "The inheritance of property", *North American Review*, 153, pp. 54-66.

ENFANTIN, B.P. (1970): *Economie Politique et Politique*, New York (Burt Franklin).

ERREYGERS, G. (1994): *Eugenio Rignano and the Inheritance Tax Debate of the 1920s* (Paper presented at the 21st Annual Conference of the History of

Economics Society, Babson College, Boston, Massachusetts), University of Antwerp (UFSIA-SESO), mimeo.

ERREYGERS, G. (1995): *The Economic Theories and Social Reform Proposals of Ernest Solvay (1838-1922)* (Paper presented at the 22nd Annual Conference of the History of Economics Society, University of Notre Dame, South Bend, Indiana), University of Antwerp (UFSIA-SESO), mimeo.

FERRERO, M. (1990): *A Blueprint for Intergenerational Socialism* (Paper presented at the Third International Conference of B.I.E.N. "Economic Democracy and Citizenship Income", Firenze, European University Institute, September 19-21), Università di Torino, (Dipartimento di Economia), mimeo.

FOURIER, C. (1890): *Œuvres Choisies*, Paris (Guillaumin)

GINI, C. (1921): "Problèmes financiers d'après guerre. Troisième partie: D'un nouveau principe de progressivité pour les impôts de succession et de ses développements possibles", *Scientia*, 30, pp. 127-44.

HALÉVY, E. (1901): *La Formation du Radicalisme Philosophique* (Vol. I, "La Jeunesse de Bentham"), Paris (Félix Alcan).

HART, H.L.A. (1982): *Essays on Bentham. Studies in Jurisprudence and Political Theory*, Oxford (Clarendon Press).

HOFFMANN, P. (1913): "François Huet" in: *Liber Memorialis. Notices Biographiques*, Gand (Université de Gand, Faculté de Philosophie et Lettres/Faculté de Droit, Maison d'Edition I. Vanderpoorten), pp. 104-14.

HUET, F. (1853): *Le Règne Social du Christianisme*, Paris (Firmin Didot Frères); Bruxelles (Librairie Polytechnique Decq.)

MEADE, J. (1988): "Outline of economic policy for a labour government" [1935], in: S. HOWSON (Ed.): *The Collected Papers of James Meade*, London (Unwin Hyman), Vol. I, pp. 33-79.

MILL, J.S. (1963): *The Earlier Letters of John Stuart Mill*, ed. by F.E. Mineka, Toronto (University of Toronto Press); London (Routledge and Kegan Paul) (= Collected Works of John Stuart Mill, Vol. XII).

MILL, J.S. (1965): *Principles of Political Economy, with Some of Their Applications to Social Philosophy*, ed. by V.W. Bladen and J.M. Robson, Toronto (University of Toronto Press); London (Routledge and Kegan Paul) (= Collected Works of John Stuart Mill, Vols. II-III).

MILL, J.S. (1981): *Autobiography and Other Literary Essays*, ed. by J.M. Robson and J. Stillinger, Toronto (University of Toronto Press); London (Routledge and Kegan Paul) (= Collected Works of John Stuart Mill, Vol. I).

PIGOU, A.C. (1912): *Wealth and Welfare*, London (Macmillan & Co).

PIGOU, A.C. (1928): *A Study in Public Finance*, London (Macmillan).

PROUDHON, P.-J. (1861): *Théorie de l'Impôt*, Bruxelles (Office de Publicité).

PROUDHON, P.-J. (1923): *Système des Contradictions Economiques ou Philosophie de la Misère*, Paris (Marcel Rivière).

Report of the Committee on National Debt and Taxation (1927), London (Her Majesty's Stationary Office).

RIGNANO, E. (1901): *Di un Socialismo in Accordo colla Dottrina Economica Liberale*, Torino (Fratelli Bocca Editori).

RIGNANO, E. (1904): *Un Socialisme en Harmonie avec la Doctrine Economique Libérale*, Paris (Girard & Brière).

RIGNANO, E. (1905): *La Question de l'Héritage*, Paris (Société nouvelle de librairie et d'édition).

RIGNANO, E. (1919): "A plea for a greater economic democratisation", *Economic Journal*, 29, pp. 302-8.

RIGNANO, E. (1920): *Per una Riforma Socialista del Diritto Successorio*, Bologna (Zanichelli).

RIGNANO, E. (1921a): "Un programme socialiste libéral", *Revue d'Economie Politique*, 35, pp. 1-10.

RIGNANO, E. (1921b): "Une lacune comblée dans la science économique", *Revue de l'Institut de Sociologie*, 1, pp. 223-32.

RIGNANO, E. (1923): *Pour une Réforme Socialiste du Droit Successoral*, Paris (F. Rieder & Co)

RIGNANO, E. (1924): *The Social Significance of the Inheritance Tax*, New York, (Alfred A. Knopf).

RIGNANO, E. (1925): *The Social Significance of Death Duties*, London (Noel Douglas).

SCHUMPETER, J.A. (1954): *History of Economic Analysis*, London (George Allen & Unwin).

SCOTT, H.C. (1926): "Some administrative aspects of the Rignano scheme of inheritance taxation [+discussion]", *Journal of the Royal Statistical Society, Series A*, 89, pp. 256-82.

SHOUP, C.S. (1968): "Taxation: Death and gift taxes", in: D.L. SILLS (Ed.): *International Encyclopedia of the Social Sciences*, New York (Macmillan), Vol. 15, pp. 555-60.

SMITH, A. (1976): *An Inquiry into the Nature and Causes of the Wealth of Nations*, ed. by R.H. Campbell, A.S. Skinner and W.B. Todd, Oxford (Oxford University Press) (= The Glasgow Edition of the Works and Correspondence of Adam Smith, Vol. II).

SOLVAY, E. (1929): *Notes, Lettres et Discours d'Ernest Solvay*, Bruxelles (Lamertin).
STAMP, J.C. (1925): "The influence of death duties on the socialisation of wealth", *Scientia*, 38, pp. 29-40.
STARK, W. (1941): "Liberty and equality, or: Jeremy Bentham as an economist", *Economic Journal*, 51, pp. 56-79.
STARK, W. (1946): "Jeremy Bentham as an economist. II. Bentham's influence", *Economic Journal*, 56, pp. 583-608.
STARK, W. (1952): "Introduction" in: W. STARK (Ed.): *Jeremy Bentham's Economic Writings*, New York (Burt Franklin), Vol. I, pp. 11-78.
WEDGWOOD, J. (1939): *The Economics of Inheritance*, Harmondsworth (Penguin Books).
WEILL, G. (1896): *L'Ecole Saint-Simonienne*, Paris (Félix Alcan).

Chapter 3

Bequests Motives and Models of Inheritance: A Survey of the Literature

ANDRÉ MASSON and PIERRE PESTIEAU

I. Introduction

The economic reality of inheritance - a factor of wealth accumulation having an appreciable effect on wealth distribution - is very different from conventional wisdom. One need only recall the stereotyped image of those elderly parents who do without their entire working lives so that they can leave each of their children a small patch of land. Literature offers up anecdotal images: the myth of the uncle in America as rich as Uncle Scrooge, the moral legacy that La Fontaine's farmer bequeaths his three sons, the inheritance which star-crossed lovers will never receive, oblivious to the fact that 'the postman always rings twice', the heir in Labiche's comedies whose major asset lies in having parents and uncles who are both wealthy and elderly. Besides those stereotypes, inheritance is for the majority associated with the loss of a beloved one and its ensuing consequences for the surviving family. Is inheritance only a private matter like marriage or a mere subject for crime novels, moralizing tales or light comedies - i.e. without economic implications?

This image is rather reductive and somehow inappropriate. Inheritance is not an incidental phenomenon; its function is equally as important as those of other intergenerational transfers such as retirement benefits or educational spending. Through the complex network of family relations, it plays a central role in the economic world.

The extended family has traditionally been a preferential domain for transfers or exchanges, either in competition with or as a complement to the state or the market. Family *transfers* are most often free and voluntary and *a priori* do not presuppose a reciprocal arrangement whereas *exchange* is based on the principle of give and take, although generally formulated in vague terms: 'I'll help you *now*, but I'll come to you *later* when I need help'. Admittedly, this distinction between exchange and transfer within the family is not that all clearcut. Even though 'pure' transfers do not imply explicit counterparts, the simple fact that they bring utility to the donor makes it less free than it sounds.

Our concern here is with exchanges or transfers between parents and children, which may be monetary or in kind. In addition to wealth transfers such as bequests and gifts, there is also the education which parents provide to their offspring through an investment in both time and money, not to mention the transmission of intangible social capital. There are also different types of assistance, often in the form of services: these may be descending (providing accommodation or care to grand-children) or ascending (care, visits or accommodating elderly parents).

This paper focuses on the most traditional type of intergenerational transfer: *inheritance*. It will be contrasted at times with two other forms of descending transmissions: *inter vivos gifts*, which differ from bequests in not being bound to the donor's death; and *education*, which is provided at a particular moment of a child's life and whose rate of return varies greatly from one family to the next, even from one child to the next. Inheritance will also be related to public intergenerational transfers such as social security. The issue here is that of complementarity or substitutability between bequests and these public transfers.

The average age of an heir in most advanced countries is above 45, an age at which people are already thinking of retirement and no longer need that helping hand so necessary at the beginning of their professional and family lives. If parents' intergenerational transmissions were motivated only by the altruistic desire to help their children at the right moment, they should be executed earlier and in the form of gifts. This is clearly an interesting empirical question.

How then can we account for the frequency and size of inheritances? We shall attempt to answer this question by introducing a taxonomy of the main types of bequests and models of inheritance developed by economists over the last decades. Each one of these models focusing on specific *motivations* for wealth transmission, is characterized by the kind of relations existing within the family, the structure of preferences, the type of information held by each member of the family, and of course his or her own characteristics such as ability or life expectancy. It will become apparent that this taxonomy is very different from the popular image of inheritance and that the economic approach does not follow the same track as the one adopted by other social scientists[1], despite the use of similar concepts (exchange, reciprocity, altruism, ...).

More importantly, we shall point out the multiple and divergent *implications* which each of these types of inheritance may have. We will focus on two types of implications, those pertaining to the effects of inheritance on *distribution* and those related to the behavioural reactions to *fiscal policy*. Distribution will be dealt with from an inter- as well as an

1 See on this MASSON (1995).

intragenerational viewpoint. Fiscal policy will comprise both intergenerational public transfers such as public debt or social security and wealth transfer taxation.

II. Models and Types of Inheritance

Inherited wealth is generally quite unequally distributed (nearly as much as wealth and a great deal more than income). In countries like France, it accounts for a large part of all wealth possessed (generally estimated at around 40%) and represents the largest descending monetary transfer, three times as much as wealth received in the form of *inter vivos* gifts for example.

Although the inheritor may very well not know the motivations behind the decision to leave him or her a bequest, it is clear that they may be diverse and sometimes contradictory. In fact, there exist three large categories of inheritance:

- *accidental* or *unplanned bequests,* characterized not primarily by the desire to transmit wealth to offspring but out of precaution or consumption deferred over an uncertain life span;
- *voluntary* or *planned bequests*, falling into different categories depending on the motive for the transmission. They range from *pure altruism* to *paternalistic* behaviour all the way to the most self-interested *strategic* exchange (cf. Table 3.1);
- *capitalist* or *entrepreneurial* bequests which are the outcome of accumulation for its own sake.

Table 3.1 presents our taxonomy of bequests with some key references. This taxonomy is based on two dividing lines: the consumer's horizon and the concern for family. Accidental bequests are typically limited to the consumer's life cycle. Voluntary bequests are essentially based on *family* considerations. Capitalist bequests have generally an horizon that extends well over the lifetime of the wealth holder; they are not primarily motivated by family considerations even though the dynastic family is used as the channel allowing for the perennity of the estate.

Table 3.1
Wealth Accumulation and Models of Inheritance

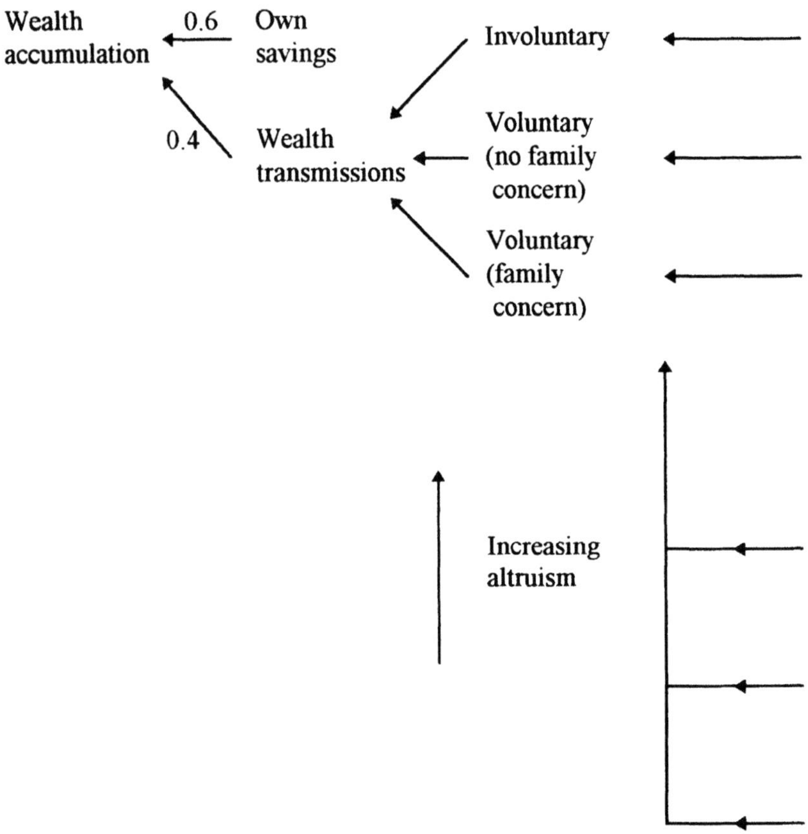

Table 3.1 (continuation)

Bequests		**Authors**
Accidental		Davies (1981)
Capitalist		Ricardo (1817), Moore (1979)
Altruistic (pure)		Becker & Tomes (1979, 1986), Barro (1974)
Retrospective (stable society)		Bevan & Stiglitz (1979), Bevan (1979)
Paternalistic		Blinder (1974, 1976b), Modigliani & Brumberg (1954), Modigliani (1975, 1986)
Motivated by exchange	← Pure exchange	Cox (1987, 1990), Desai & Shah (1983), Kotlikoff & Spivak (1981)
	↖ Strategic exchange	Bernheim et al. (1985)

These distinctions may sound ludicrous. Yet, as we hope to make it clear, they are of crucial importance. The implications and consequences that a bequest may have on the growth and distribution of income (for example) largely depend on the category it belongs to.

1. Accidental Bequests

Even if parents accumulate wealth only in provision for old age, as the theory of the life cycle claims, and have no particular desire to leave something to their children, the latter will probably still receive an inheritance. This kind of bequest, termed accidental, is generally associated with the concepts of precautionary savings and deferred consumption. It owes its existence to three factors: the uncertainty over one's lifespan, the imperfection of capital markets (pertaining to, e.g., annuities or housing) and the impossibility of leaving a negative inheritance. In a world of certainty, savings would be adjusted to match the needs of the life cycle only; if annuities were available at an actuarially fair rate, one could protect oneself against the risk of an excessively long and penniless existence. Under these conditions, there seems to be no purpose in leaving a bequest which is of no particular use in itself.

To illustrate the accidental bequest[2], let us take the case of a couple of retirees; they are only entitled to a small pension and have not taken out annuities. Anticipating a long and comfortable retirement, they have accumulated financial and real estate assets which they hope to live on. They subsequently die in a car accident, leaving their children, if any, an inheritance they were not counting on.

Other things equal, the accidental inheritance is maximal if death occurs at the moment in the life cycle when wealth is at its peak, i.e. generally at the end of the person's working life. In this type of inheritance, there is no exchange or altruism between parents and children. The children inherit only because their parents did not happen to live as long as they had expected to and had not invested their saving in a life annuity.

Accidental bequests are consistent with the logic of the life cycle model and may be illustrated simply by taking the case of an individual whose life is divided into two periods. The first is that of his working life during which

2 See, e.g., DAVIES (1981).

his income (equal to y) is used for his immediate consumption (c_1) or for consumption in the second period, that of retirement (c_2). Unfortunately, he is not certain to live on into retirement (his probability of survival is equal to s). With an interest rate of r and a logarithmic utility function, his problem consists of choosing the value of c_2 which guarantees maximum expected utility: i.e. $\log (y - c_2/(1+r)) + s \log c_2$. This optimal value is given by:

$$c_2^* = \frac{s}{1+s} y(1+r) \qquad (1)$$

with the constraint of non negative wealth.

If the individual dies before retirement (the probability of this is $1-s$), c_2^* is the amount of accidental bequest he involuntarily leaves. Expression (1) above is not difficult to interpret. If it were certain that death would occur at the end of the person's working life, everything would be consumed during this period ($c_2^* = 0$). On the other hand, if it were certain that the individual would live a maximum number of years, savings would be equal to one half of his income. These two cases preclude an accidental bequest. However, the latter will exists if s is positive but less than 1 as long as there is no effective annuity market (which is the case here). The higher the probability of survival is, the greater the amount is, although its frequency ($1-s$) is proportionally lower.[3]

If it were possible to receive a life annuity equal to $(1+r)/s$ for each unit of premium paid in period 1 (e.g., if there were such a thing as actuarially neutral life insurance), accidental inheritance would cease to be and the consumption path would be $c_1 = c_2/(1+r) = y/(1+s)$.

One could raise the question of why annuity markets are not that developed. There might be no such a demand for them because of some social norms. This leads to another point about accidental bequests. Suppose that parents are altruistic towards their children but would not leave them anything if fair annuities were available because their children are well-provided for through the secular growth in wages. In the absence of annuities these parents know that some bequest will inevitably be left and may find this highly desirable.

---

3 Within the simple example, the average level of accidental bequests is maximized for $s = 1/2$ and then equal to $y(1+r)/3$.

2. Voluntary Bequests

In accidental inheritances, neither the presence of children nor even of heirs is really required. Voluntary inheritances, on the other hand, depend on the presence of children. It was long held that intentional inheritances were the norm and, even more so, were motivated by altruism. The anthropology and sociology of the family have since taught us, however, that many different forms of voluntary bequests and family models exist. At one extreme, there is the family where solidarity and generosity prevail, while at the other there is the model of give and take where exchange is sometimes equitable and sometimes not. In this survey of intentional inheritance models, we will move gradually from pure altruism to strategic exchange which gives rise to an arrangement rather unfavourable to children.

a) Altruistic Bequests[4]

The stereotyped representation of inheritance clearly corresponds to the model based on *pure altruism*; i.e. parental love and filial piety. When making decisions on consumption and savings, parents take into account their children's preferences while anticipating their income and future needs. The property of concavity of their utility function implies that in the absence of constraints they will attempt to distribute their incomes and those of their children over time so as to *smooth* out the consumption of both parties. The concept of smoothing is already present in the life cycle hypothesis where the consumption path is independent of the income path but it is here extended to the infinite duration of a dynasty.

In this context, parents have two ways of raising their children's resources: human capital (education) transfers increase their wages and non human transfers their financial wealth. They choose the amount they wish to invest in their children's education and that to be given then in the form of *inter vivos* gifts or bequests. Their sole objective is to ensure that consumption will be divided up equitably either between them and their children or amongst the children themselves. Insofar as the return of education is variable - at first it is a great deal higher than that of financial assets before it diminishes - parents cover educational costs until the return

4 The classical references are BECKER and TOMES (1979, 1986) and BARRO (1974).

on education is equal to that of physical assets; thereafter, they make *inter vivos* gifts or bequests so as to maximize the utility of the extended family.

Choices such as these have immediate implications. If inequalities of talents or fortune exist between parents and children or between children themselves, intergenerational transfers will be tuned so as to reduce them if not eliminate them entirely. Let us take the case of two brothers: one is gifted and will have no problem acquiring a top-flight education, while his brother, unable to obtain a qualification of any kind, will be forced to take a menial job. In an altruistic environment, the latter should receive a great deal more overall from his parents than his brother; however, it is probable that strictly in terms of education costs, the opposite will be true. In a model where differences in talent are contingent on circumstances and where the brothers enjoy the same standard of living thanks to their parents' *compensatory* transfers, the members of the following generation all start from the same stand. Thus, if parents are not prevented from exercising free choice for reasons connected to their wealth, altruism or luck itself, there should be great social stability within the dynasty. Intrafamily transfers insure each of its members against the vagaries of fate or nature.

Yet, there are limits to parental choice; problems of incentives, moral hazard and adverse selection cannot be avoided. In making their transfers, parents would like to be sure that their kids really need them and will not rely on them to shirk the rest of their life.[5] But it is often argued that even though parents cannot forgo problems linked to asymmetric information, they are in a much better position than the government. This relative superiority is often viewed as a key argument against any public interference with private intergenerational transfers.

Moreover, parents may not be able to transfer as much as they might wish. In this case, they will give priority to investments in human capital where the return is greater than that on physical investments. The latter will thereby not be able to perform their role as buffers, and parent-children as well as children-children inequalities may subsist. To illustrate this inheritance model, let us suppose that an individual's utility function depends on his life cycle consumption C_p and that of his only child C_k. His resources are given and equal to W_p, while his child's depend on the inheritance to be bequeathed to him (I_k) and his earned income $Y_k(X)$, which

5 See on this Bruce and Waldman (1990), Lindbeck and Weibull (1988), Cremer and Pestieau (1996), Richter (1992).

is a function of his education X. It is assumed that the child's resources are entirely consumed. Given a logarithmic utility function for the consumption of the two generations and a simple exponential function for the return on education, the parents' problem comes down to maximizing the following expression:

$$U = \log C_p + \beta \log C_k = \log(W_p - X - \frac{I_k}{(1+r)}) + \beta \log(4\sqrt{X} + I_k) \tag{2}$$

where r is the intergenerational interest rate, β the rate of altruism and $Y_k(X) = 4\sqrt{X}$, the earnings function. First-order conditions are written as follows:

$$\frac{\partial U}{\partial I_k} = -\frac{1}{(1+r)C_p} + \beta\frac{1}{C_k} = 0\ (>0), \qquad I_k > 0\ (=0) \tag{3}$$

$$\frac{\partial U}{\partial X} = -\frac{1}{C_p} + 2\beta\frac{1}{C_k\sqrt{X}} = 0, \qquad X > 0 \tag{4}$$

As the marginal return on human capital is infinite when $X = 0$, education will always be positive. Moreover, investment in human capital has priority as long as its return is greater than $1+r$, which is the case as long as education is below a threshold equal to $X^* = (2/(1+r))^2$. All transfers beyond this threshold are material. Let us consider the case where $W_p = 16$, $r = 0$ and $\beta = 1$ (pure altruism). It results that $C_p = C_k = 10$, $X = X^* = 4$ and $I_k = 2$. There are no constraints and the investment in human capital is optimal with its marginal return being equal to 1, like that of financial capital.

This case of 'unconstrained' altruism led Becker (1974) to the famous *rotten kid* theorem. Let us imagine that a child such as the one described can increase his resources by A and that, as a consequence, his parents' resources would be diminished by $B > A$. For example, he could force his parents to move closer to his secondary school, which would cost them more than it would bring him. Even if he were totally indifferent to his parents' welfare, such a decision would be counterproductive, causing a fall in dynastic income S_p, which is equal here to $W_p - X + (Y_k(X)/(1+r)) = 20$ (if

$X = 4$), and a consequent drop in his own consumption C_k (here equal to $S_p/2$). This 'rotten kid' theorem has led to a number of theories on the *neutrality* of public policy to which we shall come back. But let us return to the issue of bequest.

The choice between education and inheritance is represented in Figure 3.1. It is immediately clear why investing either more or less than the amount of 4 in education would not be optimal in the example given above.

Figure 3.1: Education and Inheritance

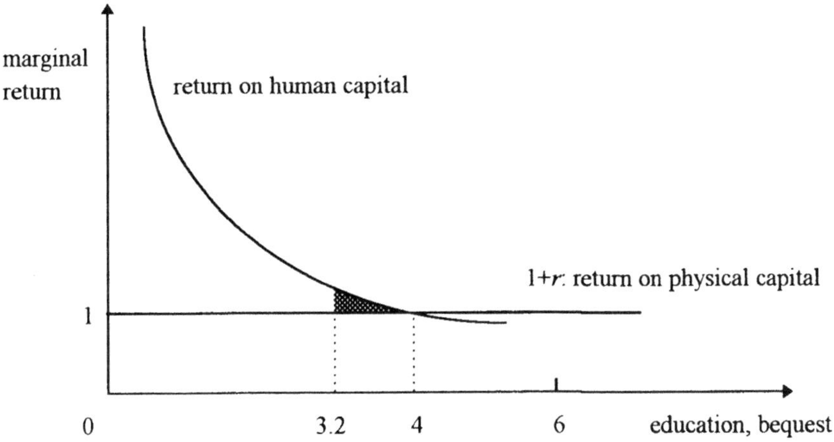

Let us within our example suppose that altruism is less than pure ($\beta = 0.5$). With $W_p = 16$, the bequest then falls to 0 and the optimal level of education must satisfy the following conditions:

$$-\frac{1}{C_p} + \frac{1}{C_k\sqrt{X}} = 0; \quad C_k = 4\sqrt{X}; \quad \text{and} \quad C_p + X = 16 \tag{5}$$

This gives $X = 3.2$, $C_p = 12.8$ and $C_k = 7.16$. If the parents' initial resources were greater, it would be possible to avoid this constraint on education while keeping $\beta = 0.5$. Let us suppose, for example, that $W_p = 20$, yielding $X = 4$ and $I_k = 0$. This clearly illustrates the two factors leading to altruistic bequests: substantial parental resources and as high a rate of altruism as possible.

It has been presumed that where education is not able to reach its optimal level, there is no inheritance. The condition $I_k \geq 0$ is crucial here. If children could borrow from a financial organization or from their parents the amount enabling them to reach the threshold $X^* = 4$, they would seek a loan of 0.8. This education loan would bring in more in present value than it would cost: the net profit is represented by the shaded triangle in Figure 3.1 which is equivalent to 0.04 (with C_k equal to 7.2 instead of 7.16). However, this type of loan is rare in practice. Furthermore, a negative bequest or a loan on uncertain future income raises problems of credibility. How can we be sure that our own children will pay off our debts, even if they have been incurred to provide them with the best education possible?[6]

The consequences of altruistic behaviour in the context of such loans raise an interesting question. In fact, the solution obtained is not what is optimal from the parents' viewpoint. Indeed, if the non-negativity constraint of bequests were to be dropped and thus if parents could force their children to pay them the amount corresponding to their maximal utility (and not only the education loan) they would be imposing a negative inheritance equal to 1.3 in the preceding example ($W_p = 16$; $\beta = 0.5$). Such a bequest corresponds to condition (3) when no constraint has been placed on the sign of I_k.[7]

In other words, if parents cannot impose negative bequests and if children can borrow the amount required for their education not provided by their parents, the consumption levels obtained do not correspond to maximum parental utility, regardless of how altruistic this utility may be. Instead, they favour the children to the detriment of the parents.

This illustrates again that altruism in the neo-classical sense of the term is not to be confused with generosity nor disinterest. Quite often, one makes a distinction between altruistic households who leave positive (operative) bequests and those who are constrained by the non negativity constraint on bequests (if they could, they would force their children into giving them some resources) and thus do not leave any. One cannot say that the former are more altruistic than the latter.

6 For a discussion of this issue, see BARHAM et al. (1995).

7 In this case, $C_k = \beta C_p = (0.5)C_p$, and finally: $C_p \approx 13.3$; $C_k \approx 6.7$; $I_k = C_k - Y_k \approx 6.7 - 8 \approx -1.3$.

Finally, in the above example, we have used a two period model. In the standard model of Becker (1974, 1991) and Barro (1974), generations are linked together through an infinite dynastic chain that is only viable if every link of that chain leaves a positive bequest (which means that parents care for their children's utility and not just for their income or consumption). We shall come back on this approach.

b) Paternalistic Bequests

The paternalistic bequest is closely related to the altruistic one. Paternalistic parents also accumulate savings with the intention of transmitting them to their children. Yet the amount and structure of the bequest are based not on their children's preferences but rather on their idea of what is good for their children, or uniquely on the pleasure they might derive from giving. Models dealing with paternalistic bequests are often referred to as bequest-as-consumption models because bequest appears in the parents' utility function as any other consumption goods. While it is possible for paternalistic and altruistic bequests to coincide, generally speaking this is not the case. Paternalistic bequests consist of assets which the heir does not really need, such as family possessions bequeathed inopportunely, i.e. without the economic situation of the children being taken into account.

Formally, one can write the parents' problem as maximizing:

$$U(C,B) = U(W - nB(1+\tau), B) \qquad (6)$$

where $U(C,B)$ is their utility function, C denotes their own lifetime consumption, B is the net amount of bequests per child, W their lifetime income, n the number of children, and τ the rate of estate taxation.[8] In other words, the gross-of-tax estate is $nB(1+\tau)$. It is often assumed that the elasticity of B with respect to W is higher than 1 and that with respect to τ and n it is negative (although total gross-of-tax estate is increasing with n).

A variant of the paternalistic bequest, put forward in particular by Modigliani (1986), assumes that the amount of the bequest does not depend on the *absolute* amount of the family's resources but rather on its *relative* value within the generation to which it belongs, the idea being that a family's consumption needs tend to increase with economic growth from one generation to the next.

---

8 See, e.g., BLINDER (1974, 1976b).

c) Retrospective Bequests

We now come to a category of models that share a number of common features: (i) bequest is motivated by some altruism that is labelled *ad hoc* relative to pure altruism à la Barro-Becker; (ii) information is limited and forecast imperfect so that parents decide to leave their children a bequest commensurate to what they themselves received; (iii) this implicit rule 'Do unto your children as you would have liked your parents to have done unto you' is rooted in social norms of *deferred reciprocity* as if bequests were made to one's children *in return* for received inheritance from one's parent. This social or rather family norm is related to what sociologists call *habitus*.

In general these models are cast in a three-generations setting and lead to social optimality if not the golden rule. However, this optimal equilibrium is not a market one but one that is based on a commitment to a perennial norm. Even though this commitment is Pareto optimal, one cannot exclude the possibility of rupture in the intergenerational social compact. Bevan (1979), Bevan and Stiglitz (1979), Cigno (1995), Cox and Stark (1994) have developed models which belong to this category of bequests.

d) Bequests Based on Pure Exchange

Intergenerational exchange was common in traditional societies. Parents took care of their children until they reached adulthood and promised to leave them an inheritance (often their work tools). In exchange, children promised to look after their parents once they reached old age, or even earlier in the event of failing health. This type, known as bequest for exchange, is still practiced in rural areas and is related to the *old-age security* hypothesis that is used to explain fertility.

There are a wide variety of bequests-as-exchange models; they have in common that parents care about some service or action undertaken by their children especially to secure old-age needs, and that the education and bequests are the payment for this service or this action. They differ in the nature of what is exchanged, in the timing of the exchange and in the enforcement mechanism (courts, altruism, economic punishment or rewards). Why not always rely on the market? When the market option is rejected, it is primarily because of higher transaction costs. The family is capable of carrying out the tasks of middlemen or insurers much more cheaply than commercial companies. In addition, family members have more complete information on the risks of illness or death when financing retirement and on individual talents and motivations when financing education. In the traditional family, for instance, the weight of custom and geographic immobility helped to ensure that these engagements were honoured.

In Kotlikoff and Spivak (1981), exchange leads to annuity-type contract; in Cox (1987), one has an exchange of services; in Cox (1990), one finds a scheme of loans by parents that are mutually advantageous; Desai and Shah (1983) study the old-age security hypothesis within traditional families.

In the same vein, Stark (1995), Becker (1993) and Cremer and Pestieau (1994) have introduced the idea of 'preference shaping' through education as a means to facilitate and secure exchange in general and support in particular. They consider a two stage model. In the first, parents attempt to inculcate values in their children; in the second, when those values (guilt for misbehaviour) are planted, children are ready to trade attention for bequests in terms that are quite favourable to their parents.[9]

e) Strategic Bequests

In the modern family, it is easy and unfortunately common for children not to come to the aid of their elderly parents. However, filial ingratitude is hardly a new phenomenon. Two famous literary representations come to our mind. Shakespeare's King Lear's misfortunes are well-known, but Balzac's Père Goriot experienced a hardly less tragic fate: "He had given his heart and soul for twenty years, his fortune in one day. When the lemon had been squeezed dry, his daughters dropped the peel at the corner of the street". These two works show why more than one parent try to eschew premature bequeathing.

This leads us quite naturally to a particular type of bequest, the strategic bequest, that in many respects belongs to the bequest for exchange category. It is one of the ways of enforcing exchange within the family when there is a time lag between the giving and the receiving and there is no credible recourse to the legal power of the courts and the state.

As formalized by game-theory economists[10], strategic inheritance brings parents at the beginning of retirement face to face with their children who

---

9 See also on this the critique by ALTONJI et al. (1995).

10 Here we present the model of BERNHEIM et al. (1985). There are other bequest-as-exchange models with strategic features, although less pronounced. See, e.g., COX (1987).

are just starting their working lives. The parents possess wealth A_p which they intend either to spend themselves or bequeath to their children. They want each of their children to help them and pay additional attention to them (a_k). Each child wishes to receive as large an inheritance as possible; at the same time, spending time with his aging parents is costly (at least beyond a certain threshold) in terms of forgone leisure or earnings on the market. The game follows a precise chronology. First, the parents make a commitment as to the total amount of the bequest and to a rule whereby this amount will be divided according to the level of attention provided by each child. For these promises to be credible, the commitment must be binding. Throughout this period, the children do not cooperate with each other and each gives his parents the amount of attention he considers optimal given the inheritance he will derive from it. At the end of this period (i.e. following the death of both parents), the inheritance is divided as stipulated. It is clear that the trump card in this game is held by the parents. Operating according to the adage 'Divide and rule', they extract the maximum from each of their children under the threat of disinheriting them.

Let us now represent the problem facing two children in the form of a graph. At first, each has one unit of leisure time endowment. Without inheritance, each would spend the amount c_0, the balance of his income and savings. The parents, banking on the lack of collusion between their children and the possibility of disinheriting one to the advantage of the other, will choose the points on their indifference curves which brings them the greatest satisfaction (represented in Figure 3.2 by E_1 and E_2). In fact, the second child has more leisure time than his sibling (whose career is more time consuming) and/or his attention is, other things being equal, more coveted by his parents. (There may be a prior bargaining procedure between parent and child over the *price* of attention.) Consequently, he will be likely to receive a larger inheritance in return for less attention. In spite of these differences, however, neither child will ultimately be better off than before the exchange.

Figure 3.2: Strategic Inheritance

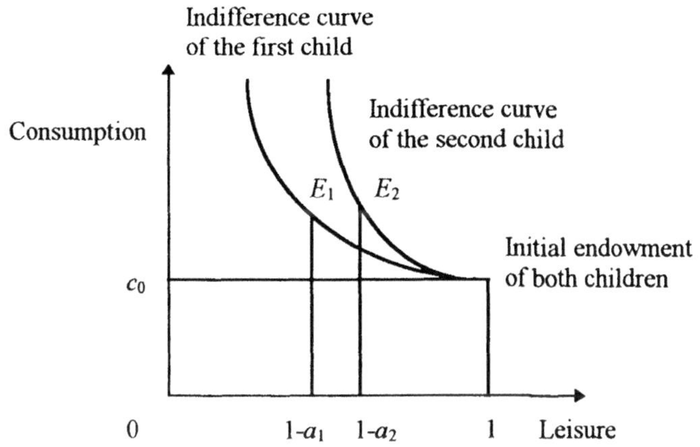

3. Capitalist Bequests

The term *capitalist* or *entrepreneurial bequests* evokes the image of the entrepreneur found in Ricardo (1817) and classical economists in general[11]: an austere individual infused with the *Weberian Protestant ethic*, investing everything he earns and extending his scope of decision-making beyond his own existence. While accidental inheritance touches all classes of society, this type concerns only the well-to-do[12]. The famous American billionaire Howard Hughes, who left behind a vast financial empire but no direct heir upon his death 20 years ago, comes to mind. This is the prototype of wealth so great that it may not be consumed in a single lifetime. It has an existence of its own which in a certain way exceeds its owner's control. Even access to the annuity market and knowledge of one's lifespan would not change the situation in the least. Parents in possession of such wealth, even those devoid of any concern for their family, have no choice but to bequeath it, most

11 See also MOORE (1979).

12 For an empirical test, see ARRONDEL and LAFERRÈRE (1996) who distinguish the behaviour of wealthy households from that of the 'top heavy' ones.

likely to their children in societies where the latter may not be disinherited. In any event, there will be an estate whether there are children or not.[13]

So far, we have focused on one factor: the very impossibility of spending an excessive amount of wealth in one generation (this applies to the 1% richest families who, in most countries, possess nearly one quarter of all wealth). There is another motivation in capitalist bequest: the desire to leave a perennial trace, like a financial or industrial dynasty. One thus thinks of individuals such as John D. Rockefeller.

Children and grandchildren are then needed not so much out of altruism but as a necessary means of perpetuation. But as will appear below, there is a formal analogy between this type of bequest and those left out of altruism within the Becker-Barro model.

In the next Section we will look at the implications of the various models we have presented here. Before we do so, we have to mention a couple of limitations in particular to the altruistic model. First, one has to do with the fact that households of married children have two sets of parents. Bernheim and Bagwell (1988) point out that if both sets choose positive bequests, all parents would be connected, which does not seem to be persuasive in practice. Accordingly, Laitner (1991), following Becker (1991), models the process of assortative mating as a non-cooperative (Nash) equilibrium. Parents adjust their bequests to help their children compete for desired mates and, in the end, only parents of similar economic standing get linked. This suggests that the standard formulation with one child per family and no marriage produces the same outcome as one with two children per household and assortative mating. A second limitation is *two-sided* altruism: children may care about their elderly parents as well as parents about their grown up children. One good reference on this is Laitner (1988) who concludes that the standard theory remains valid only for forward bequests, from parents to children.[14]

---

13 There is the example of Alfred Nobel who left his wealth not to his family but to the well-known Nobel Foundation.

14 See also KIMBALL (1988).

III. Economic Implications

Lying behind these types of bequests is a whole range of behaviour, all the way from pure altruism to selfish manipulation and absolute indifference to the children. From a normative point of view, many will prefer altruistic behaviour but in reality, one finds a little of everything (reality is not as schematic as our categories).

What might the economic interest of this typology be? Is it important to know if certain types of behaviour become more frequent and others less so in time and space? Might the likely shift in behaviour in the direction of exchange and strategic attitudes be indicative of a change in values? This is not the economist's most immediate concern. He is interested in the different types of inheritance because each has specific *implications*. For example, it may be shown that the effectiveness of economic policy may be entirely different depending on which type of behaviour predominates.

Here we only address two series of implications: that on both intergenerational and intragenerational redistribution within and across families and that on the effectiveness of fiscal policy. So doing, we restrict the analysis to four types and models of bequests: accidental, altruistic, paternalistic and strategic. We now discuss the two series of implications summarized in Table 3.2.

Table 3.2
Implications of the Four Basic Inheritance Models

	Implication	Nature of bequest
		Accidental
Effects of bequest on *intrafamilial* inequality	1 - *Inter*generational disparities of well-being between parents and children	no intentional effect
	2 - *Intra*generational disparities of well-being between co-inheritor children	no intentional effect
	3 - Is there *a priori* equal sharing of inheritance between children ?	no
Effects of bequest on social inequalities	4 - Degree of instantaneous concentration of wealth	weak negative effect
	5 - Intergenerational immobility of wealth: degree of correlation between inheritances left by fathers to sons	quasi-absence of correlation
	6 - Intragenerational inequality of life cycle resources	absence of overall effect
Effects of fiscal policy	7 - Effect of a public loan paid back by the following generation on current consumption	positive
	8 - Effect of an increase in retirement coverage on steady-state capital accumulation	negative
	9 - Effect of estate taxation on saving	nil

Table 3.2 (continuation)

Nature of bequest		
Altruistic (unconstrained)	Paternalistic	Strategic
reduces or eliminates the inequality	no intentional effect	no intentional effect
reduces or eliminates the inequality	no intentional effect	no intentional effect
no	yes	no
very marked positive effect	moderate and variable effect	weak and variable effect
very strong correlation (greater than that of income)	very weak correlation	very weak correlation
weak and rather negative effect	weak and variable effect	absence of overall effect
absence of effect (hypothesis of neutrality)	positive	positive
nil	negative	negative
negative	negative	nil

1. Distributive Implications

a) Intergenerational Family Redistribution

Starting with the issue of intergenerational redistribution, one can raise the question of whether or not bequests help reduce differences in the standard of living from one generation to the next within the family.

One might expect inheritances based on pure altruism to have a smoothing effect of this kind, especially if a choice need not be made between education and a material bequest. After all, the main function of the altruistic model is to bring parents' and children's standards of living closer together or, to be more precise, to generate an optimal intergenerational redistribution of resources. The desired smoothing out of consumption does not necessarily entail equalization; wealthy parents may indeed wish to reduce the gap in resources between themselves and their children but not to eliminate it altogether. What can be said is that *at given parental resources and level of education*, the probability of transmission as well as the amount of the bequest decline with the life cycle income of the child (independent of inheritance) or with the *average* level of this income for all children. There is thus a *double compensation* between parents and children and between children.

In the other forms of inheritance, parents adopt no particular position on intergenerational inequality: they wish neither to reduce nor to reinforce it. *Ex post* however, the models in which bequest is a luxury may also induce a compensation effect, albeit less pronounced than in the case of altruism, if there is some regression towards the mean income: wealthy parents will leave large inheritances to children who on average are less privileged at the outset. Thus the existence of a compensation effect, although clearly in keeping with the altruistic model, does not necessarily exclude other forms of bequests. However, it is difficult to reconcile it either with accidental bequests or those based on certain kinds of exchange.

In an attempt to develop a more discriminating test of the altruistic model, Cox (1987) proposes a form of strategic exchange inheritance model different from the pure sort put forth by Bernheim et al. (1985)[15]. At a given

15 The reader wishing further details is referred to COX's article (1987). In fact, his is a two-tiered transfer model (altruistic and strategic) depending on whether the child extracts a useful gain from the 'game' (attention in exchange for the

level of parental income, both models predict that the decision to transmit or the *probability* of transmitting are negatively correlated with the child's personal resources. However, the altruistic model is the only one to predict that the effect of a child-beneficiary's resources on the *amount* received will always be negative. On the other hand, Cox states that an exchange bequest will be either compensatory, neutral or anti-compensatory depending on the elasticity of parental demand for the child's attention; it will be more likely *anti-compensatory* if the implicit price of child's services increases with child's income. In any case, within bequest-as-exchange models, whether they are strategic or not, the issue of compensatory bequests has to be dealt with carefully. What really matters is comparing utility levels. A large bequest does not necessarily imply high utility as there is a price for it: attention given or services provided.

b) Intragenerational Family Redistribution

The other issue concerns *intragenerational redistribution*. One can in that respect ask whether or not bequests reduce income disparities between heirs. The answer to this question is similar to the response above. Bequests prompted by pure altruism will indeed reduce certain disparities between children; this is not true, however, for other types of bequests. As noted above, in an asymmetric information setting with either moral hazard or adverse selection, the capacity of parents to redistribute resources across generations or among their children can be eroded.

In the case of strategic behaviour, for example, it is conceivable that children of limited ability may not be able to help their parents and hence have no chance of receiving an inheritance from them. A child who is well-off and whose work places excessive demands on his time may receive a

---

promise of an inheritance) with his parents or not. COX and RANK (1992) and COX (1987) find that *inter vivos* transfers are more likely to be exchange-motivated. There are, however, several pitfalls with these findings. First, as ALTONJI et al. (1995) emphasize, this test may be biased against the altruism hypothesis, owing to selection problems: for given parental income, increasing child's income means also considering parents with stronger degree of altruism in order to get a positive transfer. Second, some *inter vivos* transfers, especially received when young, are likely to increase *human* capital and child's *income* rather than wealth. Third, there may be substitution or complementarity between *inter vivos* transfers observed and future ones, especially bequests at death.

great deal if his parents value his attention, whereas his unemployed brother will receive a relatively small inheritance given the time he spends with his parents. This leads to the issue of *equal sharing*.

In the altruistic and strategic models, equal sharing is likely only if the children are identical in all respects. As this is most often not the case, unequal sharing is to be expected. In the accidental or paternalistic models, there is nothing to prevent equal sharing, especially if this is the social norm. In any event, none of the models automatically leads to equal sharing, which is thus not a product of individual choices.

It is widely believed that mandatory equal sharing among children reduces the amount of inheritance. The effect of mandatory equal sharing may be considered analogous to that of inheritance taxation: both represent obstacles to the freedom of making out one's will. Forcing parent-savers to leave a portion of their wealth to a child they would prefer to disinherit has the same depressive effect as high inheritance taxes: it discourages saving. We may then surmise that altruistic bequests are discouraged by mandatory equal sharing (less, however, than if the rule of primogeniture prevailed). Accidental or paternalistic bequests are not affected by this type of constraint. Strategic bequests are most penalized by this measure, since it totally deletes the parents' threat to disinherit their children.

c) Transmission of Inequality

More generally, one can look at the role of inheritance in the transmission of resources and wealth inequality.

The altruistic model has very specific consequences for the transmission of income and wealth inequality as detailed in Becker and Tomes (1986). A considerable percentage of families leave virtually nothing behind them, investing only in their children's human capital. The intergenerational immobility of wealth (i.e. the correlation between the father's and son's wealth) in the inheriting population is great whereas incomes regress much more rapidly towards the mean. The amount transmitted is particularly large for the wealthiest parents who use it as a *buffer* to prevent their children's standard of living from being too low in comparison to their own (their offspring are generally not as well off in human capital). Finally, owing to the possibilities of substituting human capital and material wealth and the compensating role ascribed to inheritance, the correlation between inherited wealth and income in human capital must be limited.

On the contrary, accidental or strategic inheritance models produce almost total mobility of wealth from one generation to the next. The same is true of paternalist bequests, even when they are luxury goods.[16] Conversely, capitalist and especially retrospective bequests, as in the altruistic model, lead to a substantial immobility of wealth.

The intergenerational correlation in income for the United States is in the order of 0.20 to 0.25 for the whole of the population (see the survey in Becker and Tomes, 1986). The correlation between the inheritance (ultimately) left by the child-inheritor and the amount left to him by his father is approximately 0.70 on a sampling of wealthy families. The correlation between the amount inherited and human capital income is in the order of 0.12 (Tomes, 1981) to 0.20 (Davies, 1982). Finally, nearly 40% of families do not appear to leave a significant inheritance (Tomes, 1981). These results are entirely consistent with the scenario envisaged by the altruistic model but are not incompatible with either the retrospective type or a combination of, for example, accidental and capitalist bequests (the latter being the prerogative of the wealthiest families). Recently, Zimmermann (1992) and Solon (1992) have reached a quite different conclusion. They show that intergenerational mobility is less than was previously thought in the U.S.. Solon, for instance, obtains an estimate of the order of 0.40 for the intergenerational correlation in long run income. This is more in line with British findings where income correlation is nearly 0.40 while that of wealth varies between 0.48 and 0.59 (Harbury and Hitchens, 1979). This result has been confirmed by Dearden et al. (1995) who obtain for the UK a wealth correlation ranging from 0.44 to 0.58.

2. Fiscal Policy

We now turn to the implications of inheritance models on the efficacy of fiscal policy. Fiscal policy is here understood in two ways: wealth transfer

---

16 Based on a paternalistic transmission motive, BLINDER's simulation model (1976b) does not succeed in producing a significant degree of intergenerational wealth immobility for a range of (plausible) values of the bequest elasticity with respect to resources. DAVIES' simulation model (1983) does manage to do so by focusing on the compensatory role of the altruistic bequest.

taxation (inheritance and gift tax) and intergenerational public transfer (debt and social security).

a) Wealth Transfer Taxation

Wealth transfer taxation, typically an estate tax, will have allocative (efficiency) and redistributive (equity) implications that heavily depend on the type of bequest one has in mind. We start with the redistributive implications. The clear dividing line on this matter is between (unconstrained) altruistic bequests and all others. In an altruistic world consisting of identical (dynastic) families, we should let the *pater familias* redistribute resources *across* and *within* generations. Estate taxation is then undesirable. However, if income differences are wider across families than within families, one then faces a delicate tradeoff between two types of redistribution: public and private. The case for estate taxation will be enhanced if between-families inequality is higher than within-family one and if the efficiency cost of public redistribution is not much higher than that of private redistribution. This remark concerns only altruistic bequests. For all the other types of bequests, estate taxation is always desirable on redistribution grounds.

Let us now turn to efficiency considerations and analyze the allocative effects of a distortionary estate tax. We assume that the government runs a balanced budget and that the tax revenue is spent on public goods that enter agents' utility in an additive way. In other words, we focus on just the uncompensated price effect of wealth transfer taxation. In the altruistic model, when bequests are operative before and after the tax change, estate taxation discourages capital accumulation.[17] In the case of accidental bequests, estate taxation has no effect on saving. In the other models, bequest-as-consumption or bequest-as-exchange, taxing bequests is equivalent to taxing a particular type of future consumption. Under an assumption of gross substitutability, one can show that an uncompensated transfer tax has a depressive effect on capital accumulation.[18]

Does that mean that in general it is not desirable to tax wealth transfers? Not at all. Even when such a tax has a depressive effect on the capital-labour ratio, it can still increase welfare, granted that the overall economy is dynamically inefficient, namely there is too much capital. Further, even with

17 See CABALLE (1991).

18 CABALLE (1991), IHORI (1994).

dynamic efficiency, the desirability of a wealth transfer tax is a general equilibrium matter that ought to be dealt within the framework of optimal taxation theory.

b) Intergenerational Public Transfer: Social Security and Debt

Dynamic models of equilibrium can be divided in two streams depending on whether households are finite or infinite lived. In models of overlapping generations of *finite* agents, such as initially developed by Samuelson (1958) and Diamond (1965), the balanced growth path may be dynamically inefficient if agents happen to save 'too much'. Then, there is a case for fiscal policy such as public debt or pay-as-you-go social security that will improve the welfare of current and future generations by depressing capital accumulation. In models of *infinite* lived agents *à la* Ramsey (1928), the balanced growth path is efficient and there is no case for fiscal policy aimed at discouraging capital accumulation. There are two reasons for this. First, such fiscal policy is ineffective. Second, it is not needed on efficiency grounds at least; it is only desirable on optimality grounds if the planner's rate of time preference is lower than that of the households.

Implicitly bequests play an important role in this debate. Indeed, the infinite lived agents model can be shown as formally equivalent to a model of overlapping generations with altruistic preferences. To do that, one needs to be sure that each generation leaves positive (operative) bequests. With this assumption, one talks of a dynastic allocative problem whereby any exogenous change in the intergenerational allocation will be corrected by appropriately adjusting the flow of bequests in order to leave the utility path unaffected (Barro, 1974).

Thus the ineffectiveness of fiscal policy is guaranteed by forever unconstrained altruistic bequests. Take the example of an increase in public spending aimed at stimulating the economy and financed by borrowing instead of taxation. This technique will not work in families where intergenerational altruism is operative. Indeed, parents will not be taken in by this manoeuvring for they know that this public *manna* will ultimately have to be paid for by their children. Accordingly, they will increase the amount of their bequest proportionally. Unfunded public pensions have the same effect as public borrowing: they give to the present generation (pensioners) while making the following generation (the active contributors) pay. Any variation in public pensions should thus be neutralized in a society where altruistic bequests are the norm.

All the other forms of inheritance - strategic, paternalistic and accidental - do not generate this infinite dynastic chain. They are in that respect not really different from the life-cycle model or from the altruistic model with no bequests. They thus imply the same fiscal policy as in the models *à la* Samuelson-Diamond.

This does not mean that fiscal policy has the same effect regardless of the non altruistic models considered. Consider, for instance, the effect of increasing social security benefits. This will imply less precautionary saving and thus less accidental bequests. It will also depress savings in the other inheritance models but without so clearcut incidence on the level of bequests.

Real society comprises households exhibiting all sorts of behaviour towards inheritance. It is unlikely to expect that the vast majority of individuals either voluntarily makes or receives intentional bequests and that these bequests are motivated by altruism. Does that imply that the neutrality proposition does not hold as Bernheim (1989) argues? Michel and Pestieau (1994) show that it suffices that some individuals make altruistic bequests and thus constitute infinite dynasties to keep the standard result of infinite-life models: efficient dynamic path and ineffectiveness of intergenerational transfers.[19] However, even though macroeconomically neutral, debt policy and social security have real effects at the microeconomic level: they are shown to benefit the unconstrained altruistic households and hurt all the others households whether or not they leave bequests.

The intuition of this finding is as follows: in the steady-state, an ascending transfer such as generated by public borrowing decreases savings and thus the level of welfare of households whose bequests are either accidental, strategic or paternalistic. This drop in savings forces the altruistic households to save and bequeath more than before to keep the economy on the desired path. Such a 'forced savings' makes them wealthier and brings them more welfare.

This finding well illustrates the real meaning of unconstrained altruism in wealth accumulation. In fact, these altruistic dynasties are not much different from very wealthy dynasties that leave what we called earlier capitalist bequests. After all, the only difference between the two is the

19 The fact that the results hold only in equilibrium must be emphasized. If altruistic agents are very few in proportion, it may be necessary for them to hold unrealistic high amounts of wealth in order to keep the steady-state going.

motive: the welfare of children for the former and the perennity of wealth for the latter. In either case, one has a minority of agents who control wealth accumulation. There is also an analogy with Becker and Tomes's (1986) division of society in two classes: constrained and unconstrained altruists. Only the first need social security; the second can easily do without it.

A key objection to Michel and Pestieau's (1994) approach is that they assume that some individuals and their descendants are altruistic and make operative bequests for ever. Dutta and Michel (1995) and Gevers and Michel (1996) modify this assumption and assume that each individual has some probability of being selfish even though the proportion of altruists and of non-altruists in the population is constant over time. In that case, neutrality does not hold.

IV. Conclusion

In this paper we have presented a number of alternative models of inheritance, and we have shown the implications of each of them on the effectiveness of fiscal policy and on wealth and income distribution across and within generations.

These models can be divided in two categories: those which are well structured and have received a lot of attention in the theoretical literature: altruistic, exchange, accidental and strategic bequests; and those which are considered as rather *ad hoc* models even though they are quite intuitive and have received some empirical validation[20]: capitalist, paternalistic, and retrospective bequests. Moreover, each of these models has been presented in its purest version. This was for the clarity of the argument. Mixture of motivations can be and has been introduced. For example, Friedman and Warshawsky (1990) have studied the accidental inheritance models with some bequest motive; Kotlikoff and Spivak (1981) assume mutual altruism to enforce annuity-type contracts among family members.

As far as policy and distributional implications are concerned, it clearly appears, however, that the dividing line is between models with altruistic bequests that are fully operative and all the other inheritance models. With

20 See ARRONDEL, MASSON and PESTIEAU (1997).

altruistic bequests, we get neutrality of fiscal policy, income redistribution within each family and quite a lot of immobility of wealth across generations. With the other types of bequests, fiscal policy is not neutral. The distributive effects vary but overall they are not as conducive of intergenerational immobility of wealth as altruistic bequests.

The only exception to this rule occurs with estate taxation. Estate taxation has efficiency costs for all types of bequests except for the accidental ones.[21]

References

ALTONJI, J.G., HAYASHI, F. and KOTLIKOFF, L.J. (1995): *Parental Altruism and Inter Vivos Transfers: Theory and Evidence*, NBER Working Paper No. 5378.

ARRONDEL, L. and LAFERRÈRE, A. (1996): *Capitalist Versus Family Bequest: An Econometric Model with Two Endogenous Regimes*, Paris (DELTA), Doc. 96-06.

ARRONDEL, L., MASSON, A. and PESTIEAU, P. (1997): "Bequest and inheritance: Empirical issues and France-U.S. comparison", *this volume*.

BARHAM, V., BOADWAY, R., MARCHAND, M. and PESTIEAU, P. (1995): "Education and the poverty trap", *European Economic Review*, 39, pp. 1257-75.

BARRO, R.J. (1974): "Are government bonds net wealth?", *Journal of Political Economy*, 82, pp. 1095-117.

BECKER, G.S. (1974): "A theory of social interactions", *Journal of Political Economy*, 82, pp. 1063-93.

BECKER, G.S. (1975): "Human capital and the personal distribution of income: An analytic approach" (Woytinsky Lecture 1967), in: G.S. BECKER, *Human Capital*, New York (Columbia University Press), pp. 94-144.

21 We wish to thank Luc Arrondel, François Gardes, Anne Laferrère, Philippe Michel, Erik Schokkaert and Philippe Van Parijs for their comments on earlier versions of this paper. This paper is partly based on MASSON and PESTIEAU (1991).

BECKER, G.S. (1989): "On the economics of the family: Reply to a skeptic", *American Economic Review*, 79, pp. 514-8.

BECKER, G.S. (1991): *A Treatise on the Family*, Cambridge (Harvard University Press).

BECKER, G.S. (1993): "The economic way of looking at behavior", *Journal of Political Economy*, 101, pp. 385-409.

BECKER, G.S. and TOMES, N. (1979): "An equilibrium theory of the distribution of income and intergenerational mobility", *Journal of Political Economy*, 87, pp. 1153-89.

BECKER, G.S. and TOMES, N. (1986): "Human capital and the rise and fall of families", *Journal of Labor Economics*, 4, part 2, S1-S39.

BERNHEIM, B.D. (1989): "A neoclassical perspective on budget deficits", *Journal of Economic Perspectives*, 3(2), pp. 55-72.

BERNHEIM, B.D. and BAGWELL, K. (1988): "Is everything neutral?", *Journal of Political Economy*, 96, pp. 308-38.

BERNHEIM, B.D., SHLEIFER, A. and SUMMERS L.H. (1985): "The strategic bequest motive", *Journal of Political Economy*, 93, pp. 1045-76.

BEVAN, D.L. (1979): "Inheritance and the distribution of wealth", *Economica*, 46, pp. 1153-89.

BEVAN, D.L. and STIGLITZ, J.E. (1979): "Intergenerational transfers and inequality", *Greek Economic Review*, 1, pp. 8-26.

BLINDER, A.S. (1974): *Towards an Economic Theory of Income Distribution*, Cambridge, MA. (MIT Press).

BLINDER, A.S. (1976a): "Intergenerational transfers and life cycle consumption", *American Economic Review. Papers and Proceedings*, 66, pp. 87-93.

BLINDER, A.S. (1976b): "Inequality and mobility in the distribution of wealth", *Kyklos*, 29, pp. 607-38.

BRUCE, N. and WALDMAN, M. (1990): "The rotten kid theorem meets the Samaritan's dilemma", *Quarterly Journal of Economics*, 105, pp. 1165-82.

CABALLE, J. (1991): *Endogenous Growth, Human Capital and Bequests in a Life-Cycle Model*, University of Barcelona, mimeo.

CIGNO, A. (1995): *Saving, Fertility and Social Security in the Presence of Self-Enforcing Intra-Family Deals*, University of Florence, mimeo.

COX, D. (1987): "Motives for private transfers", *Journal of Political Economy*, 95, pp. 508-46.

COX, D. (1990): "Intergenerational transfers and liquidity constraints", *Quarterly Journal of Economics*, 104, pp. 187-217.

COX, D. and RAINES, F. (1985): "Interfamily transfers and income redistribution", in: M. DAVID and T. SMEEDING (Eds.): *Horizontal Equity, Uncertainty, and Economic Well-Being*, Chicago (University of Chicago Press), pp. 393-425.

COX, D. and RANK, M.R. (1992): "Inter-vivos transfers and intergenerational exchange" *Review of Economics and Statistics*, 74, pp. 304-14.

COX, D. and STARK, O. (1994): *Intergenerational Transfers and the Demonstration Effect*, CENTER, Tilburg University, Progress Report No. 37.

CREMER, H., KESSLER, D. and PESTIEAU, P. (1991): "Intergenerational transfers within the family", *European Economic Review*, 35, pp. 359-75.

CREMER, H. and PESTIEAU, P. (1993): "Education for attention: A Nash bargaining solution to the bequest-as-exchange model", *Public Finance*, 48 (supplement), pp. 85-97.

CREMER, H. and PESTIEAU, P. (1996): "Bequests as a heir 'discipline device'", *Journal of Population Economics*, 9, pp. 405-14.

DAVIES, J.B. (1981): "Uncertain lifetime, consumption and dissaving in retirement", *Journal of Political Economy*, 89, pp. 561-77.

DAVIES, J.B. (1982): "The relative impact of inheritance and other factors on economic inequality", *Quarterly Journal of Economics*, 97, pp. 471-98.

DEARDEN, L., MACHIN, S. and REED, H. (1995): *International Mobility in Britain*, Institute for Fiscal Studies, Working Paper W95/20.

DESAI, M. and SHAH, A. (1983): "Bequest and inheritance in nuclear families and joint families", *Economica*, 50, pp. 193-202.

DIAMOND, P.A. (1965): "National debt in a neoclassical growth model", *American Economic Review*, 55, pp. 1126-50.

DUTTA, J. and MICHEL, PH. (1995): *The Distribution of Wealth with Imperfect Altruism*, Louvain-la-Neuve (UCL, Core), CORE DP No. 9558.

FRIEDMAN, B.M. and WARSHAWSKY, M.J. (1990): "The cost of annuities: Implications for saving behavior and bequests", *Quarterly Journal of Economics*, pp. 135-54

GEVERS, L. and MICHEL, PH. (1996): *Economic Dynasties with Random Intermissions*, Louvain-la-Neuve (UCL, Core), mimeo.

GOLDBERGER, A.S. (1989): "Economic and mechanical models of intergenerational transmission", *American Economic Review*, 79, pp. 504-13.

HARBURY, C.D. and HITCHENS, D.M.W.N. (1979): *Inheritance and Wealth Inequality in Britain*, London (George Allen & Unwin).

IHORI, T. (1994): "Bequests, fiscal policy and social security" in: T. TACHIBANAKI (Ed.): *Savings and Bequests*, Ann Arbor (Michigan University Press), pp. 137-66.

KIMBALL, M.S. (1987): "Making sense of two-sided altruism", *Journal of Monetary Economics*, 20, pp. 301-26.

KOTLIKOFF, L.J. and SPIVAK, A. (1981): "The family as an incomplete annuities market", *Journal of Political Economy*, 89, pp. 372-91.

LAITNER, J. (1988): "Bequests, gifts, and social security", *Review of Economic Studies*, 55, pp. 275-99.

LAITNER, J. (1991): "Modeling marital connections among family lines", *Journal of Political Economy*, 99, pp. 1123-41.

LINDBECK, A. and WEIBULL, J.W. (1988): "Altruism and time consistency: The politics of *fait accompli*", *Journal of Political Economy*, 96, pp. 1165-82.

MASSON, A. (1995): "L'héritage au sein des transferts entre générations: Théorie, constat, perspective" in: CL. ATTIAS-DONFUT (Ed.): *La Solidarité Entre Générations*, Paris (Nathan), pp. 279-325.

MASSON, A. and PESTIEAU, P. (1991): "Types et modèles d'héritage et leurs implications", *Economie et Prévision*, No. 100-101, pp. 31-72.

MASSON, A. and PESTIEAU, P. (1994): "L'héritage et l'Etat" in: P. PESTIEAU (Ed.): *Héritage et Transferts Entre Générations*, Bruxelles (De Boeck), pp. 15-44.

MICHEL, PH. and PESTIEAU, P. (1994): *Fiscal Policy in a Growth Model with Both Altruistic and Non-Altruistic Agents*, Louvain-la-Neuve (UCL, Core), CORE DP No. 9449.

MODIGLIANI, F. (1975): "The life cycle hypothesis of saving twenty years later" in: M. PARKIN (Ed.): *Contemporary Issues in Economics*, Manchester (Manchester University Press), pp. 2-36 (also in *The Collected Papers of Franco Modigliani*, ed. by A. Abel, Cambridge (M.I.T. Press), 1980, Vol. 2, pp. 41-75).

MODIGLIANI, F. (1986): "Life cycle, individual thrift, and the wealth of nations", *American Economic Review*, 76, pp. 297-313.

MODIGLIANI, F. and BRUMBERG, R. (1954): "Utility analysis and the consumption function: An interpretation of cross-section data", in: K.K. KURIHARA (Ed.): *Post-Keynesian Economics*, New Brunswick, NJ (Rutgers University Press), pp. 388-436 (also in *The Collected Papers of Franco Modigliani*, ed. by A. Abel, Cambridge (M.I.T. Press), 1980, Vol. 2, pp. 79-127).

MOORE, B.J. (1979): "Life cycle saving and bequest behaviour", *Journal of Post Keynesian Economics*, 1, pp. 78-99.

PESTIEAU, P. (1991): "Formes d'héritages dans le débat macroéconomique contemporain", *Economie et Prévision*, No. 100-101, pp. 201-6.

RAMSEY, F.P. (1928): "A mathematical theory of saving", *Economic Journal*, 38, pp. 543-59.

RICARDO, D. (1817): *Principles of Political Economy and Taxation*, London (Murray).

RICHTER, W.F. (1992): *Bequeathing Like a Principal*, University of Dortmund, mimeo.

SAMUELSON, P.A. (1958): "An exact consumption-loan model of interest with or without the social contrivance of money", *Journal of Political Economy*, 66, pp. 467-82.

SHORROCKS, A.F. (1979): "On the structure of inter-generational transfers between families", *Economica*, 46, pp. 415-26.

SOLON, G.R. (1992): "Intergenerational income mobility in the United States", *American Economic Review*, 82, pp. 393-408.

STARK, O. (1995): *Altruism and Beyond*, Cambridge (Cambridge University Press.

TACHIBANAKI, T. (Ed.) (1994): *Savings and Bequests*, Ann Arbor (Michigan University Press).

TOMES, N. (1981): "The family, inheritance and the intergenerational transmission of inequality", *Journal of Political Economy*, 89, pp. 928-58.

TOMES, N. (1982): "On the intergenerational savings function", *Oxford Economic Papers*, 34, pp. 108-34.

TOMES, N. (1988a): "Inheritance and inequality within the family: Equal division among unequals, or do the poor get more?", in: D. KESSLER and A. MASSON (Eds.): *Modelling the Accumulation and Distribution of Wealth*, Oxford (Clarendon Press), pp. 79-104.

TOMES, N. (1988b): "The intergenerational transmission of wealth and the rise and fall of families", in: D. KESSLER and A. MASSON (Eds.): *Modelling the Accumulation and Distribution of Wealth*, Oxford (Clarendon Press), pp. 147-65.

WEIL, P. (1987): "Love thy children. Reflections on the Barro debt theorem", *Journal of Monetary Economics*, 19, pp. 377-91.

ZIMMERMANN, D.J. (1992): "Regression towards mediocrity in economic stature", *American Economic Review*, 82, pp. 409-29

Chapter 4

Bequest and Inheritance: Empirical Issues and France-U.S. Comparison

LUC ARRONDEL, ANDRÉ MASSON and PIERRE PESTIEAU

I. Introduction: the Economic Approach to Inheritance

Inheritance has long been a favoured research topic in the social sciences. Marxists viewed it as a privileged channel of class reproduction from one generation to the next. In anthropological studies of traditional or primitive societies, it plays a major role in revealing the structure of kinship relations and in the exchange of words, women and goods. Psycho-sociologists consider it first of all as a moment of crisis, but also one of truth, when hidden family links and relations to siblings, lineage and marriage are suddenly brought to light; moreover, they insist upon the double dimension, 'symbolic' (or sentimental) and economic, of inherited goods, and upon their process of 'appropriation' - how the heir must 'identify' himself with these family goods and then decide what to do with them (either keep them, or sell them, or whatever).

Economists have a peculiar and more distant approach to inheritance. On the one hand, it has been defined simply as intergenerational savings, and analysed as a factor of wealth accumulation that contributes to economic growth, and must be judged mainly from *efficiency* considerations; in this line, it has been contrasted with another means of securing growth and future generations' well-being, namely *education* assimilated with investment in children's human capital (call this the Marshallian view). On the other hand, inheritance - or rather its regulation - has been viewed, on *equity* as well on efficiency grounds, as an opportunity to redistribute wealth and resources *within* or *across* families, especially through estate taxation and division rules (call this Bentham's or Mill's view).

Modern economics of inheritance, most often framed in the neoclassical paradigm, share and develop both these views. Agents are assumed to make *rational* choices, based upon an extended and subjective analysis of (monetary and non monetary) benefits and costs, including opportunity costs of alternative uses of *time*, the most scarce resource. Moreover, the analysis of inheritance has benefitted from two theoretical developments.

The first one concerns *family economics*, which deals with both market and non-market activities: the family unit is essentially viewed as a network of exchanges and transfers among its members, whether in cash, in kind or in time; moreover 'family behaviour is active, not passive', reacting to changes in the environment and being able to reinforce or offset the effects of public action (Becker, 1988).

The second development concerns *overlapping-generations* models which focus simultaneously on the *two dependency periods* of life, childhood and old age: the family and/or the State have to see that the optimal investments have been made on the next generation - especially in the context of endogenous growth where human capital plays a key role - while ensuring that rising old-age needs are simultaneously secured.

For the economist, then, inheritance and bequest cannot be studied in isolation. One must take into account the potential relations of substitutability or complementarity between inheritance or gifts and other *private* transfers such as children's education, or *reverse* transfers, from children to parents: to what extent, for instance, 'exchange' relations take place over time within the family, where parents, in order to secure old-age needs, rely on children's attention or support provided in return to human and non human bequests; or what is the more profitable investment, education or inheritance, for 'altruistic' parents who desire to increase children's well-being. But one also has to consider complementarity or susbtitutability between inheritance and intergenerational *public* transfers (debt and social security in line of ascent, education and family allowances in line of descent), and more generally to predict private (family) responses to fiscal policy - whether estate taxation or transfer policy.

To carry out this comprehensive approach to inheritance, economists have elaborated formal and abstract *models* of inheritance and bequests, based on different assumptions concerning the personal *motivations* for intergenerational transfers. Hence, as recalled in Section II, each model pictures a 'possible world' with specific economic *implications* which, ideally, should fully characterize the role of inheritance on growth and distribution, as well as the impact and relevance of miscellaneous fiscal policies (see Masson and Pestieau, 1997).

Microeconomic data (whether estate data, cross-sectional sample surveys or even panels) are then used to convey a general picture of inheritance and bequests - their relative quantitative importance, their unequal diffusion within the population... -, and to focus on the main empirical issues, which have often generated hot debates: e.g. is inheritance the major factor of wealth inequality? Or does the less favoured child receive the largest transfer (gift or inheritance)? The results obtained should moreover allow us to test and to disentangle the different bequest models, that is to determine in which possible world we are more likely to be, or if the dominant type of bequest varies from one sub-population to another.

The analysis concentrates first on recent results obtained for France, and second, on empirical American studies (since 1979) - which are clearly the most numerous in this area. This international comparison brings additional insights about the determinants of bequest behaviour. The presentation focuses on main conclusions, avoiding technicalities (data characteristics, econometric specification, problems of interpretations...) which are particularly intricate in this domain (see Masson and Pestieau, 1991).

Section III deals with the role of bequests in wealth accumulation and concentration, and their relation to the bequeathor's life resources. Section IV focuses on the diffusion of the different forms of wealth transfers (either given or received, *inter vivos* or *post mortem*...). Section V concerns the relation of bequests (existence, amount) to the presence, number or 'qualities' of children. Section VI tackles additional issues, such as the likely influence of parental bequest behaviour on that of children. Finally, Section VII draws separate conclusions concerning the dominant motivations for bequests in the U.S. and in France, suggesting that the income or wealth disequalizing role of inheritance and the effectiveness of fiscal policies may be more important in the latter country.

II. Are the Alternative Models of Bequests Testable?

Although it does not pretend to be exhaustive, the literature has proposed different bequest models, often with opposite implications concerning the role of inheritance and the effect of fiscal policies. The problem then becomes that of finding empirical ways to discriminate between them.

1. Bequest Models, Transfer Motivations and Economic Implications

Three main types of bequest have thus been introduced (see Masson and Pestieau, 1997):

- *exchange*-motivated bequests where gifts or inheritance are (possibly deferred) payment for child services;
- *altruistic* bequests used by parents who care about the well-being of their progeny in order to obtain a desired distribution of resources and well-being within the family, between themselves and their children as well as among their children;
- *accidental* bequests due to precautionary motives against lifetime uncertainty in the absence of annuities: they are left by 'selfish' parents who do not want to trade with their children, and are therefore considered 'involuntary'.

This emphasis on motivation may appear quite psychological, but is not really so. Economists are not so much interested in personal motivations (nor in reproducing the complexity of real life). As Lucas (1981) emphasizes, they want the predictions of their abstract models to *mimic observed behaviour* and people's reactions to various individual or aggregate observable factors, at least on average and for a given *range* of environments and policies. If this is so, it is provisionally assumed that people behave *as if* they followed the logic of rational choice described by the model: they may well have multiple or mixed (conscious or unconscious) motivations for bequest, but the model is alleged to reveal the statistically predominant one. Consequently, it allows to assess the role of inheritance on growth and distribution as well, and to determine under what conditions, either hypothetical or not, a given policy measure may be highly recommended or, to the contrary, totally unsuitable.[1]

To be more specific, suppose that the economist may perform an *ideal experiment* where the estate tax rate is (unexpectedly) increased from 6% (the average French rate) to say 20%.[2] If this reform has little bearing on accumulation patterns and (before-tax) transfers, bequests are mainly accidental. If behaviour is driven by altruism, parents will try to share the burden of the tax between themselves and their children, so that both parents' and children's consumption will be similarly reduced: if they are rich and/or altruistic enough (interior solution), the before-tax transfer will then increase, but the after-tax inheritance will be reduced.[3] Finally, the tax increase is likely to be most distortionary if bequests are motivated by exchange: the before-tax transfer will probably decrease, at least if now parents can find (on the market) cheaper ways to secure old-age needs. The experiment may thus permit the disentanglement of the three main types of bequests.[4]

---

1 The economist admits that the point of view on the institution of inheritance - whether, say, it is a beneficial factor of economic progress or a harmful and unfair mechanism of social reproduction - is largely conditioned by personal values or experience and political preferences. People may thus have different views as to the trade-off between efficiency and equity, or the concept of equity itself. Nevertheless, a thorough empirical analysis, allowing to identify the dominant model of bequest in the society considered, would certainly restrict the possible range of acceptable opinions by making certain (extreme) positions untenable (MASSON and PESTIEAU, 1994).

2 Contrary to MASSON and PESTIEAU (1997) we deal here, as in the following examples of fiscal policy, only with naive comparative statics in a *partial equilibrium* framework, thus neglecting steady-state implications, tax incidence, and macroeconomic consequences of alternate uses of the tax revenue.

3 Alternatively, altruistic parents who do not have the required means will increase their investment in children's education but will not anymore leave bequests.

4 Yet, the analysis should be pursued one step further. Suppose that savings rates are found to be insensitive to the increased estate taxation from 6% to 20%, so that bequests of an accidental type seem to prevail. This does not imply that the same conclusion will obtain when tax rates are increased to 80% or even 100%, meaning partial of total confiscation of inheritance. In these circumstances, it may well be that the same people resort to the purchase of life annuities, even on very unfavourable terms (due to moral hazard, adverse selection, fraud,

Two other ideal experiments could do just as well. The first one would be a welfare transfer program targeted at indigent (grown-up) children. This policy measure would have no impact on accidental bequests driven by precautionary motives. Altruistic parents would cut transfers to indigent children who can tap government aid. But the effect on exchange-motivated gifts or bequests would be ambiguous: in this case, "public transfers need not 'crowd out' private ones", and indeed the latter "can actually reinforce rather than offset the effects of public income redistribution" (Cox and Rank, 1992, p. 305).[5]

The other experiment would be a rise in social security benefits: precautionary needs and accidental bequests would be reduced, but the amount of transfers made by altruistic parents in order to neutralize the redistribution engendered by the transfer policy increases. And one can show that the effect on exchange-motivated bequests would, once again, be ambiguous (depending on the specific form of exchange considered and on the degree of substitutability or complementarity between parental consumption and children's services).

2. Testing Bequest Models and Empirical Issues about Inheritance

There are two important caveats against this highly stylized analysis. The first one concerns the possibility of *heterogeneous* behaviour within the group considered. Indeed, the profusion of theoretical bequest models may reveal our difficulty in grasping the underlying motivations which could explain observed transfers, but may also correspond to a real heterogeneity in bequeathing patterns, from one country or social category to another - in the same way as anthropologists have shown family behaviour to vary a lot from one primitive tribe to another. One problem we shall encounter in

---

administrative costs...), leaving then no bequests. The model of accidental bequests may thus be valid only within a certain *range* of taxation policies, and one would like to use a general model of bequests with several regimes (altruistic, exchange, accidental), in which "only one motive determines behavior at the margin" (COX and RANK, 1992, p. 307).

5 They show that public redistribution will have a negative impact on the probability of *existence* of a transfer (as in the altruistic case), but a positive one on the *amount* of the transfer, whenever the implicit price of a child's services provided in exchange increases with a child's pre-transfer income.

empirical analysis consists then of isolating sub-groups for which specific dominant motives can be identified.

The second caveat is that ideal experiments like those presented above do not exist in the real world. Most of the economic implications of bequest models, concerning the role of inheritance on growth and distribution or the effects of various fiscal policy measures, are not generally testable, at least not directly. For instance, in the case of an increase in social security benefits, the models predict what will result, *ceteris paribus*, in comparative statics, i.e. in hypothetical time: they may have less to say about the consequences on actual savings behaviour engendered by the *historical* development of social security systems after the Second World War.[6]

The indirect way out is to look at the *individual determinants* of bequest choices within a given population, that is to determine how household differences in age or level of resources, in the number of children, in the level of education of parents and children... or even in (observable) family values, translate into differences in behaviour concerning the existence, amount and composition of bequests, the form taken by the transfer (whether helping out, *inter vivos* or *post mortem*), and estate division practices. The results obtained through statistical or econometric analysis will then be compared, as far as possible, with the alternative predictions of the theoretical models envisaged.

The tests will be conducted for France and the U.S. on the basis of *micro-data*. These are essentially of two types.

The first one is *estate duty data*, concerning *inter vivos* or *post mortem* transfers and collected on a yearly basis by the tax administration (see for the U.S., Menchik, 1980 and 1988; Bennett, 1990). Their main drawbacks are threefold: certain assets are tax exempt; some transfers (gifts handed over directly, bequests of modest value) are excluded, so that, in France for instance, official estate duty records involve only *half* of the people who died

6 The best empirical study devoted to that issue is American, conducted on a cohort of Wisconsin males, born between 1890 and 1899 (DAVID and MENCHIK, 1985): contrary to FELDSTEIN's view and the predictions obtained with accidental bequest models, individuals with a better social security coverage saved before retirement as much as the others; but contrary to the predictions derived from altruistic compensatory bequest models, social security benefits have been largely consumed, with little being left to the next generation. Of course, these results may owe a great deal to specific historical circumstances and expectations.

during the year; finally, individual information on the donor or the deceased, and even more on the donee or the heir are limited. This last shortcoming may be partially overcome by additional information, obtained through the administration, as in France (see Laferrère, 1988; Arrondel and Laferrère, 1991, 1992 and 1994) or, in the U.S., by merging estate data with social security files (Menchik and David, 1983; David and Menchik, 1985), matching estate tax and income tax return (Wilhem, 1996), or making interviews of recent heirs (Adams, 1980; Tomes, 1981, 1982 and 1988). This type of data, which is quite representative of the wealthier part of the population, has been collected for a longer period of time in the U.S. than in France, allowing then to compare parent's and child's bequests in order to assess the degree of intergenerational wealth immobility.

The second type of data comes from *households sample surveys*, wich cover a larger scope of transfers between parents and independent children households, including helping out through monetary or in kind (house) loans and regular financial aids, as well as small or undeclared gifts. These surveys may include a rich set of demographic and socioeconomic variables concerning parents and children, including levels of education, occupation and incomes, portfolio composition and amounts, gifts already received and bestowed, inheritance receptions and expectations, or even opinions and *intentions* concerning wealth transmission. There are two main problems with such data: information collected from households may not be fully reliable, and samples of limited size do not allow to cover the richest households. French studies using survey data include Arrondel and Masson (1991), Laferrère (1994), and more specifically on households' intentions with respect to wealth transmission, Arrondel and Perelman (1994) and Perelman and Pestieau (1991). American studies deal mainly with *inter vivos* transfers, given or bestowed over a given period of time (Cox, 1987 and 1990; Cox and Rank, 1992; Gale and Scholz, 1994).[7]

How have these data been used? It is wise to recognize that facts are always 'theory laden', and indeed economists' preconceptions - linked to the

7 See MASSON and PESTIEAU (1991) for more details. Moreover, American authors have sometimes used wealth *panel* data, either drawn from the 'Longitudinal Retirement History Survey', which allows notably to reconstitute intertemporal accumulation profiles (HURD, 1987; BERNHEIM et al., 1985), or from the 'Panel Study on Income Dynamics' (PSID), which gives detailed information on the extended family - parents and independent children (ALTONJI et al., 1989 and 1996; BEHRMAN et al., 1989).

specific predictions of the bequest models - have influenced the kind of questions being asked as well as the interpretation of the results. However, we shall try to take a fresh look at empirical issues about inheritance, since some of them clearly have independent interest. For instance, anyone who does not believe in individual rational choice with respect to estate division would nevertheless want to know if equal sharing is still the dominant pattern in countries like the U.S., where there is no constraint on estate division: children, if any, can be disinherited and transfer taxation is neutral, being of the estate taxation type (contrarily to the French case).

3. A Brief Review of the Different Types of Bequests

A quick reminder of the alternative bequest models may be useful at this level (see Masson and Pestieau, 1997). In view of the following empirical analysis, we will especially emphasize three kinds of predictions concerning: the effects of parental *resources* (whether it is mainly the rich who make important transfers); the influence of the number or characteristics of *children* on the amount of bequest or inheritance; the specific *form* of the transfers (*inter vivos* or *post mortem*).

Accidental bequests, representing deferred consumption, are proportional to the amount of life resources, do not depend upon the presence or quality of children, and are received only through inheritance.

Altruistic bequests are a luxury good (their share of life resources increases with the size of the latter), and are *compensatory* in two ways: first, bequests tend to compensate intergenerational differences, with lower average earnings of children eliciting larger bequests from parents; second, parents bequeath unequal amounts to their offspring, compensating children who have relatively lower earnings than their siblings. Moreover, a large part of transfers should be *inter vivos*, and bestowed especially when the children need them most, i.e. when they are liquidity constrained (although parents' loans to children may be also driven by exchange considerations).

Exchange-motivated bequests allow for different forms of exchange, from a '*pure*' one, when the transaction is 'fair', to a '*strategic*' type, where the parents capture the entire gain from trade using the threat of disinheritance to manipulate their children, playing each one against the others. Exchange-motivated bequests require the presence of children, but have otherwise more ambiguous predictions, depending on the type of exchange: bequests may be a necessity (their share decreases with the size of life resources) if the service provided by children, such as 'attention', is assumed to be so (because of saturation effects); strategic bequests can work only if there are at least *two* children; more importantly, bequests-as-exchange may often be *anti-compensatory*, perhaps among siblings but especially between parents and children.

Other types of bequests, which are not so well defined or modelled, will be also used in the empirical analysis.

Capitalist bequests concern well-to-do people or families and are usually part of a self-sustained accumulation process, children being primarily considered as a means of achieving the desired path of wealth accumulation (as in industrial or financial dynasties). They are usually of a very large size. Moreover, they do not depend upon the presence and quality of children, but may be received through gifts as well as inheritance.

Bequests are '*paternalistic*' when people derive direct utility from the size of bequest (perhaps owing to the 'joy of giving'), the latter being simply considered like an additional, albeit luxury consumption good. This type of bequests leads often to the same predictions as capitalist transfers, the main difference (apart from the size of the estate) being that they require the presence of children and increase with the number of them.

Bequests are '*retrospective*' when, for different reasons (perennity of family values or norms, transmission of *habitus*, limited information on descendants...), bequeathing patterns tend to be *reproduced* from one generation to the next: what is left is then commensurate to what has been received, and children are inclined to use the same form of transfer (helping out, loan of a house, *inter vivos*, inheritance with or without a will) as their parents. Otherwise, predictions are similar to that obtained for paternalistic bequests.

III. Inheritance, Accumulation and Concentration of Wealth

Before inquiring into the precise motivation for bequests, the first requisite is to have an idea of their relative importance. We have to know the shares of *inherited* and *self-accumulated* wealth in total existing assets: if the share of inherited wealth was found negligible, inheritance would be of limited interest for economists. The next question concerns of course the relation between inheritance and (wealth) inequality: in Atkinson's (1983) words, how relevant is "the man in the street's view of inheritance", associated with "the Rockefellers, the Rothschilds, and the Dukes of Westminster"? Or more generally, who is concerned by inheritance, and for how much?

1. The Quantitative Importance of Bequests in Wealth Accumulation

This issue has raised a hot debate between Kotlikoff (1988) and Modigliani (1988), the former claiming that the share of inherited wealth in the U.S. is close to 80%, the latter estimating it below 20% (it would be nil if there was only saving for retirement). How to account for such a huge discrepancy which shows that empirical measures are also 'theory laden'? Indeed, the two authors do not agree on: (i) the relevant unit of decision and the definition of a transfer; (ii) the way to evaluate the actual contribution to wealth accumulation of a transfer received in the past (Kessler and Masson, 1989; Kessler et al., 1991).

On the first point, Modigliani considers only inheritance and *major* gifts (i.e. that "add to children's wealth, not to consumption") between *independent* households, whereas Kotlikoff wants to add all transfers received above *18 years of age* ('adulthood'), including notably college education fees, which means twice as much transfers. Given our conventional definition of bequest, we have to side rather with Modigliani, while allowing for the fact that his evaluation may be somewhat underestimated.

On the second point, Modigliani wants to impute to the *contribution* of bequests to total saving only the sum *in real terms* of received transfers, whereas Kotlikoff wants to add to this the *accumulated interest* on transfers - once again doubling the figures (hence the discrepancy in the results, in the order of one to four). Who is right? Apparently no one since each convention relies on an arbitrary, *accounting* decomposition of wealth in inherited and self-accumulated shares (Blinder, 1988).

The right question to ask concerns the reduction of total saving engendered by a confiscation of bequests, or a uniform reduction of x% of their amounts. To perform such a thought experiment, one needs a *behavioural* and 'comprehensive' simulation model of accumulation, capable of reproducing the aggregate level and the distribution of wealth over time (from one generation to another). Estimates derived with this method are comprised between 35% and 40% for France, and should be slightly lower for the U.S. (Kessler and Masson, 1989). The contribution of bequests to wealth accumulation appears therefore substantial but not overwhelming.[8]

2. The Diffusion of Private Transfers and Their Relation to Saver's Life Resources

Who is concerned by inheritance? There are first important life-cycle factors. Table 4.1 shows that the average age at which inheritance is received during a given year is around 48 in France; however, one inherits earlier from parents, around the age of 42 (39 for the father, 46 for the mother) and a third of the transfers comes from other relatives. Gifts are naturally received earlier: at 38 on average (Laferrère, 1988 and 1991).

These timing effects make it difficult to infer the proportion of people expecting to eventually receive an inheritance during their lifetime. For France, using data on inheritance expectations and parental wealth, or considering subsamples where individuals have already lost both of their parents, it can be evaluated at around 60% for individuals, corresponding to *two thirds of the households* (owing to mating patterns). This proportion has certainly risen over time, and especially during the after-war period where old people have benefitted from a rapid growth in their income and wealth (and also from the development of social security).

The results appear roughly consistent with the percentage of deceased people *leaving no bequests* (taking into account previous transfers to children or wealth transmitted to the surviving spouse): although always difficult to assess, it seems to be around a good third, in France as in the U.S.. The majority of these have low incomes. It remains to be determined whether, among bequeathers, those leaving large estates are concentrated in

8 It is likely that this contribution of bequest has declined. In the 19th century, it was more difficult to build a fortune without a sizeable inheritance. Things have changed after the destructions of the first World War and the steady growth following the second one, although the last twenty years may have altered this secular trend.

high income strata, or more precisely, whether bequests are a *luxury* good. To test this, economists usually refer to the *elasticity* of bequests with respect to life resources. If this elasticity is constant, it must be superior to one for bequests to be a luxury good.

Table 4.1
Beneficiary Average Age

	Beneficiary						
	Spouse	Father or mother	Grand-father or grand-mother	Brother or sister	Other relatives	No relatives	**Total**
According to the sex of the beneficiary							
man	68	42	29	61	46	50	**46**
woman	65	42	29	67	50	51	**50**
Total	**66**	**42**	**29**	**65**	**48**	**51**	**48**
According to the sex of the deceased							
man	65	39	26	60	50	48	**47**
woman	68	46	31	70	47	52	**50**

Source : DGI-Insee, 1984 French estate data

For the U.S., estimates of this elasticity of bequests (or of received inheritance) among bequeathers are fairly scattered but generally superior to one: 1.3 for Adams (1980), 1.7 for Tomes (1981), a wide range from 0.9 to 2.9 for Tomes (1982) - depending on the functional form used and other parameters. Moreover, using estate data statistics relative only to wealthy people, Menchik (1980b) finds a higher elasticity of 2.5, while on the basis of the Longitudinal Retirement History Survey, Kotlikoff (1989), who substitutes bequeathable wealth for the amount of bequests, finds a much lower elasticity, in the range of 0.5 to 0.8 (depending on permanent income estimation). Methodological and empirical pitfalls aside, such a difference in estimates might also reflect the *heterogeneity* of the populations studied: e.g. Kotlikoff considers only the middle class to the exclusion of the well-to-do, while only the latter are represented in Menchik's sampling.

Hence arises the idea that the elasticity of bequests may *vary* (increase) along the income scale. Menchik and David (1983), clearly the most reliable study in this field, do corroborate this hypothesis while merging estate duty files and social security files: in each cohort, bequests are of a limited amount and of an elasticity inferior to one for the 80% lower incomes, but become much larger for the top 20% in permanent income, with an elasticity comprised between 2 and 3.

A similar procedure has been applied for France, with comparable although less striking results *both* on estate data (Arrondel and Laferrère, 1991) and sample survey (Arrondel and Masson, 1991). In the former case, for instance, the dividing line obtained through alternative functional forms is again between the 80% lower income and the top quintile of bequeathers: the elasticity of bequests is between 0.6-0.7 for the first group but around 1.6 for the second one.

Interestingly enough, these results may receive different interpretations. They are roughly compatible with altruistic behaviour throughout the entire population, but could also reveal an heterogeneity in accumulation patterns, as suggested by Modigliani (1986): the bottom 80% would be mainly life-cycle savers, whereas the top 20% would have a much longer horizon that extends to future generations.

3. The Effect of Bequests on Wealth Concentration and Inequality

The fact that the share of inherited wealth in total saving amounts to 40% may correspond to very different situations: a homogeneous society where the share of bequests is the same for everyone; or a society of castes, where the top wealth decile, owning half of total assets, has an inherited share of 80% and the rest of the population receives no bequest. Moreover, one cannot tell the effect of inheritance on wealth inequality simply from the fact that the distribution of inheritance is highly skewed like the distribution of wealth, the top 10% of estates representing each year more than half of total wealth transmitted: one has still to know *who receives what*, e.g. whether already wealthier households receive the largest transfers. To assess the role of inheritance, one should indeed compare the actual distribution of wealth with the one that would be obtained in a hypothetical situation where inheritance would be abolished or equally distributed among the population; but once again, one needs a behavioural simulation model to explore such a situation.

Anyhow, simple statistical descriptions and simulation models results seem to agree on several well accepted facts about inheritance (both in France and in the U.S.). Inheritance is probably the main factor of wealth concentration among the richest part of the population, and of its intergenerational reproduction. Thus, more than half of American citizens who have died rich (the top 1%) have received a sizeable inheritance. On the other hand, the role of inheritance on wealth inequality appears more modest for the rest of the population. In France for instance, the degree of wealth inequality remains large among non heirs, whether one considers households who have not yet received any wealth transfer, or only those who will never inherit; moreover, a significant part of this inequality (more than one third) does not seem to be explained by observable individual differences - in age, (permanent) income, level of education, occupational group... (see Kessler and Masson, 1990).

Some French data allow also to better understand the importance of inheritance in wealth inequality while comparing the average situation of blue-collar workers and (wealthy) self-employed. The inequality with respect to wealth transfers can thus be divided in three components:

- inequality in *diffusion* over the entire lifetime, between those who will never receive anything (of significant value) and the others: the proportion of those who will inherit one day is only 40% for blue-collar workers, but near 95% for self-employed professionals;
- inequality in the *timing* of capital receipts, between those who have not yet received anything (but will in the future) and those who are already heirs or donees: owing to differential mortality and intergenerational social immobility, blue-collar workers should inherit earlier than others, but this advantage is largely compensated, at least among wealthy self-employed, by *inter vivos* transfers;
- inequality, *among beneficiaries*, in the *total amount* of transfers received over the lifetime: the ratio is of the order of 1 to 12 between blue-collar workers whose parents were also blue-collar workers, and self-employed, whose parents were also self-employed. Since the former have a probability to inherit (30%) which is at least three times lower than the

latter (almost 100%), the total *quantitative* discrepancy in inheritance (diffusion *and* amount) between the two groups is finally given by the ratio of *1 to 30 or 40*... (see Arrondel and Laferrère, 1991).

IV. The Diffusion of the Different Forms of Wealth Transfers

Cox and Rank (1992) rightly emphasize that "Inter vivos transfers are more likely to be intentional and therefore more informative about transfer motives." (p. 306), and moreover that there are ways to disentangle between the two main motivations for intentional bequests, altruism and exchange. There are however two pitfalls with this statement: first, in sample surveys like the one used by Cox and Rank, gifts are observed only over a truncated period of the lifetime (only the last five years in their case); second, there may be important *interactions* between gifts and post-mortem transfers that could bias the results obtained while studying *inter vivos* transfers in isolation.

In any case, it is useful to have an idea of the quantitative importance of gifts and of their diffusion within the population. Another issue is to know whether *inter vivos* transfers are compensatory, i.e. decreasing, everything equal, with the beneficiary's income. Finally, we shall investigate the relations between different forms of transfers (helping out, gifts, inheritance) bestowed or received.

1. What is the Relative Importance of Gifts with Respect to Inheritance?

The importance of *inter vivos* gifts is a very controversial issue in the U.S., the differences in definition being not sufficient, far from it, to account for conflicting conclusions. In different papers, Tomes mentions that gifts, on which he has no information, will not invalidate his results since they are probably only of minor importance, with the possible exception of the wealthiest individuals. Bernheim et al. (1985) see 'the apparent insignificance of gifts' as an element supporting their model of strategic bequest. On the other hand, Kurz (1984), Cox (1987, 1990), and Cox and Raines (1985) claim that an enlarged conception of *inter vivos* transfers, including in kind or in cash transfers received by any adult child (above 18) even in the same household, make them more important than inheritance (in the ratio of 3 to 2). More surprisingly, Gale and Scholz (1994), considering only inter-household transfers worth more than $3,000, find yet that *inter vivos* transfers "account for at least 20 percent of U.S. wealth and possibly more" (p. 156) (and inheritances for roughly 30%).

In France, estate duty statistics indicate that the total amount of *declared inter vivos* transfers represents each year approximatively *one third* of the total amount of *declared* inheritances (or one quarter of total transfers). This evaluation is however incomplete, since small inheritances as well as many gifts (especially those handed over directly) and various parental aids (sometimes important) are not declared.

In any case, it is clear that the rate of diffusion of gifts, and their relative importance with respect to inheritance, have increased over the last 40 years in France: beyond the increase of average household's wealth during that period, other reasons for the long-term development of gifts may include the rise in life expectancy and the lengthened period where generations (parents and adult children) overlap, and perhaps also the development of social security. Over the short run however, the frequency of gifts appears quite sensitive to changes in *taxation*: their number was greatest in 1981, before the introduction of the wealth tax, declined afterwards until 1986, and rose again when tax advantages of gifts relative to inheritance were re-established (Laferrère, 1991).

2. Gifts in France: an Upper Class Phenomenon

This sensitivity of gifts to various tax incentives suggests that they are mainly concentrated among the richest households. Based upon estate data, Table 4.2 shows that it is indeed the case, the amount of wealth held being the main explanatory factor of the existence and amount of (declared) *inter vivos* transfers. Among the people who died in 1987, less than 10% had made gifts before, but the corresponding proportion is more than half among the top 1% of the bequest distribution; moreover, this privileged group accounts for 19% of total bequests, but for more than 54% of the total amount of gifts (Arrondel and Laferrère, 1994).

Table 4.2
Frequency and Amount of Gifts
According to the Level of Total Bequests

Bequest amount (bequests and previous *inter vivos* transfers)	Share in total bequests (%)	Share in total fiscal income (%)	Percentage rate of donors (%)	Share in total gifts (%)
Decile 1	0,7	4,9	1,0	0,1
Decile 2	1,7	6,3	6,0	0,5
Decile 3	2,5	5,8	3,2	0,2
Decile 4	3,4	7,5	6,0	0,7
Decile 5	4,3	8,2	5,7	1,0
Decile 6	5,5	9,1	4,7	1,0
Decile 7	7,0	9,0	5,5	1,6
Decile 8	9,5	10,8	8,9	2,1
Decile 9	14,2	13,7	19,8	10,6
Decile 10	51,2	24,7	31,9	82,3
Total	**100,0**	**100,0**	**9,3**	**100,0**
Top 5 %	39,0	16,9	43,2	73,8
Top 1%	19,4	5,5	54,3	50,4

Source: DGI-Insee, 1987 French estate data

Gifts appear also more frequent among farmers and wealthy self-employed, who bequeath their professional assets, and also among widow(er)s; a great number of these gifts are of small value, especially landed property. They are less frequent among wage-earners, especially blue-collar workers, where they mainly correspond to an anticipation of inheritance.[9]

9 On the other hand, helping out children is more common among wealthy wage-earners and professionals who give more weight to education than other categories.

3. 'Compensatory' *Inter Vivos* Transfers?

Are *inter vivos* transfers, considered in isolation, dependent upon the economic situation of the recipient, namely the size of his income or the fact that he is liquidity-constrained? The answer must be twofold: it concerns first the probability of a transfer, and second its amount.

For the U.S., Cox (1990) and Cox and Jappelli (1990) claim that transfers between parents and adult children (i.e. loans and gifts) are meant for consumers who are *liquidity-constrained*, insofar as their *permanent* income (and therefore their consumption needs) exceeds their *current* resources (income or assets). They thus find that, *for a given permanent income* of the child, the probability of receiving a transfer decreases both with current income and the ratio of financial assets to income; on the other hand, these variables have no significant (statistical) effect on the amount of the transfer received.

However, the picture is different when one does not control for child's permanent income. Cox (1987), and especially Cox and Rank (1992) conclude that the transfer *decision* is *compensatory*, the probability of receiving a transfer declining, other things equal, with recipient's income; but the transfer *amount* is *anti-compensatory*, increasing with child's current income. On the other hand, McGarry and Schoeni (1994) find that *inter vivos* transfers are greater when given to less well-off children.

There is only one French study (Arrondel and Masson, 1991) which tackles this last issue. It reaches similar results: the frequency of gifts is compensatory, but the amount bestowed is anti-compensatory. Such conclusions could be more in favour of exchange-motivated than altruistic models of transfers (but see Altonji et al. 1996, for further qualifications).

4. Strong Complementarity among the Different Forms of Transfers in France

This French study is apparently the only one to consider the relation between different forms of transfers, whether bestowed or received. Results are striking. Parents who have helped out their children are more likely to make a gift later... and to leave a significant bequest at death; also, the probability to help out children is higher for donors. Finally, repeated aids or gifts over the lifetime are quite common. Likewise, already helped out children are more likely to receive a gift or to benefit from another aid, and donees are more likely to be helped out or to receive a second gift; moreover, the probability to receive an inheritance is higher for donees and heirs. However, this complementarity does not extend to amounts: for instance, the amount of gifts bestowed (received) is not significantly higher for helpers (helped out children).

In other words, the same subpopulation of French families appears to monopolize private intergenerational transfers whether received or bestowed, combining the different forms of transfers and multiplying them - a result we shall use later.

V. Children and Bequests

The relation between bequests and the presence, number or characteristics of children is certainly the most studied issue in the literature. It allows to discriminate between intentional transfers, depending on family composition, and others (accidental, capitalist), as well as to test for the 'compensatory' effects of altruistic bequests.

We shall first consider the influence on the size of bequests of the existence or number of (independent) children. We shall then see if the altruistic predictions that bequests are meant for reducing intergenerational differences in incomes is warranted - which would lead to fewer or smaller transfers with higher economic growth. Finally, we shall examine estate division practices in France, where equal sharing is enforced by law and inheritance taxation, and in the U.S. where there is freedom to bequeath and estate (neutral) taxation.

1. Does the Presence or Number of Children Influence the Existence and Size of Bequests?

Few studies deal specifically with the effect of the *existence* of children in itself. Using U.S. *panel* data, Hurd (1987) has found that on average couples with independent children *dissave* during retirement proportionally *more* than childless couples, other things equal (including the amount of wealth and annuities at retirement). This striking conclusion, which is in favour of accidental bequests, is not entirely warranted, however, for two reasons: first, couples without children may continue to save for precautionary motives against major catastrophies (illness, invalidity), whereas children may provide a 'safety net' in other families; second, altruistic parents could decumulate more rapidly during their retirement period because they make (partly unobserved) *inter vivos* transfers to their liquidity-constrained children rather than to pass their wealth only at death (see Bernheim, 1991).

On the basis of French estate data, Arrondel and Laferrère (1994) have focused on the specific behaviour of the *rich* (top 1% or so), who are mainly (former or actual) self-employed, own most of stocks, and make much more gifts (see Table 4.2 above) and wills (see Table 4.3 below) than others. The idea is that "The very wealthy (...) may not have an operable bequest motive (...) because they already consume as much as they want (or can); (...) changing the concern they have for the welfare of their heirs will not change their consumption behavior or wealth holdings." (Hurd, 1990, p. 621) - in other words, they make *capitalist* bequests. The empirical analysis corroborates this prediction: below the top 1%, the size of bequests is *lower* for childless couples and increases with average children's income (anti-compensation); but among the richest centile, the size of bequests does not depend anymore on the presence of children (neither on their income).

On the other hand, the relation between bequest left and the *number* of children is not clear, both in the U.S. and in France: the only exception is the Bernheim et al. (1985) study, which finds that bequests are much more important and sensitive to the level of children's attention when there are at least two of them. In any case, most American studies (Adams, 1980; Tomes, 1981; Wilhem, 1996) as well as French ones (Arrondel and Laferrère, 1991; Arrondel and Masson, 1991) find a significant negative correlation between the amount of inheritance or transfers *received* by a child and the number of his/her siblings, which is often interpreted as the consequence of the quantity-quality trade-off in the 'demand' for children.

2. Do Bequests Reduce Intergenerational Differences in Well-Being?

We have already discussed the case of *inter vivos* transfers. We consider now the relation between the size of bequests (including gifts) - or of bequeathable wealth at old age - and the average pre-transfer income of children.

On U.S. estate data, Tomes (1981) obtains a significant compensatory effect, both for the probability of the existence of (a minimal) bequest and its amount: however, the negative correlation between bequest and children's average earnings depends crucially on the estimation of parents' income. Wilhem (1996) is the only study with direct information on current incomes of the deceased as well as of all his or her children. Dealing with well-to-do families with several children, he concludes that the amount of bequests *increases* with the average level of children's resources, although the effect is not always significant. Of course, one may still object that permanent instead of current incomes should be used...

The same remark applies to French studies. Using different sample surveys as well as estate data, they however reach a uniform conclusion (Arrondel and Laferrère, 1991; Arrondel and Masson, 1991): as far as intergenerational differences in resources are concerned, bequests are (slightly) *anti-compensatory*, increasing for given parents' income with the average level of education or income of children.

3. Equal or Unequal Shares: Does Bequest Division Compensate for Children's Unequal Incomes?

Bequeathing patterns play an important role in shaping wealth distribution - at least if the contribution of bequest to wealth accumulation is substantial. Their analysis allows, furthermore, to assess the specific role of legislation on individual behaviour by a comparison of the French and American situations. In France, people are forced by law to share their estate equally among their children, except for a limited part (called 'quotité disponible') they can allocate more freely by writing a will. In the U.S. equal sharing is the rule in intestate cases, but people are free to divide their estate as they wish by making a will; moreover, estate taxation is not distortionary.

The first difference between the two countries is that the proportion of testate cases is two thirds in the U.S., but less than 10% in France, although the proportion increases strongly for the richest people as well as for the childless deceased (see Table 4.3).

Table 4.3
Estate Division Practice and Frequency of Testate Cases According to the Level of Total Bequests

Distribution of total bequests	Frequency of French marriage settlement: 'separate properties' (%)	Frequency of unequal sharing (%)	Frequency of testate cases (%) when there are:	
			children	no children
75%-100%	3,1	3,0	4,7	38,1
50%-75%	3,5	4,2	4,3	31,5
25%-50%	6,6	4,7	5,2	40,9
Top 25%	15,0	19,9	9,7	32,7
Total	**7,1**	**7,9**	**6,0**	**35,9**
Top 10%	20,4	28,0	13,9	40,3
Top 5%	26,6	41,5	12,5	39,8
Top 1%	43,0	53,3	21,3	55,6

Source : DGI-Insee, 1987 French estate data

Let us first consider the U.S. testate cases. Tomes (1981, 1988), whose work is based on *heirs' declarations*, concludes that exact equality is achieved in one-fifth of the cases and 'approximate' equality in less than half. Other authors, who confine themselves to information contained in *probate records,* find a much greater incidence of equal sharing. In families with two children, for example, exact equality is observed in approximatively 70% of the cases (63% in Menchik, 1980a; 87% in Menchik, 1988; 69% in Wilhem, 1996; 81% in Bennett, 1990; 63% in Joulfaian, 1993) versus only 22% in Tomes. Moreover, primogeniture represents less than 10% of the cases, and the frequency of equal sharing is *higher* among wealthy households. Finally, the transmission of an indivisible professional asset leads often to unequal sharing only if there is no other wealth that can compensate children deprived of the professional bequest.

There is thus hardly any doubt that equal sharing is the most frequent official practice in the U.S.. But it remains to be seen whether heirs' subjective responses are truly biased or if they reflect the fact that parents use unofficial means (aid and undeclared gifts) to favour a particular child...

In France, less than 8% of the estates are unequally divided (see Table 4.3 and Arrondel and Laferrère, 1992). These cases concern mainly the *rich* (contrarily to the U.S. case) and the self-employed with several children and an illiquid or indivisible bequest (professional assets, real estate). Moreover, inheritance shares remain generally equal, the redistribution between siblings being mainly achieved through previous gifts (80% of the cases).

There remains the question whether unequal shares compensate the less privileged child. There is some evidence in the U.S. that girls, assumed to receive less education or to care more for parents, are slightly advantaged (Menchik, 1980a; Bennett, 1990). Otherwise, evidence is mixed. Tomes (1981, 1988) finds significant compensatory effects, but other authors (Menchik, 1988; Wilhem, 1996) do not find any significant correlation between children's *observable* characteristics and the relative amount of inheritance received. This ambiguous conclusion is also found for France by Arrondel and Laferrère (1992). Indeed, the French or American studies (apart from Tomes') can explain why unequal estate division occurs, but not the rationale underlying the distribution observed.

VI. Additional Issues

We shall consider here other tests of the alternative models. A strong influence of parental bequeathing behaviour on that of children would be really in favour of retrospective bequests. A positive relation between the frequency or the amount of bequests and the existence or volume of attention or aid provided by children would back up exchange-motivated models. A decrease in the frequency or amount of bequests with the level of parents' education would be more compatible with Beckerian altruism, which assumes substitution between human and non human bequests.

1. Are Bequeathing Patterns and Behaviour Strongly Influenced by those of the Parents?

Most models predict that bequest behaviour does not depend *per se* on parents' behaviour, nor on the composition (human and non-human) of life resources. Only the 'retrospective' model establishes a specific link between the amount of inheritance received and the amount of bequest left (although such a relation is often assumed in growth models), and more importantly, acknowledges the possibility that parents' bequeathing practices may strongly influence the ones of children.

Most of the American studies which relate bequests left to inheritance received are not relevant because they do not take into account life earnings. The main exception is Menchik (1980b) who on the basis of somewhat flimsy composite data obtains an elasticity of bequests with respect to human resources of approximatively 2.5, and an elasticity of 0.33 to 0.38 with respect to inheritance received. If there was complete substitutability between the two components of resources, the second elasticity would be less than 0.25 (since wealth received represents less than 10% of human resources). The propensity to bequeath out of capital receipts is thereby significantly higher than the one out of life earnings.

For France, Arrondel and Masson (1991) have applied the same methodology, using bequeathable wealth at old age as a proxy for bequests. They reach a comparable conclusion: the elasticity of 'bequests' with respect to inheritance is 0.5 to 0.6 for all households, and still between .35 and .4 for households with children, whereas the corresponding one with respect to human resources is only 1.5;the first elasticity is therefore at least twice as high as the one that would be obtained if there was complete substitutability.

But the most striking information in the French data concerns the high degree of transmission of bequeathing practices from one generation to the next. Households who have been helped out by their parents are more likely to help out their children 'in return'. Likewise, donees are more likely to become donors, and heirs more often to become bequest-leavers. This intergenerational correlation extends even to more specific practices: inheritance received through a will increases the probability to make a will; parents who have benefitted from a loan are more likely to do the same for their children...

2. Is There any Relation between the Level of Aid or Attention Provided to Parents and the Size of Inheritance Received?

The relation between the amount of aid or attention provided to parents and the size of inheritance received or inheritance expected allows for a test of exchange-motivated models. It is essential, however, to make a clear distinction here between the implications of the strategic and the insurance models. The difference does not lie so much in the nature of the services obtained by parents ('aid' or 'attention'). The strategic inheritance aims to obtain attention *today* in return for *bequeathable* wealth (excluding for instance life annuities), and is only truly operative if there are several children: there is virtually no link between attention and inheritance expectations if there is a sole presumed heir. Conversely, insurance bequests occur in families with one heir as well as many, but only guarantee *potential* aid (financial or in kind) in case of parental need (unexpected longevity, disability or illness, etc.): for that reason, they may be more difficult to test.

On the other hand, inheritance models not based on exchange predict no specific relation between aid or attention and the size of bequeathable wealth or inheritance.

Empirical results are only available for the U.S.[10]. As far as aid is concerned, Menchik et al. (1986) recall that the NLS survey asked households whether they thought they could call on their children in case of need for financial or other assistance. The authors obtain no relation between 'the intention to bequeath' and the fact of counting on one's children for financial or other help. Although this result seems to contradict the insurance model, it is only a preliminary one: the test requires more reliable and more extensive data.

Consider next the case of attention. In Tomes (1981), the frequency of visits paid has a significant *negative* effect both on the amount of inheritance received and on the child's human capital income. Similarly, an equation which attemps to explain the number of visits by the characteristics of both the deceased and the beneficiary reveals that the amount of the

---

10 French results should soon be available, based upon a new survey of 1992 dealing with family (time or money) exchanges and transfers between *three* adult generations (cf. ATTIAS-DONFUT, 1995). These *inter vivos* transfers seem to be quite frequent in France and to flow in both directions, from parents (and grandparents) to children and from children to parents.

inheritance received by the child enters with a negative but not significant coefficient. On the other hand, Menchik et al. (1986) obtain a positive correlation between the parents' intention to bequeath and the frequency of their children's telephone calls and visits. Yet, these results do not directly pertain to the strategic bequest model since they do not distinguish between single and multiple heirs.[11]

Bernheim et al. (1985) compare the average amount of attention provided by children (telephone calls or visits) with the parents' bequeathable and non bequeathable wealth (controlling for the age and state of health of parents, or whether they were retired or not). In families with two or more children, bequeathable wealth has a decisive positive influence on the amount of such attention, while the effect of retirement or pension rights is negative but not significant. In families with only one child, the effect of the size of bequeathable wealth on the level of attention is on the contrary not significant (and negative). These conclusions are very favourable to the strategic model but are somewhat less clear when the number of letters received is used instead as a measure of children's attention.

More recently, Altonji et al. (1996), using the 1988 PSID, have considered *inter vivos* time and money transfers running both ways between parents and children. Such data allow only for a partial test of bequest models since they only consider *realized* transfers, and not expected future ones, especially bequests at death. Nevertheless, the results of this thorough study are worth mentioning: "In contrast to simple exchange models of transfers, there is little evidence (...) that parental income or wealth raises time transfers from children (...)." (p. 29). The latter decrease sharply with geographical distance but are otherwise weakly related to income differences within the family or to the existence of money transfers (from parents). On the other hand, money transfers are not an implicit payment for services but tend to reduce inequality in household incomes: "Richer siblings give more

11 Moreover, MENCHIK et al. (1986) point out that a positive correlation between the volume of attention and the intent to bequeath may be given an entirely different interpretation than that of the strategic bequest. People may simply wish to leave an inheritance to those they love : if this is the case, the intent to bequeath and the attention received would only be the concomitant signs of harmonious and close families. In testing the strategic model, it is thus essential to compare behaviours in families of one and more than one child.

to parents and receive less." (*ibid.*). These equalizing effects are quite small, however, and do not fit a simple unidirectional altruism model.

3. Other Ways of Testing Bequest Models

Empirical studies of bequest still use additional information concerning the composition of wealth, opinion or intention variables, or the influence of the level of parental education.

The *composition* of bequest or bequeathable wealth should provide some information as to the cause or motive of the transmission. But clearcut cases - e.g. an estate consisting mainly of life annuities (accidental bequest), a widower declaring an important life insurance (altruistic model), a large fortune composed primarily of stocks and shares and other high-yield assets (capitalist bequest) - are quite rare. Moreover, the nature of the asset must be precisely determined to be of any value: for instance, the beneficiary of the life insurance should be known.

It is thus not surprising that very few studies use information on the nature of assets held to test inheritance models. Bernheim (1991) does find, on U.S. panel data, that higher social security old-age insurance benefits tend to be associated with a higher level of *life insurance* purchase. Moreover, the purchase of life insurance is more frequent among older couples with independent children, and especially so when children are worse off than parents. Clearly, these results are evidence of the presence of altruistic compensatory motives for bequest.

The most simple and direct way of determining whether future bequests correspond to a genuine transmission motive consists of questioning households on their *intentions* or *opinions* on this matter. It is known that economists are often reluctant to use such subjective information in their analysis. However, such variables appear in several American studies (Menchik et al., 1986; McGarry, 1996), as well as in French ones.

Several lessons are to be drawn from these works. First, in the absence of any in-depth psychological interview, it is essential, at the very least, that this information be obtained in a favourable context, when people are actually faced with the question. This is one reason explaining that intentions work better than opinions. Also, asking a person, in the abstract, for her general opinion on transmission is likely to lead to poor results: this is amply shown by the little econometric significance of the regression in the

Menchik et al. (1986) American study. On the other hand, asking a retired person, who has just been questioned on her different assets, as to how she intends to dispose of her estate will undoubtedly provide more satisfactory results, as in the French wealth surveys Insee 1986 and 1992 (Perelman and Pestieau, 1991; Arrondel and Perelman, 1994).

Second, opinions and intentions give more significant results when used as explanatory variables rather than as dependent ones, although the 'bequest intent' in French surveys can be quite successfully explained by household characteristics: wealth, income, self-employed status, and especially inheritance received. Third, the bequest intent is found in France to increase the amount of bequeathable wealth, the level of portfolio diversification and the probability to hold homes and other illiquid or indivisible assets. But opinions in French surveys, used as explanatory variables, can also have significant effects on the amount of wealth, especially those referring to '*retrospective*' behaviour: "Would you be upset to leave to your kids a lesser amount of wealth than you have received from your parents?".

Finally, if human and non-human transfers are substitutable, the *level of parental education* should, other things equal (notably the level of parental resources), *reduce* the amount of bequests, because more educated parents are more efficient at producing learning or earning skills in their children.

For the U.S., Tomes (1981) obtains a specific negative effect of parents' education on the inheritance received by the child. Tomes (1982) shows more specifically that the overall amount of the estate and of intergenerational savings are negatively correlated, at given parental resources, with the father or mother's education. These results, which lend support to the altruistic model, have however been obtained only by members of the Chicago (Beckerian) school.

For France, Arrondel and Masson (1991) get mixed or opposite results: a higher level of parental education increases the amount of gifts bestowed; on the other hand, it has an ambiguous effect on the size of bequeathable wealth, depending on econometric specification and population selection.

VII. Conclusions

At the end of this overview, it is time to go back to the theoretical models and to evaluate their performances with respect to the battery of tests conducted in both the U.S. and France.

1. Bequest Motives in the U.S.: the Unsettled Debate

In the American case, one might be disappointed by the overall results, for they do not seem to enable one to draw up a clear and definitive philosophy as to the validity of the different bequest models. The first difficulty is the fact that studies devoted to the same test often lead to opposite conclusions; furthermore, it is not always possible to determine the reason for the contradictions (quality of data, method used...) or to evaluate the reliability of the different studies. This may give rise to a feeling of unease which is further reinforced by the observation that the supporters of a given model too often arrive at a total or almost total corroboration of their theoretical hypotheses, and, on some occasions, are even alone in their conclusions.

A second problem in interpreting results lies in the same models eliciting highly variable performances from one test to another. The most patent example is that of compensatory altruism, which achieves a series of dazzling successes, especially in the two reference papers of Tomes (1981) and Becker and Tomes (1986), at the same time as it experiences a number of resounding failures, for instance in Cox and Rank (1992) and Wilhem (1996). This difficulty of interpreting results concerning altruism allows indeed for widely divergent positions, especially in the macroeconomic literature. In a recent debate concerning the consequences of public deficits, Bernheim (1989) asserts not to know of any test (on individual or aggregate data) favourable to the altruistic (or Ricardian) model, while Barro (1989) considers that the Ricardian equivalence principle is borne out by American (macro-) data, even if the latter do not lead to definitive conclusions...

At the microeconomic level at least, one can however find a certain coherence in the American literature, characterized over the years by a gradual change of opinions concerning the leading bequest model. In the seventies and early eighties, *altruism* was the dominant hypothesis, its main competitor being rather accidental bequests. But since, its fame has somewhat declined, and Becker (1993) himself in his Nobel lecture admits that "many economists, including [him], have excessively relied on altruism to tie together the interests of family members" (p. 400).

Taking advantage of this decline, exchange-motivated bequests have gained more and more in credibility in recent years although they do not occupy yet, far from it, the dominant position that altruism used to have. Indeed, they have often been considered simply as a remedy to the shortcomings of altruism, instead of being a genuine alternative leading to original predictions. Moreover, there are quite different forms of exchange which do not yet provide a coherent framework. But a promising move of the recent literature is precisely to develop more elaborated models of exchange, which give more emphasis on the process of inculcation of family values in children and focus much more on the determinants and the role of transfers in line of *ascent*, from children to parents (see Masson and Pestieau, 1997, for references).

This gradual change has implications concerning the views of the profession concerning the effectiveness of public policies. It is likely that more and more American economists questioned the once popular belief that public transfers are bound to 'crowd out' private transfers.

2. The Heterogeneity of Bequeathing Patterns in France: a Widening Gap between Heirs and Non Heirs?

By contrast, in the case of France, the battery of tests conducted on different surveys and estate data leads to conclusions that reveal a large *consensus*... perhaps because they have been performed by a rather coherent and small group of people. Unlike most U.S. economists, these authors adopt a more pragmatic and piecemeal approach, and are ready to admit that households with different preferences or motivations may coexist in the same population. Not surprisingly, their main conclusion concerns the great *heterogeneity* in behaviours.

A sizeable fraction of the population (almost one third, mainly modest wage earners) leave no bequest at all and accumulate few and small assets (liquidities, durables) over their life-cycle. At the other end of the social spectrum, the rich (mainly self-employed) behave in a specific *capitalist* way: within the top 1% richest households, the frequency of gifts, wills, unequal sharing... is far higher than for the rest of the population. Note that these conclusions may not be so different from those obtained for the U.S..

The remaining bulk of the population (70% ?) could be divided into two groups:

- a *'heir' group*, i.e. households who have received or who will most likely be receiving a sizeable property transfer, where transfers are dominantly intentional but not compensatory and appear more compatible with the model of *retrospective* bequests: what is left is largely dependent of what has been received, and bequeathing practices have a strong tendency to reproduce from one generation to the next;
- a larger *'non heir' group* of households who have received none or little inheritance, make few gifts and leave transfers of a smaller size, mainly corresponding to precautionary savings in order to secure old-age needs, as claimed by the model of *accidental* bequests; this group includes a large fraction of modest or intermediate wage-earners.

Two remarks are in order about these results. The first one concerns the theory. Retrospective bequests are not very well defined, having received different interpretations and constituting probably a hybrid type, between altruism and exchange. Once again, a promising way to model such bequests would be to emphasize the perennity of family values or norms, and to study sophisticated mecanisms of reciprocity involving often three generations.

The second remark concerns distribution and policy. The heterogeneity of bequeathing behaviours, the rather anti-compensatory effects of bequests, and the concentration of transfers received or left in the hands of a privileged minority of households (making capitalist or retrospective bequests) are likely to induce strong discrepancies between potential beneficiaries, concerning the existence, timing, and amount of received transfers. Moreover, these factors could well reinforce the income and wealth *disequalizing role* of inheritance and other private transfers in France. In this respect at least, there may be more scope and justification for redistributive fiscal policies in France than in the U.S..

References

ADAMS, J.D. (1980): "Personal wealth transfers", *Quarterly Journal of Economics*, 95, pp. 159-79.

ALTONJI, J.G., HAYASHI F. and KOTLIKOFF, L.J. (1989): *Is the Extended Family Altruistically Linked? Direct Tests Using Micro Data*, NBER Working Paper No. 3046.

ALTONJI, J.G., HAYASHI F. and KOTLIKOFF, L.J. (1996): *The Effects of Income and Wealth on Time and Money Transfers Between Parents and Children*, NBER Working Paper No. 5522.

ANDO, A., GUISO, L. and TERLIZZESE, D. (1993): *Dissaving by the Elderly, Transfer Motives and Liquidity Constraints*, NBER Working Paper No. 4569.

ARRONDEL, L. and LAFERRÈRE, A. (1991): "Successions et héritiers à travers les données fiscales", *Economie et Prévision*, No. 100-101, pp. 137-59.

ARRONDEL, L. and LAFERRÈRE, A. (1992): "Les partages inégaux des successions entre frères et sœurs", *Economie et Statistique*, 250, pp. 29-42.

ARRONDEL, L. and LAFERRÈRE, A. (1994): "La transmission des grandes fortunes", *Economie et Statistique*, 273, pp. 41-52.

ARRONDEL, L. and MASSON, A. (1991): "Que nous enseignent les enquêtes sur les transferts patrimoniaux en France?", *Economie et Prévision*, No. 100-101, pp. 93-128.

ARRONDEL, L. and PERELMAN, S. (1994): "Les opinions des Français sur l'héritage sont-elles compatibles avec leurs comportements de transmission?" in: P. PESTIEAU (Ed.): *Héritage et Transferts Entre Générations*, Bruxelles (De Boeck), pp. 45-67.

ATKINSON, A.B. (1983): *Social Justice and Public Policy*, Cambridge, London (MIT Press).

ATTIAS-DONFUT, CL. (1995): "Le double circuit des transmissions", in: CL. ATTIAS-DONFUT (Ed.): *Les Solidarités Entre Générations*, Paris (Nathan), pp. 41-81.

BARRO, R.J. (1989): "The Ricardian approach to budget deficits", *Journal of Economic Perspectives*, 3(2), pp. 37-54.

BECKER, G.S. (1988): "Family economics and macro behavior", *American Economic Review*, 78, pp. 1-13.

BECKER, G.S. (1993): "The economic way of looking at behavior", *Journal of Political Economy*, 101, pp. 385-409.

BECKER, G.S. and TOMES, N. (1986): "Human capital and the rise and fall of families", *Journal of Labor Economics*, 4, part 2, pp. S1-S39.

BENNETT, S.K. (1990): *Economic and Non-Economic Factors Motivating Bequest Patterns*, Trinity University, mimeo.

BEHRMAN, J., POLLACK , R. and TAUBMAN, P. (1989): *The Wealth Model: Efficiency in Education and Equity in the Family*, University of Pennsylvania, mimeo.

BERNHEIM, B.D. (1989): "A neoclassical perspective on budget deficits", *Journal of Economic Perspectives*, 3(2), pp. 55-72.

BERNHEIM, B.D. (1991): "How strong are bequest motives? Evidence based on estimates on the demand for life insurance and annuities", *Journal of Political Economy*, 99, pp. 899-927.

BERNHEIM, B.D., SHLEIFER, A. and SUMMERS, L.H. (1985): "The strategic bequest motive", *Journal of Political Economy*, 93, pp. 1045-76.

BLINDER, A.S. (1988): "Comments on Chapter 1 and Chapter 2", in: D. KESSLER and A. MASSON (Eds.): *Modelling the Accumulation and Distribution of Wealth*, Oxford (Clarendon Press), pp. 68-76.

COX, D. (1987): "Motives for private transfers", *Journal of Political Economy*, 95, pp. 508-46.

COX, D. (1990): "Intergenerational transfers and liquidity constraints", *Quarterly Journal of Economics*, 104, pp. 187-217.

COX, D. and JAPPELLI ,T. (1990): "Credit rationing and private transfers: Evidence from survey data", *Review of Economics and Statistics*, 72, pp. 445-53.

COX, D. and RAINES, F. (1985): "Interfamily transfers and income redistribution", in: M. DAVID and T. SMEEDING (Eds.): *Horizontal Equity, Uncertainty, and Economic Well-Being*, Chicago (University of Chicago Press), pp. 393-425.

COX, D. and RANK, M.R. (1992): "Inter-vivos transfers and intergenerational exchange", *Review of Economics and Statistics*, 74, pp. 305-14.

DAVID, M. and MENCHIK, P.L. (1985): "The effect of social security on lifetime wealth accumulation and bequests", *Economica*, 52, pp. 421-34.

DAVIES, J.B. (1982): "The relative impact of inheritance and other factors on economic inequality", *Quarterly Journal of Economics*, 97, pp. 471-98.

GALE, W.J. and SCHOLZ, J.K.: (1994), "Intergenerational transfers and the accumulation of wealth", *Journal of Economic Perspectives*, 8(4), pp. 145-60.

HURD, M.D. (1987): "Savings of the elderly and desired bequests", *American Economic Review*, 77, pp. 299-312.

HURD, M.D. (1990): "Research on the elderly: Economic status, retirement, and consumption and saving", *Journal of Economic Literature*, 28, pp. 565-637.

JOULFAIAN, D. (1993): *The Distribution and Division of Bequests in the U.S. Evidence from the Collation Study*, Office of Tax Analysis, mimeo.

KESSLER, D. and MASSON, A. (1989): "Bequest and wealth accumulation: Are some pieces of the puzzle missing?", *Journal of Economic Perspectives*, 3(3), pp. 141-52.

KESSLER, D. and MASSON, A. (1990): "Le patrimoine des Français: Faits et controverses", *Données Sociales 1990*, Paris, pp. 156-66.

KESSLER, D., MASSON, A. and PESTIEAU, P. (1991): "Trois vues sur l'héritage: La famille, la propriété, l'Etat", *Economie et Prévision*, No. 100-101, pp. 1-29.

KOTLIKOFF, L.J. (1988): "Intergenerational transfers and saving", *Journal of Economic Perspectives*, 2(2), pp. 41-58.

KOTLIKOFF, L.J. (1989): "Estimating the wealth elasticity of bequests from a sample of potential decedents", in: L.J. KOTLIKOFF, *What Determines Savings?*, Cambridge, London (MIT Press), pp. 404-28.

KURZ, M. (1984): "Capital accumulation and the characteristics of private intergenerational transfers", *Economica*, 51, pp. 1-22.

LAFERRÈRE A. (1990): "Héritiers et héritages", *Economie et Statistique*, 214, pp. 33-9.

LAFERRÈRE, A. (1991): "Les donations: Surtout de l'immobilier", *Insee Première*, No. 169.

LAFERRÈRE, A. (1994): "Les mesures volontaires de transmission du patrimoine et la protection du conjoint survivant", in: P. PESTIEAU (Ed.): *Héritage et Transferts Entre Générations*, Bruxelles (De Boeck), pp. 69-89.

LUCAS, R.E. (1981): *Studies in Business Cycles Theories*, Oxford (Blackwell).

MASSON, A. and PESTIEAU, P. (1991): "Tests des modèles d'héritage: Un inventaire critique", *Economie et Prévision*, No. 100-101, pp. 73-92.

MASSON, A. and PESTIEAU, P. (1994): "L'héritage et l'Etat", in: P. PESTIEAU (Ed.): *Héritage et Transferts Entre Générations*, Bruxelles (De Boeck), pp. 15-44.

MASSON, A. and PESTIEAU, P. (1997): "Bequests motives and models of inheritance: A survey of the literature", *this volume*.

MCGARRY, K. (1996): *Patterns of Inter Vivos Transfers and Intended Bequests*, Los Angeles, University of California, mimeo.

MCGARRY K. and SCHOENI R.F. (1994): "Transfers behavior: Measurement, and the redistribution of resources within the family", *Journal of Human Resources*, 30, pp. S184-S226.

MENCHIK, P.L. (1979): "Intergenerational transmission of inequality: An empirical study of wealth mobility", *Economica*, 46, pp. 346-62.

MENCHIK, P.L. (1980a): "Primogeniture, equal sharing and the U.S. distribution of wealth", *Quarterly Journal of Economics*, 94, pp. 299-316.

MENCHIK, P.L. (1980b): "Effect of material inheritance on the distribution of wealth", in: J.D. SMITH (Ed.): *Modelling the Distribution and Intergenerational Transmission of Wealth*, Chicago (University of Chicago Press), pp. 159-85.

MENCHIK P.L. (1988): "Unequal estate division: Is it altruism, reverse bequests, or simply noise?", in: D. KESSLER and A. MASSON (Eds.): *Modelling the Accumulation and Distribution of Wealth*, Oxford (Clarendon Press), pp. 105-16.

MENCHIK, P.L. and DAVID, M. (1983): "Income distribution, lifetime savings, and bequests", *American Economic Review*, 73, pp. 672-90.

MENCHIK, P.L., IRVINE, F.O. and JIANAKOPLOS, N.A. (1986): *Determinants of Intended Bequests*, Michigan State University, Discussion Paper A-197.

MODIGLIANI, F. (1986): "Life cycle, individual thrift, and the wealth of nations", *American Economic Review*, 76, pp. 297-313.

MODIGLIANI, F. (1988): "The role of intergenerational transfers and life cycle saving in the accumulation of wealth", *Journal of Economic Perspectives*, 2(2), pp. 15-40.

PERELMAN, S. and PESTIEAU, P. (1991): "Les legs volontaires en France: Evaluation et explication", *Economie et Prévision*, No. 100-101, pp. 129-36.

TOMES, N. (1981): "The family, inheritance and the intergenerational transmission of inequality", *Journal of Political Economy*, 89, pp. 928-58.

TOMES, N. (1982): "On the intergenerational savings function", *Oxford Economic Papers*, 34, pp. 108-34.

TOMES, N. (1988): "Inheritance and inequality within the family: Equal division among unequals, or do the poor get more?", in: D. KESSLER and A. MASSON (Eds.): *Modelling the Accumulation and Distribution of Wealth*, Oxford (Clarendon Press), pp. 79-104.

WILHEM, M.O. (1996): "Bequest behavior and the effect of heirs' earnings: Testing the altruistic model of bequests", *American Economic Review*, 86, pp. 874-92.

Chapter 5

Bequests and Inheritance Taxation: A Comment

ERIK SCHOKKAERT

The traditional economic approach to policy evaluation is dominated by consequentialism. The consequentialist reasoning goes as follows. First, describe or predict the effects of the policy measure. Secondly, evaluate these effects with a well-specified social objective function. To simplify matters one usually introduces additional assumptions in both steps. In the first step, effects are analysed within an equilibrium model with self-interested agents. The broad institutional structure is kept constant when the value of a policy instrument is changed. In the second step the social objective function is usually specified in a welfarist way, i.e. it is assumed that social welfare is dependent on the welfare levels of the individual households and on these welfare levels only.

It is my personal conviction that the consequentialist approach is very useful for the ethical analysis of economic policy. But often I have more problems with the set of simplifying assumptions. Abstraction and simplification are necessary when we want to get a better understanding of reality but the acceptability of these simplifying assumptions depends on the specific problem analysed. I feel that the analysis of inheritance taxation is an example of a problem where there are severe limitations to the traditional assumptions. My brief comment will focus on three aspects: motivations and behaviour (Section I); the interrelationship between social structures and policy instruments (Section II); the welfarist evaluation (Section III).

This comment should in no way be read as a criticism on the papers by Luc Arrondel, André Masson and Pierre Pestieau. Quite the contrary: these papers give an extremely useful and interesting survey of theoretical and empirical findings on bequests and inheritance and explain clearly the most important aspects of the problem. The summary tables in the paper of Masson and Pestieau (1997) are so transparent that they can give even the non-specialised reader the impression that he or she has a good overall view of the literature. Moreover, the papers go a long way into the direction of my general remarks. My comment should therefore be read as a (quite ambitious) agenda for future research.

I. Motivations and Behaviour

The crux of the problem is the fact that it is not straightforward to explain bequests with a model based on narrow self-interested behaviour. At least at first sight, bequests seem to reflect either altruistic motivations or sheer accident. Recently the analysis of strategic behaviour has also become popular in the literature, although it has not yet gained the dominant position that altruism used to occupy. The importance attached to these motivational differences by the literature on bequests is extremely untypical for the economic approach, where there often is a tendency to denounce explanations in terms of preference differences as ad hoc. Things become even more unconventional (from the economist's point of view) when reference is made to the phenomena of retrospective and capitalist bequests and to the importance of social and family norms.

As is illustrated clearly in the theoretical survey of Masson and Pestieau, differences in the nature of motivations are absolutely crucial to understand the effects of government policy in general and inheritance taxation in particular. If we want to gain useful insights from such theoretical models, it is important not to introduce unnecessary complications. But when we turn to the empirical facts, we should keep in mind that reality is not as schematic as the theoretical categories used, to borrow a phrase from the authors. I will first give some examples and then turn to some implications for the research strategy to be followed in empirical work.

Most economic agents do not belong unambiguously to one of the theoretical categories but are characterised by mixed motivations. They may be reasonably altruistic, but at the same time sensitive to strategic considerations. They may care for all their children, but at the same time favour some of them over the others. They may judge that the personality of some children makes them more efficient caretakers. The last point indicates that behaviour does not only depend on motivations, but also on the available information and on the expectations of parents, e.g., about the future earnings power of their children. For the strong neutrality results with respect to public debt to hold, it is not sufficient that parents are pure altruists: in addition it is necessary that they are informed about the consequences of the fiscal policy. Since nobody can predict the future perfectly, bequest behaviour and investment in the human capital of the children are decisions under uncertainty. Parents do not have exact knowledge about the productive talents of their children (and hence about the return of their investment in the human capital of their offspring). Only in some simple economic models can they perfectly foresee the future course of the economy. To conclude: mixed motivations, expectations and uncertainty all play a role in the parent's decisions.

All this is quite obvious but it is important to see the consequences for empirical work. Given the complexity of the decision problem of the parents, it is dangerous to infer their motivations directly from observed behaviour, a strategy which is basically advocated in the empirical survey of Arrondel, Masson and Pestieau (1997). When motivations are simple (e.g., narrowly defined self-interest), expectations unimportant and information almost perfect, it is fruitful not to concentrate on these aspects and to explain behaviour with a simple model in which preferences are reasonably stable and economic decisions are linked to the features of the economic environment (the constraints). Many consumption decisions can be analysed in this way. But it is hard to accept these simplifications in an explanation of bequest behaviour. And as if-assumptions - Arrondel et al. write that "it is provisionally assumed that people behave as if they followed the logic of rational choice described by the model" (p. 93)- may be misleading. Suppose we observe that parents do not adjust their bequests after a change in the public debt policy. They will behave as if they are not purely altruistic. But suppose now that they really are altruistic, but are imperfectly informed about the change in policy (or simply unable to calculate its consequences). In that case the as if-approach will lead to a wrong prediction of the effects of a change in that information. In the correct interpretation of the facts, parents will adjust their behaviour. The as if-model however will predict that the change in information is irrelevant. This example illustrates my conclusion that to predict bequest behaviour it is necessary to distinguish clearly between the different effects: motivations, expectations, uncertainty. In fact, I do think that wrong perceptions of reality and wrong expectations about the future are crucial to understand individual behaviour and should receive more attention from economists.

Since all these factors together determine observed behaviour, we need additional information to distinguish between them. I therefore take a more positive attitude towards survey research on opinions and attitudes, i.e. about motivations, than Arrondel et al., who claim that economists should be reluctant to use motivational statements in their explanation. Of course I agree that one should not automatically believe what respondents are saying and that the ultimate test of a theory is the explanation and prediction of observed behaviour. But I do believe that self-reported attitudes may contribute to get a better insight into the complexities of real behaviour. Moreover we should also set up surveys concerning subjective perceptions and expectations. In fact, I see no alternative for the survey approach, if we want to distinguish the various subjective variables. Actually, the difference between survey responses and 'hard' information about bequest behaviour should not be exaggerated. In the first place, response behaviour is also behaviour and can be analysed as such. In the second place, the hard information is often based on self-reports (even when it is collected by statistical institutes). This self-reported information about behaviour is not necessarily more reliable than the self-reported motivations.

Arrondel et al. are cautious enough to introduce themselves important caveats against a highly stylised economic analysis. Moreover, they do behave much less like hard-headed economists in their overview of the empirical work than in their statement of principles. All in all, the papers by Masson and Pestieau and by Arrondel et al. show that the economic literature on bequests and inheritance is rather open for broader psychological and sociological interpretations. I think that it offers extremely useful insights about bequest behaviour and I like in particular the idea of confronting well-structured theories with data on individual behaviour and attitudes. But perhaps the approach does not yet go far enough.

II. Social Norms and Government Policy

Not only do motivational differences play a crucial role in understanding bequest behaviour. Preferences vary over time and are influenced by behaviour itself. They are related to family and social norms and parents shape the preferences of their children through education. These ideas are trivial for most social scientists. But for traditional economists, who like the assumption of given and unchanging preferences, they really open up Pandora's box.

In the first place they point to the limitations of the traditional economic explanation. If motivational differences and social norms are so important, it is obviously interesting to explain where these differences and social norms come from. Preferences and social norms are not independent of the economic environment. We know from anthropological and historical research that the pattern of bequests plays an important role for the stability of the social structure. Social customs may be functional given the economic situation of the communities: think about the role of primogeniture for the division of land in agricultural societies. The legal structure regulating bequests and inheritance taxation reflects these social norms and customs, but on its turn influences actual behaviour and preferences. Also in developed capitalist societies, discussions about inheritance taxation arouse deep feelings (both among the rich and among the poor). Underneath the economic model with given preferences is the real world of preference formation. This is one of the most fascinating topics in the social sciences.

As such, this is not really a criticism on the traditional economic approach. It is a perfectly sound research strategy to develop first a model with given preferences and focus on the effects of other variables, while relegating the problem of preference formation to later research or to other social sciences. But again we must be cautious when we go from theory to reality and try to predict the effect of changes in inheritance taxation. Is it possible to make the assumption that such changes will have no effect on the broader set of social norms, i.e. on preferences? This assumption is reasonable when we analyse marginal changes in tax rates. It is much more difficult to accept when we consider proposals to abolish all inheritance taxation or (at the other extreme) to introduce a 100% inheritance tax. If preferences are influenced by the policy itself it becomes necessary to go beyond the traditional economic approach when predicting the consequences of that policy.

Let me make a side-remark here. An evaluation of concrete policy proposals should not only concentrate on the likely consequences of their implementation, but also on their political feasibility. Also from this point of view, the empirical work summarised in the paper by Arrondel et al. yields extremely useful information. But again it should be supplemented with a broader perspective on the creation of social norms in different social groups. The interrelationship between social norms and economic environment is important to understand the political feasibility of different proposals.

III. The Limitations of Welfarism

Let us look further at the contents of Pandora's box. As soon as we accept that preferences differ and a fortiori when we accept that they are shaped by the economic environment and may be changed by economic policy, we start undermining the normative basis of the welfarist approach. To repeat: welfarism means that we base our policy evaluation only on the consequences for the welfare levels of the individual households. If motivational structures differ a lot, are they all equally respectable from an ethical point of view? Are all sources of individual welfare equally good? Note that once we start 'correcting' preferences, we need a theoretical framework to justify these corrections, i.e. we have to go beyond the traditional welfarist approach to introduce other considerations into the evaluative exercise. And even if we accept that all preferences are equally respectable, how are we going to evaluate the effects of a policy instrument which influences these preferences themselves? Do we use ex ante or ex post preferences for this exercise? These are basic questions for any welfarist policy analysis, but they become especially prominent in the context of inheritance taxation because of the importance of motivational differences for the understanding of bequest behaviour.

There is another aspect to this problem. When reading the other papers in this volume and in particular when looking at the views on inheritance from the history of economic thought, as presented by Guido Erreygers (1997), it is striking that many popular arguments cannot be easily integrated in a welfarist mould. Think about the ethical distinction between children and other heirs (and the feeling that it is not fair that children get nothing, even if this is what parents prefer); the different ethical status given (e.g. by Solvay and Rignano) to self-created and inherited property; or, more generally, the productivity idea as a basic principle (as advocated by the Saint-Simonians and to be distinguished from the productivity idea as an instrumental principle, i.e. as a means to increase the value of some other objective function). I think that these intuitions are not only relevant from an historical point of view but are still well alive in our society today. While I do not claim that all these considerations are equally valuable from an ethical point of view, I do think that they should at least be taken up in the discussion on the ethical legitimacy of inheritance and inheritance taxation. Therefore the narrow welfarist approach is extremely restrictive and should not be taken as a starting point above suspicion. Quite the contrary, here, as elsewhere, there are good reasons to be extremely suspicious. For social scientists who want to make a contribution to the ethical debate it is important to elaborate a broader consequentialist framework.

References

ARRONDEL, L., MASSON, A. and PESTIEAU, P. (1997): "Bequest and inheritance: Empirical issues and France-U.S. comparison", *this volume*.

ERREYGERS, G. (1997): "Views on inheritance in the history of economic thought", *this volume*.

MASSON, A. and PESTIEAU, P. (1997): "Bequests motives and models of inheritance: A survey of the literature", *this volume*.

Chapter 6

Distributive Justice and Inheritance

D. W. HASLETT

It is often argued that a just distribution of wealth is one in which each person's wealth is proportional to his or her productivity. Let us call this the 'productivity' ideal of distributive justice. Some version of it has been held by writers with views otherwise as different as those of the arch-conservative Milton Friedman and the socialist Pierre-Joseph Proudhon.[1] In this essay I shall attempt to defend a version of the productivity ideal of distributive justice, and examine its practical implications, especially with regard to inheritance. It is usually thought that the productivity ideal of distributive justice justifies rather conservative policies, policies which, for the sake of assuring that wealth is indeed proportional to productivity, reject

---

1 See FRIEDMAN (1962) and PROUDHON (1876). The productivity ideal of distributive justice is to be contrasted with views of distributive justice such as that set out in John RAWLS' 'difference principle', which (roughly speaking) characterizes a just distribution as one in which the worst-off members of society have as much as possible. See RAWLS (1971).

governmental aid to the poor or any other interference with the market. Thus support for this ideal usually comes from conservatives.[2] I shall try to show, however, that conservative support for the productivity ideal of distributive justice is misplaced; that this ideal, as I shall interpret it at least, does not justify conservative policies.

I. Theory

1. Indirect Utilitarianism

Let me begin by revealing the general theoretical perspective from which I write. In short, it is an indirect, or rule, utilitarian perspective, a perspective that follows from two, widely accepted premises. The first premise - 'the point-of-morality' premise - is simply that, in the most general sense, the point of society's having a morality is our well-being. If the point of morality were not our well-being, then what could its point possibly be? The second premise - 'the equal consideration' premise - is that by 'our' well-being what is meant is the well-being everyone, with everyone's well-being to be considered equally important. That is, everyone's well-being is to be considered equally important in this sense: in calculating which from among alternative codes, values, virtues, ideals, or norms of morality are most conducive to well-being, equal degrees of well-being that are equally probable are to be given equal weight in our calculations, no matter whose well-being it may be. What is conducive to well-being, giving everyone's well being equal consideration, I shall refer to simply as what is conducive to 'overall' well-being.

Now anything that has a point, or purpose, is to be evaluated in terms of how conducive it is to achieving that point, or purpose. For example, the purpose of a knife is to cut; therefore, the best knife is the one most conducive to cutting. Similarly, from the above two premises concerning the purpose of morality it follows that the 'best', or most justified, codes, values,

2 See, for example, FRIEDMAN (1962), especially Chapter 10. Whenever I speak of conservatives, I refer to those, and those only, who are conservative in the sense of advocating as small a role for government in the lives of people as possible.

virtues, ideals, or norms of morality are the ones most conducive to overall well-being.[3]

Codes of morality include (1) criteria for judging the behaviour of people, and (2) criteria for judging the behaviour of political units, or governments. Criteria for judging the behaviour of people are those of 'personal' morality. These criteria include norms, such as ones that obligate people to tell the truth, and to refrain from theft. And they include personal values, or virtues, such as generosity and kindness. Criteria for judging the behaviour (acts, policies, laws, institutions) of political units are those of 'political' morality. They include norms, such as ones that obligate governments to tell the truth, and to pay their debts. They include rights against the government, such as the right to freedom of speech and the right to freedom of religion. And, finally, they include political values or ideals, such as equal opportunity and freedom. The most *fundamental* political ideal, or standard, is the general welfare. The general welfare standard, incidentally, should not be confused with the utilitarian standard, since (as opposed to the utilitarian standard which is not part of political morality) the general welfare standard gives priority to the welfare of those currently within the jurisdiction of the political unit in question.[4] All other political ideals are to serve as specific guides for determining what act, policy, or institution is most in the general welfare. As such, all other political ideals are only prima facie, not absolute, in that they are to be realized only in so far as their realization does not conflict with the realization of some other political ideal the realization of which, in the circumstances, is *more* in the general welfare. And governmental pursuit of all political ideals, including even the general welfare, should, I assume, always be constrained by rights against the government and other norms of political morality.

2. The Productivity Ideal

It is, as I see it, within the general category of 'political ideals' that distributive justice falls. Distributive justice is an ideal that is supposed to

3 This perspective is set out much more fully and defended in Chapter 1 of HASLETT (1994). See also HASLETT (1987).

4 I set out in detail what I take to be the general welfare standard, or norm, and how it differs from the utilitarian standard, in Chapter 8 of HASLETT (1987).

delineate what distribution of income and wealth throughout society should be sought. The ideal of distributive justice that I shall attempt to defend here can be stated as follows: "To all people according to the productivity of their labour, or of the property they have acquired in return for the productivity of their labour".[5] Moreover, only productivity from legal labour is to count. It is hardly just for people to acquire income and wealth from activities society has chosen to make illegal. The only exception is for those relatively rare cases in which breaking the law can, for one reason or another, be morally justified.

This ideal of distributive justice - the 'productivity' ideal - is satisfied if a person receives exactly what he or she has produced, or its equivalent. Accordingly, this ideal is satisfied by that which a person voluntarily produces for himself. Take, for example, a person cleaning his own house. What this person has produced is a clean house, and what he gets in return is exactly the same thing - namely, a clean house for himself. Thus, by his getting (i.e. consuming himself) exactly what he has produced, he has indeed received that and only that which he has produced, and therefore, assuming at least the absence of externalities (see below), the requirements of distributive justice are satisfied. The more difficult problem is that of determining what satisfies the requirements of distributive justice in the case where productivity is exchanged for money in the marketplace. Let us now turn to this problem, the solution to which requires an understanding of what, exactly, the 'ideal' monetary value of a person's productivity is.

First of all, a person is being productive in the marketplace only to the extent that he or she is producing something that people really want or need. A person producing buggy whips, for example, is not being productive, since no one wants or needs buggy whips. Second, I am assuming that what people really want or need is to be determined not necessarily by what they in fact do prefer, but by what they would prefer if their preferences were 'fully informed'.[6] This, in effect, means that what people really want and need is to be determined not by what they might (mistakenly) *think* maximizes their 'expected utility' or that of another, but by what really

5 It is to be understood, for purposes of this ideal, that people can, of course, acquire property in return for their productivity 'indirectly' by acquiring it not in return for their own productivity, but in return for the productivity of property previously acquired in return for their own productivity.

6 What I mean by preferences that are 'fully informed' is explained, in some detail, in Section 1.7 of HASLETT (1994).

does.[7] So, for example, a person producing the insidious drug, crack, is not being productive, since (I take it) people would not want crack if their preferences were fully informed.

The hypothetical, 'ideal', monetary value of a person's productivity is, I submit, best defined in terms of this concept of fully informed preferences. As a first approximation, let us say that the ideal monetary value of a person's productivity is what others would be willing to pay for that productivity if (1) their preferences were fully informed and (2) all alternative uses of their wealth were fully apparent to them. We may refer to hypothetical individuals who meet these two conditions as 'fully informed consumers'. Only a definition in terms of fully informed consumers avoids useless speculation about what, regardless of our own preferences no matter how fully informed, is *'really'* good for us.

But the monetary value of a person's productivity cannot be defined *solely* in terms of what fully informed consumers would pay for it. First of all, for the amount that fully informed consumers would pay for it to represent the ideal monetary value of a person's productivity, this amount cannot have been affected by unnecessary limitations upon people's *opportunities* to be productive, or use their property productively.

Let me explain. An 'unnecessary' limitation upon a person's opportunity is a limitation that is the result of something such as discrimination against him, special-interest rules and regulations that exclude him, or educational requirements that he is not given a chance to attain, all of which are limitations imposed, maintained, or deliberately not removed by other human beings. A 'necessary' limitation upon a person's opportunity, for purposes of distributive justice, is a limitation that either cannot be removed by human beings given our present knowledge (i.e. it is one that is 'empirically' necessary) or else, although it could be removed, to the extent that it was removed it would undermine distributive justice itself (i.e. it is a limitation that is a necessary consequence of a just distribution). The limitations on opportunities that are a necessary consequence of a just distribution are financial in nature. Obviously a person who has justly become wealthy as a result of his productivity has, from this wealth, certain opportunities that someone whose productivity has not made him wealthy does not have, and to the extent that this wealth were confiscated by the

7 For my analysis of the concept of 'expected utility', see Sections 1.7-1.10 of HASLETT (1994), and HASLETT (1990).

government or otherwise coercively removed, wealth would thus, by hypothesis, be distributed less justly. Finally, the most important *empirically* necessary limitation on a person's opportunity to be productive is that of a person's inborn talents and abilities. Now in a supply and demand economy, the more scarce demanded talents and abilities are, the higher the payment for their use will be. If the scarcity of certain demanded talents and abilities is attributable to a scarcity of people born with these talents and abilities, then higher than average payment resulting from this scarcity does, I submit, represent payment for productivity. Using talents and abilities that few others have been born with, or are willing to use, is indeed socially valuable and thus represents genuine productivity. (A similar argument applies to the use of scarce property.) On the other hand, if the scarcity of certain demanded talents and abilities is merely a consequence of *unnecessary* limitations on people's opportunities to develop and use these talents and abilities, then higher than average payment resulting from this scarcity does not represent payment for productivity. It represents, instead, monopoly-like income. Likewise, any payment that is *lower* than average merely as a result of unnecessary limitations upon opportunity does not represent *lower* productivity, but (if the limitations cannot be justified) it represents, instead, exploitation. Thus a full definition of the ideal monetary value of a person's productivity must exclude any affect upon the payment the person gets for it that is merely the consequence of unnecessary limitations upon people's opportunities. This is crucial and worth emphasizing. What it means is that distributive justice can be realized only to the extent that each person has complete, and equal opportunity to develop fully his or her *potential* for productivity. Accordingly, any increase in equal opportunity will, other things being equal, bring about more distributive justice as well.

Next, a full definition of the ideal monetary value of a person's productivity must also exclude payment that is merely the result of failing to internalize negative externalities. A negative externality is a cost of a good or service for which the producer or consumer of that good or service does not pay. The most common negative externality is pollution, which imposes tremendous costs upon society not paid for by those producing or consuming what causes the pollution. To the extent that the payment a person gets for his or her productivity is inflated because the external costs of that productivity have been neglected, this payment does not, therefore, represent the true value of the productivity. Similarly, a person is underpaid for productivity that has positive externalities. So a full definition of the ideal monetary value of a person's productivity must also exclude any effect upon the payment the person gets for it that is merely the consequence of failing to internalize (i.e. pay for, or be paid for) externalities.

Still other adjustments must be built into the definition as well - namely, whatever other adjustments are necessary to exclude from the ideal monetary value of a person's productivity any payments the person gets merely because of departures from maximum efficiency. Payments that are greater (or less) than they otherwise would be *merely* because of departures from maximum efficiency surely do not represent accurately a person's productivity. Thus, for example, the definition must be adjusted so as to exclude any effect upon the payment a person gets that is merely a result of imperfect competition, a well recognized source of inefficiency. Still other such adjustments must no doubt be made as well. One approach is simply to incorporate into the definition those conditons for optimal *Pareto* efficiency that economists have already formulated,[8] but this raises complex issues beyond the scope of this essay. Here I need only note, without trying to formulate them, that additional adjustments must be made for the sake of excluding effects upon payment from mere inefficiency. So we may conclude, finally, that, for purposes of distributive justice, the ideal monetary value of a person's productivity, or that of their property, is what fully informed consumers would pay for this productivity, adjusted so as to exclude any effect upon this payment from (1) unnecessary limitations upon people's opportunities, (2) externalities that have not been internalized, and (3) any other departures from maximum efficiency. The ideal of distributive justice I am defending is satisfied to the extent, and only to the extent, that, whenever people's productivity, or that of their property, is exchanged for money in the marketplace, they are paid precisely this amount.

3. The Rationale

Before concluding this Section on theory, let us take a very brief look at the rationale for the productivity ideal of distributive justice. One might be tempted to seek a rationale merely in terms of the intuitive idea that we

8 For a useful summary of the conditions economists have formulated for maximum (Pareto) efficiency, see Chapter 2 of BUCHANAN (1985).

'own' ourselves, and our productivity is, so to speak, simply an extension of ourselves. But, as pointed out above, the most fundamental rationale for moral norms, values, and ideals, according to the theoretical deep-structure from which I am writing, is in terms of their conduciveness to overall well-being. A rationale in these terms proceeds somewhat as follows. People cannot put their talents and abilities, and property, to work in *all* possible ways. So what is needed is for people to put their talents and abilities, and property, to work in the most *productive* ways, which often means in ways that are most scarce. Now we cannot *force* people to use their talents and abilities in the most productive ways, since we cannot know for sure what scarce talents and abilities they may have, or whether they are really using them to the fullest. We can only *entice* people to use their talents and abilities in the most productive ways by rewarding them to the extent that they in fact do so, which is precisely what the productivity ideal of distributive justice calls for. Thus this ideal, by calling for people to be paid precisely in proportion to their productivity and that of their justly acquired property, will indeed, more than any alternative ideal of distributive justice, entice people to put their talents and abilities, and property, to work in the most productive ways. This ideal, therefore, more than any alternative, will tend to promote productivity, and, other things being equal, that ideal of distributive justice which tends most successfully to promote productivity will be the most conducive to overall well-being.

Conversely, large gifts and bequests, which are *contrary* to the productivity ideal of distributive justice, tend to *undermine* productivity. First, those who receive large gifts and bequests - that is, 'large inheritances' - need not work hard, or even at all, since they will have had the means for supporting themselves and their families simply handed to them. It is, incidentally, curious that many conservatives become highly indignant at the prospect of poor people losing their incentives to work by being given welfare, yet these same conservatives are perfectly content with the prospect of rich people losing their incentives to work by being given large inheritances.

Moreover, to the extent that those who are given large inheritances do in fact put themselves or their inheritances to productive use, these inheritances tend to undermine productivity in another, more subtle, yet important way. To the extent that a person's productivity is the result of a large inheritance, this productivity is a result of opportunities that were not equal. And, to the extent that productivity is the result of opportunities that were not equal, overall productivity suffers. The intuitive idea is this. Everyone is born with different 'inherent capacities', potentialities that may or may not be realized. Society is most productive to the extent that people's inherent capacities, once developed, are appropriate for - that is, a good 'match' for - the positions they hold in society. Take, for example, Jane, with inherent capacities appropriate for becoming a successful Chief Executive Officer (CEO), and John, with inherent capacities appropriate only for a lesser position in the enterprise. Society will be most productive if, in fact, Jane is the CEO and John holds a lesser position. The best way to assure that people's inherent capacities generally do match their positions is for everyone to have an equal opportunity at getting every position. But the more inheritance there is, the less equal people's opportunities will be and, hence, the less close the match between people's inherent capacities and their positions. And the less close the match, the less the productivity. For example, John, through inheriting the enterprise, or the funds to buy the enterprise, may then set himself up as CEO and, not having the inherent capacities for this position, end up squandering the enterprise's assets. And once John has pre-empted the CEO position for himself, Jane will have to settle for a lesser position in the enterprise, one in which much of her potential for productivity will be wasted. So even if John, through inheriting a large fortune, did not lose his incentive to work hard, productivity would probably end up being lost anyway.

II. Practice

1. Abolishing Inheritance: Answers to Objections

Let us turn now from theory to practice. The social policy that seems to follow most obviously from the productivity ideal of distributive justice is the abolishment of inheritance. And whenever I speak of abolishing inheritance, this must be taken to mean abolishing not just bequests, but gifts as well - that is, ones large enough so that they could defeat the purpose of abolishing inheritance. Nothing seems further from the ideal of 'to all people according to the productivity of their labour' than inheritance, which people get for absolutely no productive labour at all. Nor does anything seem further from the closely related ideal of equal opportunity, since, given that wealth *is* opportunity, those who inherit large fortunes have, as a result, significantly more opportunities than those who do not.

But before setting out the details of what I take to be the most justified policy on inheritance, let me first address some common objections to abolishing it.[9] The first objection often brought up is that a law abolishing inheritance is altogether unenforceable since there are so many ways to cheat on such a law - secret Swiss bank accounts, bogus jobs, bogus marriages, simply passing money under the table, and the like. The answer to this objection is that, without broad public support, almost any law is unenforceable, while with broad public support, almost any law, including this one, can be enforced. With broad public support, enough people will comply with the law *voluntarily* to make it work, just as is the case with current income tax law. The only question is whether, for a law abolishing inheritance, there ever will be broad public support, which, in turn, depends upon whether such a law is (*aside* from its public support) justifiable. And the latter is, of course, precisely the question at hand here.

The next objection often brought up against abolishing inheritance is that no longer being able to leave one's money to one's children will significantly reduce people's incentives to be productive.[10] But empirical

---

9 Incidentally, I hope no one is tempted to raise the following objection to abolishing inheritance, an objection based on so-called property rights. The objection is that our right to property includes the right to give our property to whomever we please, and therefore abolishing inheritance clearly violates this fundamental right. This objection is weak simply because it begs the question. Our right to property should be delineated in whatever way is most justified, and one way of putting the very point at issue in discussing the abolishment of inheritance is whether or not it is justified to make our right to property so rigid that it excludes any constraints whatever upon the capacity to give. This issue can only be resolved through rational argumentation; not dogmatic proclamation.

10 It is, I think, a rather perverse consequence of the institution of inheritance that so many people seem to view what parents can give their children primarily in terms of wealth. My own view is that there are far more important things that parents can give their children, such as their time and love, and the skills, capacities and values that will enable their children to succeed in life on their own, rather than having to live largely off the success of their parents. By abolishing inheritance, perhaps parents will then concentrate more on giving

studies,[11] as well as common sense, suggest otherwise. After all, people with no children to inherit their wealth are certainly no less productive, on average, then those who do have children. The fact is that people are motivated to be productive for many reasons other than merely that of leaving their money to their children; these reasons include that of supporting their children well while their children remain dependents, saving for old age, and, of course, enjoying their wealth by spending it on themselves. Moreover, another, very fundamental reason for being productive is simply that of *succeeding*, and thereby gaining respect from others, as well as self-respect. Just as a professional athlete will surely try just as hard to win, regardless of whether or not he can leave his wealth to his children, so also will a business executive, doctor, lawyer, engineer, or research scientist try just as hard to "win" - if for no other reason than for the sake of respect from others and self-respect.[12]

But, it might now be objected, even if abolishing inheritance would not decrease productivity by decreasing people's incentives to be productive, would it not decrease productivity by decreasing people's incentives to save and invest? Would not people simply reason that, since they cannot either take their wealth with them when they die or give it to loved ones, they might as well spend it? Moreover, with the abolishment of inheritance, would not the number of ultrarich people with the capacity for really big-time savings and investment be fewer? Therefore would not abolishing inheritance significantly undermine the very savings and investment upon which the creation of new capital, and thus productivity growth, depends?

---

their children not mere wealth, but what is more important: love, capacities, values, and strength of character.

11 See, for example, McClelland (1961, pp. 234-5) and Fiekowsky (1959, pp. 370-1).

12 Also, consider the following 'race' analogy, which suggests that abolishing inheritance will actually tend to *increase* people's incentives to succeed. In which of the following 100 meter races will each of two competing runners have the most incentive to run hard: one in which both start equally, or one in which one starts with a 50 meter head start (thereby making his victory virtually a foregone conclusion)? Clearly *both* will have the most incentive in the race in which they start equally. What is true about footraces is probably true about the 'race of life' as well: the more equal people's starting points, the greater will tend to be their incentives to succeed, and, of course, abolishing inheritance helps equalize starting points.

In fact, no one really knows for sure how, if at all, abolishing inheritance would affect savings and investment. There are reasons to believe, however, that the effect may not, or need not, be serious. Much of society's new-capital savings and investment today is corporate savings and investment, which will be unaffected by abolishing inheritance.[13] And even if inheritance is abolished people must continue to save for the future anyway, since no one knows for how many years, and in what state of health, they or their spouse may have to live off these savings. Although abolishing inheritance will decrease the number of ultrarich people there are to save and invest, the number of moderately well-off people is likely to increase, thereby helping somewhat to take up any slack. Moreover, abolishing inheritance will give rise to an important countertendency, often overlooked, in the form of *increased* savings and investment. With no prospects for inheritance, the need for people to save for their *own* future will be greater than ever, and, accordingly, so too may be their savings. Let us also not forget that, even if inheritance is abolished, many, especially the ultrarich, will continue to cling to their fortunes merely from the sheer joy, power, and prestige they get from maintaining control over large sums of money.[14]

---

13 Conversely, much savings and investment by the rich takes the form of trading in previously-issued stock, and therefore does not create new capital. A ready market for previously-issued stock is, of course, necessary for supporting a healthy market in newly-issued stock, the funds from which typically do go to create new capital, but we cannot assume that any given percentage drop in *overall* savings and investment by the rich will necessarily result in the very same percentage drop in *new-capital* savings and investment. Perhaps more than enough savings and investment in the form of trading in previously issued stock takes place today than is actually necessary for supporting a healthy market in newly-issued stock. Indeed, perhaps it is precisely such socially superfluous trading which accounts, in large part, for why stock prices periodically become greatly inflated, thereby setting the stage for market crashes and recessions.

14 McCAFFERY (1995) argues for a progressive consumption tax in place of any tax upon not only income, but gifts and bequests (i.e. estate taxes) as well. His main argument against estate taxes seems to be that they greatly decrease savings and investment, in favour of consumption. But, to make his case against estate taxes as clear as possible, he simply assumes, *arguendo*, that these taxes greatly decrease savings and investment, not to mention hard work (p. 289). But, as I have been trying to show, this assumption is unwarranted. And if this assumption is unwarranted, then McCAFFERY's essay is left with nothing with

Finally, if, as a result of abolishing inheritance, savings and investment throughout society did prove to be inadequate, government has many measures at hand that can be used to motivate more savings and investment. These measures include a switch from taxing income to taxing consumption, or (for the U.S.) some plan for funneling one's Social Security taxes into the hands of a private investment manager of one's choice rather than merely into government coffers. Another such measure is, of course, simply to use the amounts collected from abolishing inheritance to *subsidize* investments (or, if the amounts thus collected are insufficient, to use instead amounts collected from ordinary taxes). Such a subsidy can, for example, take the form of governmental matching funds that work as follows. For any amount an entrepreneur is able to raise on his own for (and only for) creating new capital, the government is to match it with some additional sum to be set by law at whatever amount may be necessary for bringing investments in new capital throughout society up to the desired level. Governmental control over *what* investments are pursued can be avoided if the government is forbidden from picking and choosing, but instead must thus subsidize each investment in new capital equally. And thus subsidizing too many *frivolous* investments can be avoided largely by requiring that each entrepreneur put up the majority of the funds himself. (Certain other requirements of a more technical nature will, I assume, be necessary here also.) Finally, to the extent that investment in new capital is brought about through these subsidies rather than relying instead upon inheritance, investment efficiency may actually increase, since these subsidies, as opposed to inheritance, put

---

which to counter the substantial advantages, both in theory and practice, of estate taxes, or abolishing inheritance altogether. Moreover, even if his assumption were warranted - that is, even if abolishing inheritance did result in an unacceptable decline in investments - there would be, as I try to show in the following pages, better ways of reinstating the previous level of investments, ways, if you will, that would be more compatible with 'political liberalism', than bringing back inheritance as we know it today. For additional support for my claim that abolishing inheritance will not necessarily decrease savings and investment, see ASCHER (1993, esp. pp. 102-11), and DUFF (1993, esp. pp. 10-3, 28-37). Both of the above are thorough, well researched essays. More detail on my answer to the savings and investment objection, as well as my answers to other objections to abolishing inheritance as we know it today, is found in Chapter 6 of HASLETT (1994).

investment funds *directly* in the hands of those with the most creativity and initiative for creating new capital.

2. A Compromise Inheritance Policy

But what I consider to be the most justified social policy with respect to inheritance largely avoids the savings and investment problem anyway. It is time, therefore, to set out exactly what this policy is. This policy - the one that, I submit, achieves the best compromise between distributive justice and other political ideals such as freedom and equality - is not a complete abolishment of inheritance, but rather a lifetime inheritance (i.e. gift and bequest) quota.[15] The way this quota works is as follows. First, the amount of the quota is to be set at an amount that is small enough to break up large fortunes yet large enough not to impede most giving and receiving among people of ordinary means, a giving and receiving not likely to create dramatic inequalities of opportunity that have a major effect upon how justly wealth is distributed. For any given country, an amount somewhere around the current, average (i.e. mean) value of the estates of all people in that country who die over age twenty-one might be appropriate.[16] In the United States, for example, this might, today, translate into a lifetime inheritance quota of, say, $100,000. And just as one must, today, report all one's income to the government each year, likewise with this inheritance quota one is, at the same time, to report all gifts and bequests received each year. Once one's reportable gifts and bequests, throughout one's lifetime, reach the quota, then one is no longer eligible to receive further reportable gifts or bequests

15 A quota, although a more lenient one than advocated here, was also advocated by John Stuart MILL. See MILL (1965, p. 225).

16 Another, perhaps better, benchmark for the amount of a country's quota is the average (i.e. mean) *net wealth* of all individuals in that country over age twenty-five. I choose age twenty-five simply because, by then, most of those who have gone to college, and even graduate school, will have finished. In any case, once the amount of the quota is set, it should then be 'indexed' so as to change automatically with (very substantial) changes in average wealth throughout the country, whether these changes be real or merely a result of changes in the value of the country's currency. Any percentage change in the amount of the quota would, of course, be applicable only to any, as yet, unfulfilled portion of a person's quota.

from anyone.[17] Excluded from this reporting requirement, of course, will be the ordinary, relatively small gifts people get for birthdays and other special occasions.[18]

Also excluded from this reporting requirement will be any gifts or bequests falling under one of the following three exceptions to the quota. First, unlimited gifts and bequests between spouses are to be allowed. The closeness of the relationship between husband and wife, and the differing contributions and sacrifices necessary from both for the sake of overall productivity from the marriage-unit, makes an analogy to a business partnership not too far-fetched for the typical marriage, and helps justify this exception for unlimited inheritance between spouses.[19] Second, everyone is to be able to support, as luxuriously as they please, their minor children and other genuine dependants, and bequeath to them as much in trust as may be necessary for continuing to support them for as long as they remain

---

17 ASCHER (1993) suggests that, rather than a lifetime quota on how much any given person may *receive*, we establish the quota on how much any given person may *give* (he suggests $250,000). This is an interesting idea; it has the advantage of making wills simpler. The main advantage of placing the quota, instead, on how much a person may receive, and why I tend to support this alternative, is that it will tend to disperse the estates of the wealthy more widely and, for those who know a ***number*** of eligible people to whom they want to leave some wealth, it then provides more motivation for savings.

18 The general idea is to exclude from the reporting requirement those gifts, perhaps even fairly expensive ones, that depreciate in value and cannot serve to establish a significant estate. Exactly where to draw the line, for purposes of an inheritance quota, between reportable and nonreportable gifts, and how to do so without leaving open loopholes, are technical details we need not pursue here.

19 Actually, so as to prevent marriages of convenience, those merely for purposes of avoiding the quota, this unlimited exception may have to be qualified. The most reasonable way of doing so is, I suggest, something like this. Prior to marriage, each person's assets are to be evaluated. Unlimited inheritance as between spouses is then to be applicable only to any amount by which the total value of their combined assets at the time of the first spouse's death exceeds the value of the assets which the deceased spouse initially brought to the marriage. This provision might be softened with an additional provision providing that, with each passing year, each spouse is to become entitled to an additional 5 percent of what the other spouse initially brought to the marriage, so that after 20 years of marriage, but *only* after 20 years, inheritance between spouses would then be unlimited. Cf. the proposal of ASCHER (1993, pp. 123-6).

incapacitated, underage, or are making normal progress toward a higher educational, or trade school, degree. For dependents, gifts that quickly depreciate in value, such as (ordinary) automobiles, or that take the form of education of any sort, are not to count toward the quota, but large gifts that retain their value and can form the basis for a future nest egg do count. Genuine dependants cannot be expected to be highly productive. Therefore this exception for dependents will not, to any great extent, support idleness from people who otherwise would have been productive. And, assuming that all families have at least the basic necessities, including educational opportunities (see below), this exception will not create enormous inequalities of opportunity either. Thus this exception will not, to any great extent, undermine the productivity that constitutes much of the rationale for distributive justice. The third and final exception to the quota takes the form of allowing unlimited gifts and bequests for genuine charitable organizations or purposes. Like the exception for dependents, such an exception will neither be an incentive for people to remain idle nor create significant inequalities of opportunity; thus it will not undermine the rationale for distributive justice either.[20]

Finally, to the extent that one's wealth does not, upon one's death, go to people who have not already received their quota or to those, such as charitable organizations, exempt from it, then one's wealth is to go to the government. And any non-cash assets that the government, or a charity, so receives are to be sold to the highest bidder within a reasonable time - say, six months.

The inheritance policy set out above has the following advantages over the most obvious alternatives. Take, first, the alternative of leaving things as they are today. Today, in most countries, there are relatively few restrictions upon inheritance. Consider, for example, the United States. There is, to be sure, a relatively high *nominal* tax upon gifts and bequests.[21] But there are so many loopholes built into this tax that, as one authority has pointed out, it amounts to little more than a "voluntary" tax.[22] And, according to the best evidence available today, of men who qualify as "ultrarich" in the United

20 So as to avoid an obvious loophole, to qualify as a charitable organization for purposes of this unlimited exception, the salaries paid by the organization to those who manage it will have to be strictly limited, by law.

21 According to current U.S. law, after a generous exemption of $1.2 million per married couple, estate taxation rates quickly move up to a 55 percent level.

22 See COOPER (1979).

States, inheritance is primarily responsible for the fortunes of no less than sixty-seven percent.[23] Under these circumstances, a strict, lifetime inheritance quota, since it precludes people from receiving vast sums of wealth for no productivity at all, will certainly result in a distribution of wealth more in accordance with the productivity ideal of distributive justice. Moreover, by forcing the ultrarich to break up their fortunes and spread them among a far greater number of people, this quota will achieve greater equality of opportunity, which (considering the close relationship between distributive justice and equal opportunity) will contribute to a more just distribution as well. With greater equality of opportunity, more people will have the opportunity to pursue one of the higher-paying occupations, such as doctor, lawyer, business entrepreneur, and so on. And, given only that the relative scarcity of people in these occupations today is, to a significant extent, due to unnecessary limitations on opportunity (as I suspect it is), with greater opportunity to pursue these occupations, more people will in fact pursue them. More people pursuing today's higher-paying occupations will leave less people available for pursuing today's lower-paying occupations, such as assembly line work, sales clerk, and manual labourer. This, according to the law of supply and demand, will, in turn, mean that the higher-paying occupations will become somewhat less high paying and the lower-paying occupations somewhat less low paying, all of which will tend to equalize incomes, and thus opportunities, even more. With even more equality of opportunity may come even more people pursuing higher-paying occupations, and so on, all over again. In short, spreading large fortunes around more evenly may actually jump start a benevolent cycle of sorts, which is similar to a vicious cycle, except that the consequences keep getting better and better rather than worse and worse.

To be sure, we will never be able to achieve *complete* equality of opportunity, or of wealth - certainly not without doing more harm than good through abolishing the family, tinkering with genes, and other ill-conceived measures. But that in no way detracts from the gains in equality of opportunity and wealth achievable through an inheritance quota and other measures with net results that are good. Half a loaf is better than none at all. Nor, incidentally, is an inheritance quota the *only* reform that is needed for increasing equality of opportunity and wealth; reforms that make educational opportunities more available for all, that equalize health care,

---

23 See BRITTAIN (1978).

that provide every family with access to at least bare necessities, are needed also (more on this below).

Finally, although an inheritance quota will decrease somewhat the freedom enjoyed by the ultrarich today, the resulting gains in equality of opportunity, equality of wealth, and overall productivity should bring about more freedom to do what one wants for almost everyone else. Thus the *overall* amount of freedom throughout society will increase, an increase that will be experienced along a number of different dimensions. A more equal distribution of wealth, for example, promotes freedom from the constraints of poverty. It also promotes 'social' freedom by helping break down class barriers, and, in so far as political power is a function of wealth, it promotes political freedom as well.[24]

Compare now the inheritance quota set out above with that of abolishing inheritance altogether. Although by not abolishing inheritance altogether there may be some loss in distributive justice, a quota goes far toward avoiding legitimate objections against abolishing inheritance, and thereby represents, I submit, the best possible compromise. First, a quota goes far toward avoiding the potential savings and investment objection. Say the quota is, as I suggested above, set at the average value, today, of an adult's estate at the time of his or her death. Most people will probably know at least five people for whom they really care who will not yet have received any, or much, of their quota - children, grandchildren, great grandchildren, friends, close relatives, the children of close relatives, loyal employees,[25] and the like. Thus most people will be able to leave an amount to loved ones that is at least five times the value of the average estate. Accordingly, people with net wealth up to at least five times greater than average will tend to have as much motivation to save and invest as they would with no restrictions on inheritance at all. This, of course, includes almost everyone. Moreover, such a quota means that government will have to become involved in the sale of assets in only a relatively few cases, which will preclude any serious governmental red-tape problem. Another legitimate

24 In HASLETT (1994) I discuss how abolishing inheritance affects freedom in more detail (pp. 241-5) and I defend the sense in which I use the word 'freedom' (pp. 76-9).

25 Leaving wealth to loyal employees may be especially appropriate for wealth in the form of the business in which these employees have been working. Such a bequest can help workers purchase the business and transform it into a worker-controlled enterprise. On this, see HASLETT (1994, pp. 260-1).

objection to abolishing inheritance altogether is that this will prevent the passing of family heirlooms, homesteads, and small family businesses from one generation to the next, heirlooms, homesteads and businesses that might well be of far more value to family members than is their value on the market. But the lifetime inheritance quota will enable family heirlooms and, by using the amount as a down payment, all but the most expensive homesteads and small businesses to be purchased by family members who care enough. This is especially true if this quota is combined, as I think it should be, with regulations (1) that provide people with the opportunity to designate, in their wills, those who are to be given first chance at any such purchases, and (2) that provide those so designated with helpful credit terms.[26]

Finally, compare an inheritance quota with a progressive inheritance (not estate) *tax*. A progressive inheritance tax, if sufficiently rigorous, may not be altogether bad. But one disadvantage of an inheritance tax is that, like any tax, it is likely, sooner or later, to become riddled with insidious loopholes created for special interests by unscrupulous politicians. It is not, of course, certain that a quota can be any more successful in avoiding most insidious loopholes, but, contrary to a tax, it does at least succeed in placing a ceiling upon how much any one person can, throughout his or her life, receive from all sources - a ceiling that is necessarily absent with a tax. And the absence of any such ceiling is perhaps the most insidious loophole of all.

3. Other Policies and Reforms

Before closing, let us consider, briefly, how compatible the productivity ideal of distributive justice is with important social policies or reforms that do not involve inheritance. Consider, first, government programs designed to fight poverty. Even in a country as rich as the United States is today, over ten percent of all families, and one in every four children under age six, live

26 To prevent the fragmentation of farmland through governmental sale, whether to family members or not, any such sale of farmland could be limited, by law, only to its sale as a whole, with a restriction in the deed prohibiting any resale within a certain number of years except as a whole (unless, for some reason, the land no longer remained viable *farm*land).

in poverty - that is, without even enough for the bare necessities of life.[27] Formulating governmental programs that will eliminate most of this poverty without, at the same time, compromising people's incentives to work, or undermining important values such as productivity and freedom, is difficult, yet it can be done. But rather than going into the details of how it can be done, which I try to do elsewhere,[28] here I shall merely address how such programs are likely to affect distributive justice.

Somewhat paradoxically, the effect of antipoverty (or 'welfare') programs may be to bring about what, according to the productivity ideal, is both a gain and a loss in distributive justice. Antipoverty programs bring about a loss in distributive justice to the extent that these programs, coercively through taxes, take income from the rich that accurately reflected their productivity and transfer it, or its equivalent in goods and services, to the poor irrespective of their productivity. On the other hand, such programs bring about a gain in distributive justice to the extent that they help bring about the equal opportunities for all so essential if people's incomes really are to accurately reflect their productivity. Indeed, if the incomes of poor working people at present under-represent their productivity because of the very inequalities in opportunity that these antipoverty programs are designed, in part, to remedy, then at least those programs that supplement the incomes of poor *working* people may bring about a gain only, without any corresponding loss, in distributive justice. Given the vast inequalities in opportunity that exist today, income-supplementing programs almost surely do, in fact, bring about a gain only. I have in mind here programs such as the 'refundable earned income credit' (EIC) program.[29] And, as we have seen, for people's incomes to accurately reflect their productivity, it is also essential that externalities be 'internalized'. Thus antipoverty programs that help internalize certain *positive externalities* probably bring about an overall gain in distributive justice as well. I have in mind here positive externalities

27 These figures, along with other information about poverty in the United States, can be found in SHAW and BARRY (1994, pp. 128-30).

28 See Chapter 5 of HASLETT (1994).

29 For the details of an EIC program that will eliminate virtually all poverty among poor working families, see Chapter 5 of HASLETT (1994). As I try to explain in that chapter, increasing the incomes of poor working people through programs funded from tax revenue, such as this EIC program, is far superior to doing so by means of minimum wage legislation, which creates as many problems as it solves.

in the form of a healthier, better educated, and therefore more productive society for all, externalities that programs such as universal health care and educational subsidies help internalize. Yet even if, contrary to what I have been suggesting, the effect of these programs upon distributive justice were neutral, or even somewhat negative, the sheer relief from suffering that they bring to the poor would probably tip the balance in their favour anyway. Distributive justice is, after all, only a prima facie, not absolute, ideal.

Consider, finally, the compatibility of the productivity ideal of distributive justice with a revolutionary form of capitalism sometimes called 'worker control capitalism'. This is a form of capitalism in which each worker, from janitor to CEO, and *only* each worker, has an individual share in the ownership of the enterprise at which he or she works, along with an equal vote in periodically electing a management team for the enterprise. I argue elsewhere that the potential advantages of this form of capitalism over traditional capitalism are considerable.[30] Among these advantages is a more equal distribution of income. For one thing, managers who are responsible to workers as a whole will probably find it more difficult than managers do today to unjustifiably pad their own salaries at the expense of ordinary workers. This translates into a distribution that is more just. Another potential advantage is as follows. Managers, being responsible to workers who must live in the immediate area, may be more reluctant to pollute this area, or, in other words, they may be more likely to internalize certain externalities, which, to whatever extent it happens, also translates into a distribution that is more just. But it might be argued that, in at least the following respect, worker control will bring about a distribution that is less just. With worker control capitalism, just as with traditional capitalism, each worker's income is supposed to depend upon his or her productivity, which is perfectly compatible with the productivity ideal. Yet with worker control capitalism, each worker's individual share in the ownership of the enterprise, a share that serves to supplement his or her wealth, does *not* depend upon his or her productivity. So, it might be argued, to this extent at least, worker control capitalism may not be as compatible with the productivity ideal as traditional capitalism. On the other hand, this supplement to the *wealth* of working people is no different, in principle, from a supplement to the *income* of working people from an antipoverty program. Given, once again, the extent to which the distribution of income

---

30 See Chapter 4 of HASLETT (1994).

and wealth is currently distorted as a result of unnecessary inequalities of opportunity - including inequalities of 'investment' opportunity - this supplement to wealth, like a supplement to income, may well therefore bring about a distribution that is more, not less, just.[31]

References

ASCHER, M.L. (1993): "Curtailing inherited wealth", *Michigan Law Review*, 89, pp. 61-151.

BRITTAIN, J.A. (1978): *Inheritance and the Inequality of National Wealth*, Washington, DC (Brookings Institute).

BUCHANAN, A. (1985): *Ethics, Efficiency, and the Market*, Totowa, NJ (Rowman & Allanheld).

COOPER, G. (1979): *A Voluntary Tax? New Perspectives on Sophisticated Estate Tax Avoidance*, Washington, DC (Brookings Institute).

DUFF, D.G. (1993): "Taxing inherited wealth: A philosophical proposal", *Canadian Journal of Law and Jurisprudence*, 6, pp. 3-62.

FIEKOWSKY, S. (1959): *On the Economic Effects of Taxation in the United States*, Cambridge, MA (Harvard University), unpublished dissertation.

FRIEDMAN, M. (1962): *Capitalism and Freedom*, Chicago (University of Chicago Press).

HASLETT, D.W. (1987): *Equal Consideration: A Theory of Moral Justification*, Newark, DE (University of Delaware Press); London and Toronto (Associated University Presses).

HASLETT, D.W. (1990): "What is utility?", *Economics and Philosophy*, 6, pp. 65-94.

HASLETT, D.W. (1994): *Capitalism with Morality*, Oxford (Clarendon Press).

MCCAFFERY, E.J. (1994): "The political liberal case against the estate tax", *Philosophy and Public Affairs*, 23, pp. 281-312.

---

31 I have benefited from comments on an earlier version of this essay by Ken Koford, James P. Sterba, and the participants at the conference "Is Inheritance Legitimate?".

McCLELLAND, D.C. (1961): *The Achieving Society*, Princeton, NJ (Van Nostrand).
MILL, J.S. (1965): ***Principles of Political Economy, with Some of their Applications** to Social Philiosophy*, ed. by V.W. Bladen and J.M. Robson, Toronto (University of Toronto Press); London (Routledge and Kegan Paul) (= Collected Works of John Stuart Mill, Vols. II-III).
PROUDHON, P.-J. (1876): *What is Property?*, Princeton (Princeton University Press).
RAWLS, J. (1971): *A Theory of Justice*, Cambridge, MA (Harvard University Press)
SHAW, W. and BARRY, V. (Eds.) (1994): *Moral Issues in Business*, Belmont, CA (Wadsworth).

Chapter 7

The Hidden Costs of Inheritance Taxation

BARRY BRACEWELL-MILNES

I. Introduction

Inheritance is an institution of great antiquity which has been regarded with favour or even with reverence in a wide variety of cultures. In the King James translation of the Bible, there are about 125 references to inheritance, all favourable; the sense of the word is sometimes material, sometimes moral or spiritual, and sometimes a mixture of the two. The transmission to the next generation of both a moral and a material legacy is regarded as a duty; the members of the present generation are not so much the absolute owners of material possessions as their stewards. *The Lord forbid it me,* says Naboth to Ahab, *that I should give the inheritance of my fathers unto thee.* (I Kings XXI 3).

Institutions attract taxation. Inheritance taxation[1] can be traced back through the medieval *heriot* or 'voluntary' donation from the tenant to his feudal lord, to the Roman twentieth (5 per cent) or *vicesima hereditatium* and ultimately to Egypt in the first millennium before Christ.[2] The main reason for its persistence over such a long period was its convenience for governments: governments were inevitably involved in effecting the passage of title to the heirs of the deceased, and it was little extra trouble to levy a tax charge when the relevant facts were already at the government's disposal. Taxes at this level do limited damage (although 5 per cent is substantial, and it is explained below what damage is done by any tax on giving, at however low a rate). Within the last century and a half, however, two developments have served to raise rates of inheritance tax to far more confiscatory levels.

First, death duties have been used as an engine of redistribution from rich to poor. In the United Kingdom, explicitly redistributive death duties started with Sir William Harcourt's estate duty, introduced in 1894 with the slogan "We are all socialists now". Rates of tax increased over the next half century, reaching avowedly sacrificial levels in the interest of the War effort

1 *Estate duty* or *capital transfer tax* is a tax on the testator or donor. *Succession duty* is a tax on the heir or donee. Inheritance tax is usually a tax on the heir or donee; but in the United Kingdom it is a tax on the testator or donor. *Death duties* is a generic term for any tax on the occasion of death and (by extension) on lifetime gifts (gifts *inter vivos).*

2 See Max WEST (1908, pp. 12-5). Cf. also Barry BRACEWELL-MILNES (1989, p. 20).

during the Second World War. The top rate of tax remained at or above wartime levels until it was reduced from 75 per cent to 60 per cent in 1986 and to 40 per cent in 1988. On the continent of Europe, rates of inheritance tax did not generally rise so high as in Britain; and bequests in the direct line are still taxed at an average maximum rate of some 25 per cent, as compared with 40 per cent in the United Kingdom.

Second, it has come to be believed in some liberal as well as socialist circles that the economic agent is the individual rather than the family and that the suppression of inheritance, whether through taxation or otherwise, is economically and socially neutral or even beneficial, because it prevents the control of assets from passing to those whose qualifications are genetic rather than meritocratic.

Neither of these attitudes is powerful today. Confiscatory rates of tax have lost their appeal, and death duties are widely opposed as yet another tax on saving. Yet variants of these ideas provide death duties with much of the modest intellectual support they still enjoy.

The present paper argues that these intellectual supports for death duties are mistaken on their own terms. They impose too heavy a cost in their own dimensions of equality and efficiency. These costs, like the cost of not insuring against fire or theft, are not the less real for being hidden. Economic cost is opportunity cost, the cost of wealth destroyed or not created, the cost of a lower quality of life and diminished social harmony.

This paper draws on three earlier publications of mine, all mentioned in the bibliography. *Land and Heritage* examined the economic concepts of perpetual saving and stewardship. *The Wealth of Giving* discussed the creation of wealth through giving and bequest and the vulnerability of this creation to inheritance tax and other forms of death duties. *Will to Succeed* analysed the perverse consequences of inheritance tax in all the dimensions in which it operates.

The paper has a United Kingdom orientation; but the arguments are generally applicable to other countries.

Section II of the paper starts with the traditional concepts of economic indifference and consumer's surplus. Sections III and IV move on to the analogous concepts of saver's surplus and owner's surplus and Section IV considers the relationship of owner's surplus to saving in perpetuity. Section V explains the creation of wealth through donor's surplus. Section VI compares and contrasts ownership with stewardship and examines the potential for wealth creation through the latter. Section VII analyses the tax system in terms of taxes on spending and taxes on saving. Section VIII discusses the implications of the foregoing argument for the taxation of giving and inheritance. Section IX revisits the ideal of equality of opportunity, and Section X computes the amount of wealth which inheritance tax puts at risk. Section XI notes the implications of the argument for public policy.

II. Economic Indifference and Consumer's Surplus

It is argued against death duties that they are old-fashioned and form no logical part of a modern tax system; that their administrative and compliance costs are exceptionally high; that the Treasury may lose more than their nominal yield from the reductions they effect in the yields of other taxes; that they are a disproportionately heavy burden on small and medium-sized firms and that they thus increase unemployment, since these firms are principal providers of new jobs; that they cause damaging 'short-termist' distortions to the economy by artificially curtailing the time-horizons of economic agents; that they are unthrifty and anticipatory taxes that levy on the present value of future income flows; that the proceeds of taxes on capital are used to defray government spending on current account; and in general that they are inimical to the creation of material wealth in a capitalist system.

These arguments are correct and important, and I have addressed them in *Will to Succeed*. Most of them constitute hidden costs and thus fall within our terms of reference here. The present paper, however, focuses on the complementary and less familiar thesis that death duties are no less damaging through their destruction of immaterial wealth, the wealth that subsists in the mind.

Mainstream theory of economic value has derived for more than a century from the work done on marginal utility, independently of each other, by Jevons, Menger and Walras in the 1870s. Value is subjective and in the mind of the consumer, not objective and externally determined; and the value of each unit of any good or service to a given consumer tends to fall as the quantity consumed increases. This latter idea has reached the general public in the phrases 'diminishing returns' or 'the law of diminishing returns'. The main rival of marginal-utility value theory has been the labour theory of value, derived from Adam Smith, David Ricardo and Karl Marx. The labour theory of value has provided the theoretical underpinnings of socialism; and the collapse of communism in the Soviet Union and Eastern Europe constitutes the most spectacular refutation of an economic theory on record. Attempts by followers of Ricardo to develop a non-Marxist labour theory of value have not supplied marginal-utility theory with a serious competitor.

The economic value of consumption to the consumer lies in his consumer's surplus, the excess of his marginal-utility curve over the price he has to pay. When his marginal-utility curve has fallen to the market price, he is *indifferent* to further consumption of the good; no value is created for him by the purchase of another unit at this point since his gain in utility exactly matches his loss in money. Beyond the point of indifference, he loses from the purchase of additional units, since his gain in utility is less than the market price.

Similarly, producer's surplus is the excess of the market price over the cost of production in lost utility. Production ceases at the point of indifference, where this rising cost reaches the market price.

It is often assumed rather than argued that the consumer's utility curve is given, just as the market price is generally beyond the control of the consumer. This may be a useful assumption for analytical purposes, and it may be true in particular circumstances; but it is not true universally. For example, a spoilt child has a low utility curve for many goods and services, takes too many things for granted, is not grateful for presents, does not appreciate his good fortune and so on. An improvement in his upbringing might take the form of reducing the supply of goods and services; but even at his present level of consumption, wealth is created if he is induced to mend his ways and value the goods and services he is using more as he would if he were paying for them himself.

Examples could be multiplied. The argument is a general one. The curve of a consumer's utility may be fixed or it may be more or less variable. If it is variable, the consumer may gain as much (or more) from a rise in the utility curve as from a fall in the price or an increase in income that enables him to buy more units of the good or service. Although the argument is presented here in terms of economic theory, it has long been understood as a spiritual truth. *Magnum vectigal est parsimonia*, says the Latin proverb quoted by Cicero, economy is a large income. In the capital dimension,

Godliness is great riches, says St. Paul to Timothy, *if a man be content with that he hath.* (I.VI.6). We now extend the argument to saver's surplus.

III. Consumer's Surplus and Saver's Surplus

The two ultimate aims of economic activity are consumption and perpetual saving: whatever is not used for the one is used for the other. The two are equally rational sources of economic satisfaction.

It is sometimes argued that consumption is ultimately the only rational purpose of economic activity. I have shown elsewhere that this argument is mistaken.[3] It is inconsistent with the facts. If consumption were the only rational economic aim, everyone would invest his total wealth in annuities and spend to the limit, so that at the time of his death the value of his estate would be nil. But people do not behave like this. As Marshall says:

> "That men labour and save chiefly for the sake of their families and not for themselves, is shown by the fact that they seldom spend, after they have retired from work, more than the income that comes in from their savings, preferring to leave their stored-up wealth intact for their families (...). (...)
>
> A man can have no stronger stimulus to energy and enterprise than the hope of rising in life and leaving his family to start from a higher round of the social ladder than that on which he began."[4]

The argument that consumption is the end of economic activity is also strikingly refuted by the twelfth satire of Juvenal. His target was the legacy-hunters who leeched on the *orbi*, the childless men of substance who might be persuaded to make them their heirs. These *orbi* were so far from being consumption-maximisers that, in the absence of descendants of their own, they were willing to be swindled by these scroungers rather than spend their own money on themselves.

---

3 See Barry BRACEWELL-MILNES (1982, p 23-25).

4 See Alfred MARSHALL (1961, Book IV, Chapter VII, para. 6; in the margin he summarized this paragraph with the words: "A few people save for their own sakes: but the chief motive of saving is family affection."). By a similar process, an expectation of inheritance is confirmed through the passage of time in the minds of the beneficiaries.

The argument that consumption is ultimately the only rational economic aim is right in so far as consumption has logical priority over production. But the error of excluding perpetual saving appears to derive from a model of economic activity and agency that focuses on the individual and the firm and neglects the importance of the family. The economic behaviour of the family is more complex and less tidy than that of individuals and firms, but not less important or worthy of study.[5] *Atomistic individualism* may be a useful assumption for certain purposes of argument and analysis; but it is a poor guide to reality.

Temporary saving is consumption with a time dimension. As in forward contracts and futures markets, there is a specified relationship between an amount of consumption now and a larger amount at a named future date. For every individual this relationship gives his subjective rate of discount. Many children and some adults find waiting for consumption difficult or tedious and therefore have a high subjective rate of interest or discount; those who can wait without impatience have a lower subjective rate. The market rate of interest or discount is the market-clearing rate at which one can lend or borrow. Bringing consumption forward is an economic good or service which commands a market price. This price, the rate of interest or discount, makes it attractive for both the lender to lend and the borrower to borrow. The analysis is the same as for the sale and purchase of any other good or service.

It follows that the lender with a subjective rate of discount lower than the market rate enjoys a lender's surplus (or saver's surplus) strictly analogous to producer's surplus. The borrower with a subjective rate of discount higher than the market rate enjoys a borrower's surplus strictly analogous to consumer's surplus. Wealth can be created by reducing the saver's subjective rate of discount. The opposite process of wealth creation through an increase in the borrower's subjective rate of discount is subject to the severe practical constraint of his ability to service his borrowings.

Whereas temporary saving is a producer activity and temporary borrowing a consumer activity, perpetual saving is both. It is a producer activity in that it provides a service to others and a consumer activity in that it is enjoyed for its own sake. It is like paid work which people would do for nothing or would even pay to do. Work of this kind is still work to the consumer; but if the 'disutility' of work becomes a 'utility', more than the

5 See Gary S. BECKER (1981).

whole payment for work becomes producer's surplus and the wealth created per unit of payment is drastically increased.

Perpetual saving need not be planned as such. It becomes perpetual merely by virtue of never being drawn down for consumption. In every period in which it is not drawn down, the saver prefers the combination of interest (or other income) and ownership to the level of consumption obtainable through drawing down capital. This pattern of preference can last for ever. Where ownership is the motive, the saver may tolerate a negative rate of interest rather than consume his assets. If in this situation he receives a positive return, he is in the position of the producer who is paid for work that he himself would pay to do. The potential for wealth creation is correspondingly enhanced.

Although the utility of consumption is in the mind, the scope for wealth creation through the increase of consumer's surplus is constrained by the realities of the external world. We need much of what we consume. As Bolingbroke says in Shakespeare's Richard II (Act I.III):

O who can hold a fire in his hand
By thinking on the frosty Caucasus?
Or cloy the hungry edge of appetite
By bare imagination of a feast?
Or wallow naked in December snow
By thinking on fantastic summer's heat?

Who indeed? And there are likewise narrow limits on the creation of wealth through an increase in the surplus on temporary saving (or saving for consumption).

It is otherwise with saving in perpetuity. There is no longer a link with consumption. The whole process of wealth creation is in the mind. Wealth can be created by a reduction in the saver's subjective rate of discount, which now means by changes in the saver's attitude to ownership, the future and wealth itself. Wealth can be created if the saver has a long time-horizon and regards himself less as an outright owner than as a steward. And such changes in attitude can be taught and learnt.

Although value-free economics has its uses, it also has its limitations. There are areas where economics and morality are inextricably intertwined. Teaching a child to be grateful for its presents is not just a matter of inculcating good manners or good behaviour; it is also a form of wealth creation through the increase of consumer's surplus. Counting our blessings is not merely a religious exercise; it is likewise a form of wealth creation.

Although this process of costless wealth creation is subject to severe practical constraints in the enjoyment of consumer goods and services, these constraints disappear in the enjoyment of perpetual saving. This form of enjoyment is costless and better than costless to the rest of society. The saving that is enjoyed in perpetuity is to the rest of society a loan that need never be repaid.

The right attitude to saving and wealth is an important question in most religions and cultures. Economics can identify the attitude that maximizes individual wealth: it is the long-term perspective, the long time-horizon, the minimum subjective rate of discount and also the sense of stewardship and vocation rather than outright ownership which a low subjective discount rate implies. This economic analysis is entirely consistent with Biblical concepts, since a zero or negligible subjective rate of discount is attributed by several Biblical writers to God himself. *The Lord thy God (...) keepeth covenant and mercy with them that love him and keep his commandments to a thousand generations.* (Deuteronomy VII 9). *A thousand years in thy sight are but as yesterday.* (Psalm XC 4). *One day is with the Lord as a thousand years, and a thousand years as one day.* (II Peter III 8).

The miser gains satisfaction from possessing a hoard of gold which is not available for use by others. This behaviour is economically irrational, because he is denying himself the income his wealth could yield if invested. His behaviour is also condemned by Christ in the Parable of the Talents (Matthew XXV). The rational saver in perpetuity, by contrast, invests his assets: he enjoys the income (which is also available to be spent on good works), while the rest of society has the benefit of a loan which need never be repaid.

The creation of wealth through self-restraint and stewardship maintains the normal relationship between money and economic wellbeing: the richer, the better off. Religious poverty, an ideal which I respect, has the more ambitious programme of transcending economic wellbeing in a higher cause: what the individual is maximizing is no longer economic wellbeing, however sublimated, but a spiritual value. This involves an attempt to exert the dominion of mind over matter in consumer goods and services; it also involves forgoing the enjoyment of personal ownership, however committed, vocational or costless to the rest of society. Although committed ownership and religious poverty both involve the creation of value through mental exertion or a change of attitude, therefore, committed ownership and saving in perpetuity remain within the discipline of economics, whereas religious poverty falls outside.

IV. Saver's Surplus and Owner's Surplus

Saving in perpetuity is any increase in an individual's or a family's pool of saving (and thus eventually of bequest). *Active* saving in any period is the excess of income over consumption; *passive* saving is the increase in value of the portfolio over the period, exclusive of active saving.

As an example of saving in perpetuity, the individual earns 1000 in year 1 and saves 100, which yields 5 in year 1 and 10 thereafter. This investment income is spent year by year. At the time of his death the individual has an estate of 100 from his saving in Year 1. The same process may be repeated in years 2 and following which are separate and independent years.

If the saving is temporary, by contrast, the saving of 100 in year 1 brings an annuity of 10 in year 1 and 20 thereafter. The annuity is spent year by year, and at the time of death the value of the estate is nil.

There are three senses of *saving:* active saving, passive saving and the existing stock of saving (*savings*, but also sometimes referred to as *saving*). If active and passive saving are nil, savings are unchanged. It is clearer to reserve the terms *active* and *passive saving* for *incremental saving* and *savings* for the *stock of saving under ownership. Saver's surplus* cumulates into *owner's surplus.*

Why do people save in perpetuity? The only rational answer is that they prefer ownership to consumption: ownership yields them more satisfaction, utility, welfare, wellbeing. Ownership is a separate (and much neglected) dimension of welfare from consumption, and the two may be in competition. Suppose that the individual is offered a choice between *(a)* 100 yielding 10 per cent for ever with the option to encash any part of the capital at any time and suffer a corresponding fall in income and *(b)* an income stream of 11, 12, 13, 14 or more with no access to the capital. Which is preferable? Someone who chose *(a)* and never encashed would prefer a permanently lower level of consumption than all the variants in *(b)*: ownership would be preferred at the margin to consumption. An out-and-out consumer would prefer *(b)* 11 to *(a)* because it would offer a permanently higher level of consumption. An individual with an interest in ownership might prefer *(a)* to *(b)* 11; but as the level of consumption rose, he might prefer *(b)* 12 or 13 to *(a)*. But at some rate of exchange ownership is preferable to consumption at the margin, except for the logical extreme of the out-and-out consumer.

Saving in perpetuity is the voluntary renunciation of (a tranche of) consumption in the interest of ownership. It makes money work twice in a way that temporary saving does not, since society as the collective counterparty to the saver in perpetuity is never obliged to repay the loan corresponding to the saver's investment. And, since ownership has a life of its own, it is not subject to the law of diminishing marginal utility, which holds good only for consumption. Politicians do not lose interest in power as they become more powerful, nor do rich men lose interest in riches as they become richer.

The whole argument is predicated on the assumption of personal ownership - ownership by sentient, natural persons. It does not hold good for ownership by companies (though it does for ownership *of* companies *by* their individual, non-corporate shareholders). Still less does it hold good for ownership by institutions of government. Wealth is created through ownership by persons and destroyed through ownership by corporations, agencies and institutions. All this constitutes an argument against the taxation of wealth in personal hands.

V. Owner's Surplus and Donor's Surplus

Since man is mortal, saving in perpetuity implies giving or bequest. Owner's surplus leads on to the subject of the present Section, the creation of wealth through giving (charitable or otherwise, by bequest or *inter vivos)*. Owner's surplus implies a low subjective rate of discount which in turn implies a long time-horizon often extending far beyond the lifetime of a single individual. Thus wealth creation through giving is a logical complement to wealth creation through ownership; it is the purpose of the present Section to examine the relationship between the two.[6] The argument

6 The creation of wealth through giving is additional to the four methods of wealth creation discussed in Barry BRACEWELL-MILNES (1981, pp. 39, 41).

holds good equally for transfers without consideration *inter vivos* (lifetime giving) and *mortis causa* (bequest).

1. Giving Not a Zero-Sum Game

The idea that the ownership of riches confers economic enjoyment independent of the income they produce is of great antiquity as well as being conformable to common sense. By contrast, in mainstream economic doctrine, giving has been treated as a zero-sum game in which the gains of the recipient are matched by the losses of the donor. Gifts are a form of transfer payment; and in the conventions of national accounting, wealth is neither increased nor diminished by transfers from one economic agent to another.

This is wrong several times over. In an ordinary trading transaction the same amount of money or money's worth is paid by the one party as is received by the other; but wealth is created by consumer's surplus and producer's surplus: the good or service traded is worth more to the purchaser than he pays and less to the seller than he receives, and so both of them benefit. Since giving is a voluntary transaction, it shares these properties: both donor and donee are volunteers, and both gain from the process.

The gains of donor and donee are analysed in *The Wealth of Giving.*[7] The position of the donee is the simpler of the two, in that he may be assumed to gain by the market value of the gift.[8] The donor controls the funds he owns and can use them for spending, saving, investing, lending, hoarding and gambling.

These four methods are: production of goods and services; investment in second-hand assets; extension and articulation of private ownership; and entrepreneurship in ideas.

7 Barry BRACEWELL-MILNES (1989).

8 The value of the gift to the recipient may be less than its market value if it damages economic relationships or weakens incentives, as has been explained by Lord BAUER (1976, 1994) for international aid and by Charles MURRAY (1984) for welfare benefits. The value to the recipient may be more than its market value by reason of the recipient's owner's surplus; see BRACEWELL-MILNES (1989, p. 87). Wealth is also created by the two *echo effects* (*ibid.*, pp. 87-8).

It follows that, far from contributing to a zero sum in which the gains of the gainers exactly match the losses of the losers, the act of giving at least doubles the value of the gift. If A gives £100 to B, the gift is worth £100 to B; but it is worth at least a countervalue of £100 to A, since otherwise he would not have preferred giving to the various other possible uses of his money. Donor's surplus (analogous to consumer's surplus) is additional to this countervalue of £100; it is an element of bequest as well as of lifetime giving, since the testator, like the live donor, is giving away assets which he could have used to finance additional consumption.

The argument holds good only for voluntary giving and does not apply to involuntary transfers like taxation. The argument thus gives strong support to the substitution of charitable funding for the funding of public causes from pooled tax revenue. Voluntary giving is economically productive as well as having a moral or ethical dimension which compulsory payments like taxation inevitably lack.[9]

Once again, the argument of this paper corresponds closely with the teaching of the Bible. The sum of donor's countervalue and donor's surplus exceeds the market value of the gift to the recipient: *it is more blessed to give than to receive* (Acts XX 35). And the gain to the donor is most as his joy in giving is greatest: *every man according as he purposeth in his heart, so let him give; not grudgingly, or of necessity: for God loveth a cheerful giver* (II Corinthians IX 7).[10]

2. The Relationships of the Concepts

Consumer's surplus and producer's surplus are integral elements of mainstream economic teaching. Saver's surplus, owner's surplus and donor's surplus are not; but they are strictly analogous, since saving, owning and giving are voluntary activities which are not undertaken unless they yield a gain.[11]

---

9 Charitable giving is one of more than a dozen methods of funding public causes alternative to the traditional method of funding out of pooled tax revenue; see Barry BRACEWELL-MILNES (1991, pp. 73 ff., 85 ff.).

10 The principal relevant Biblical texts are cited in Barry BRACEWELL-MILNES (1990).

11 The marginal case of economic indifference or zero surplus, where the transaction or activity is scarcely worth undertaking at all, is a logical extreme

Whereas consumer's surplus and producer's surplus are independent concepts, saver's surplus, owner's surplus and donor's surplus are interrelated. Owner's surplus is the aggregate of perpetual saver's surplus and surplus value from personal assets; donor's surplus must exceed the donor's owner's surplus, since otherwise he prefers retaining the asset to making the gift; the donor's owner's surplus ceases when he makes the gift, since he is no longer the owner; and the recipient's owner's surplus may exceed that of the donor.

The value of an asset in the hands of its owner is its market value plus its owner's surplus. Its value to him in the hands of the recipient is donor's countervalue plus donor's surplus. Unless the sum of donor's countervalue and surplus exceeds the sum of market value and owner's surplus, the asset will be retained by the owner and the gift will not be made.

Donor's surplus and owner's surplus are *alternative;* the donor's owner's surplus perishes with the gift. However, the recipient may have his own owner's surplus which may be equal to the donor's owner's surplus or larger or smaller. Moreover, an increase in the individual recipient's owner's surplus is likely to cause an increase in the donor's surplus. For example, a father who wishes to hand over the family firm to his son is likely to have more satisfaction in so doing if he believes that his son will run the company as a family concern and eventually hand it on to his own heirs in his turn and less satisfaction if he believes that within a few years the son will sell the firm for cash. This is the *first of the echo effects* whereby the surplus enjoyed by one party to a gratuitous transfer between individuals itself creates additional surplus for the other party.

If the donor's and the recipient's owner's surplus both increase by the same amount, the gift is worth more to the recipient; but, unless there is a corresponding rise in donor's surplus, there is an increase in the value of the asset to the donor in his own hands relatively to its value to him in the hands of the recipient.

These relationships are illustrated in Table 7.1, which shows the gain from a gift and its composition. No gift is made unless the sum of countervalue and donor's surplus exceeds the sum of market value and donor's owner's surplus. A comparison of A and B shows how a small reduction in the recipient's owner's surplus together with a corresponding

for producers and consumers and of no economic significance; and there is no reason to believe that it is of any significance for savers, owners or donors.

reduction in donor's surplus prevents the gift from taking place and thus reduces the gain from the gift from 160 to 0: unless the sum of donor's countervalue and surplus exceeds the value of the asset to the donor in his own hands, his altruism is not effective and does no good. The realisation of the gain from a gift is thus very sensitive to the height of donor's surplus; and donor's surplus is itself likely to be increased by an increase in the recipient's owner's surplus (and may even rise by more than the latter).

Table 7.1
The Gain from a Gift and its Composition

	(1) MV=CV	(2) DOS	(3) TVD	(4) CV+DS	(5) ROS	(6) TVR	(7) GG
A	100	50	150	160	50	150	160
B	100	50	150	150	40	140	-
C	100	-	100	110	-	100	110
D	100	-	100	100	-	100	-
E	100	50	150	170	60	160	180
F	100	60	160	180	60	160	180
G	100	50	150	150	60	160	-

MV = *market value*
CV = *countervalue*
DOS = *donor's owner's surplus*
TVD = *total value to donor (value of asset in old owner's hands)*
= (1)+(2)
DS = *donor's surplus*
ROS = *recipient's owner's surplus*
TVR = *total value to recipient (value of asset in new owner's hands)*
= (1)+(5)
GG = *gain from the gift where* (4) > (3)
= (4)-(3)+(6) = (4)-(2)+(5)

In C and D the fall in donor's surplus from 10 to zero extinguishes a gift yielding a gain of 110. The loss from forgoing the gift is less than in A and B, because the original donor's surplus was lower. Similarly, the loss from the gift's extinction is reduced (but the likelihood of its extinction is increased) if the recipient's owner's surplus is small relatively to the donor's owner's surplus.

In E and F the gain from the gift is unaffected by a rise in donor's surplus accompanied by a matching rise in donor's owner's surplus. In G the gift is extinguished because donor's surplus is no more than the donor's owner's surplus, even though the recipient's owner's surplus is larger than the donor's.

The first *echo effect*, noted above, is the increase in donor's surplus resulting from an increase in the recipient's owner's surplus. There is also a *second echo effect* working in the opposite direction. The donor and recipient are on friendly or affectionate terms and not at arm's length. The pleasure of the donor in the act of giving, represented by his donor's surplus, can itself be the source of additional wealth for the recipient, as reflected in an increase in his owner's surplus. Each party derives value from the pleasure of the other. The two echo effects may between them add significantly to the wealth that can be created by giving and bequest.

This analysis shows once again the narrowness and fragility of giving as a tax base and the damage that can be done by even a low rate of tax on giving or bequest. Where a gift takes place, it creates additional wealth at least equal to its financial value, perhaps much more; and this additional wealth can easily be destroyed through taxation by a small reduction in donor's surplus.

VI. Ownership and Stewardship

Personal ownership creates wealth partly because it has a value additional to that of the income it yields and partly because ownership in perpetuity enables borrowings to be renewed in perpetuity instead of being repaid for consumption by the lender. The same money can be used three times, by saver, owner/lender and borrower, in their different capacities. Potential consumption acts as a surrogate for consumption and potential repayment for repayment. The ownership dimension of economic prosperity has been largely neglected in public policy and academic analysis.[12]

The short-term or temporary owner, who saves and invests merely to increase his spending in years to come, is Rothbard man[13], a simple or simplistic maximizer of his own satisfaction through the consumption of goods and services. But most people do not resemble this logical extreme. As Marshall says, most people accumulate capital and live on the income, in so far as taxes permit them to do so[14]; saving in perpetuity is the rule rather than the exception.

Where the owner is saving in perpetuity rather than for additional consumption in later years, he may come insensibly to regard himself as a steward rather than an outright owner and to behave accordingly: in particular, he is reluctant to draw down capital even though his heirs may well enjoy a higher standard of living than his and his needs are in this sense greater than theirs. Alternatively, he may be drawn into the role of steward by a prudential aversion to living from capital. If the estate is a house and a portfolio of financial assets, the concept of stewardship need not be formal or explicit, and leaving the capital intact may be the result of habit rather than original intention.

It is otherwise if the owner owns a historic house or a family farm or firm. Here the moral obligation is clearer and more tangible: to maintain and improve the property and hand it on to the next generation in so far as market forces, costs and death taxes permit.

The advantage of the owner's acting as steward is the economy of the arrangement. He fulfils two roles for less than the cost of one: the steward's work he does for nothing and as owner he takes less from the estate, perhaps much less, than he could. Since he is doing both jobs himself, the lines of communication are shortened, and since he is a volunteer, there is no

---

12 See Barry BRACEWELL-MILNES (1982, p. 17).

13 "All saving is directed toward enjoying more consumption in the future. Otherwise, there would be no point at all in saving." (ROTHBARD, 1970, pp. 74-5).

14 See the citation in Section III above. Inheritance tax reduces the attraction of saving by comparison with spending by up to 40 per cent. (See Section VIII.1, below.) The tax rules for pensions are also a major obstacle to accumulation: contributions are attracted by a tax-free regime, but some three-quarters of the fund so built up has to be spent on purchasing an annuity or annuities that end with the death of the pensioner or his spouse.

conflict between his two capacities. The arrangement avoids the hazards of the agency principle (that the agent always follows his own interest in some measure and never entirely that of his principal). The owner has a longer time-horizon than any other steward.

For land and family firms, the advantages of personal stewardship can extend to third parties such as employees and neighbours.[15] The reality of these advantages is shown by the regret that is often expressed when a long-term landed estate or family firm goes under, whether through death duties or for other reasons. And the reality of the financial sacrifice made by the owners of landed estates and the owner-managers of family firms in continuing to act in these capacities is attested by the substantially higher incomes or levels of personal spending that they could generally obtain by relinquishing their responsibilities, selling out and reinvesting the proceeds.[16]

A portfolio of financial assets is at the impersonal extreme of individual ownership and a family firm, farm or landed estate is at the personal extreme. In between is a gradation of personal assets, defined as assets worth more to their owners than to strangers by reason of family or other personal links. The argument of this Section holds good even for impersonal assets; but it becomes more powerful as the personal quality of personal assets intensifies, and more and more surplus value is created by their personal ownership. The removal of these assets from their owner, through taxation or otherwise, destroys that value.

There is no taxable capacity in the capital value of an asset held in perpetuity. This is illustrated by the 'farmer's paradox': if an asset is held in perpetuity and is subject to death taxes, a rise in its value that apparently makes the taxpayer richer in reality makes him poorer. Most assets passing on death are held in perpetuity[17], and attempts to levy tax on a base without taxable capacity cause disproportionate damage elsewhere.

This Section has argued that it is not only heritage assets and family firms and farms, but assets in general, that are best and most efficiently looked after by long-term family owners acting to some degree in the quality

15 See Barry BRACEWELL-MILNES (1982, Section IV). Long-term family firms are often leaders in their localities, through charitable and voluntary work and otherwise.

16 The concept of vocational ownership and the public interest therein is analysed in Barry BRACEWELL-MILNES (1982, pp. 80-94).

17 See Section III above.

of stewards. Through the operation of market forces, houses, chattels and even financial assets tend to find their way into the hands of the individuals best qualified to look after them; and links of interest, affection and personal commitment are often strengthened by the passage of time within the ownership of a single individual or family. The stewardship of the country's total wealth is best undertaken by individual owners within the aggregate of the whole.

The concepts of ownership in perpetuity and of the owner as steward are once again consonant with Biblical teaching. Inheritance, both spiritual and material, is for everybody.[18]

1. Short Term and Long Term

There are two different senses in which an individual may have a long-term outlook on business matters without being guilty of 'long-termist' overemphasis on the distant future. The first sense is a matter of rational calculation, arithmetical or even intuitive, on the basis of market and subjective rates of discount; it is primarily a matter of not leaving out distant years merely because they are distant. In the second sense, by contrast, an individual has a long time-horizon because his subjective rate of discount is low: what happens in ten or twenty years is not much less important to him than what happens next year. There is an overlap between the two senses:

18 *So Joshua let the people depart, every man unto his inheritance.* (Joshua XXIV 28). *The children of Israel went every man unto his inheritance to possess the land.* (Judges II 6). *Every one in his inheritance* (Nehemiah XI 20). The concept of inheritance is combined with that of ownership in perpetuity. *The Lord knoweth the days of the upright: and their inheritance shall be for ever* (Psalm XXXVII 18). Materially, this is achieved through the institution of bequest. *A good man leaveth an inheritance to his children's children* (Proverbs XIII 22). *Children's children* does not mean grandchildren but remote posterity: *But the mercy of the Lord is from everlasting to everlasting upon them that fear him, and his righteousness unto children's children.* (Psalm CIII 17). Personal and inherited assets are not to be alienated to strangers. *The Lord forbid it me, that I should give the inheritance of my fathers unto thee* (I Kings XXI 3). The government should not expropriate family property. *The prince shall not take of the people's inheritance by oppression, to thrust them out of their possession* (Ezekiel XLVI 18).

the man with a low subjective rate of discount looks further ahead in the first sense also, because there is a wider span of years before the future is discounted to financial insignificance.

Subjective rates of discount are morally neutral, like other economic manifestations of personal taste and preference. But a low subjective rate of discount has advantages both for the individual and for society. The excess of the market rate of discount over the subjective rate is what makes saving and investment worthwhile for the individual: the lower his subjective rate of discount, the more he gains from these activities. Society gains because he becomes in part a steward of his assets and not merely their owner.

The advantages of a low subjective rate of discount are not a new discovery. Many societies have practised the Biblical precept of looking ahead to the third and fourth generation and beyond.

In our own time, there are two groups of people which illustrate with particular clarity the advantages of a long-term outlook in the sense of a low subjective rate of discount: the owners of long-term landed estates and the owners of long-term family firms. A time horizon of over fifty years is normal in these sectors and it may extend to a hundred years or more if death duties permit. The social advantages of long-term committed personal ownership are widely recognised in the particular case of historic houses, since the owner will do for nothing work of stewardship and maintenance which would otherwise fall as a heavy charge on society; but the argument is of general application. The advantages extend from the owners to others: on the larger landed estates it is normal for the agent or factor to spend the majority of his working life in a single employment, and much of the employment there and in family firms is very long-term.

The owners of family firms, farms and landed estates are individuals acting in that capacity, investing their own money and not someone else's. Where the individual is investing his own money, the same long-term outlook can be found in portfolio investment as well. It is not unusual for an individual in his twenties to make financial dispositions from which he intends to benefit fifty years or more later, and his children after his death. But low subjective discount rates are particularly characteristic of the stewardship of heritage assets and family firms and farms.

2. Heritage Assets

Heritage estates have different values for different purposes; four different values are relevant to our argument. They are, from the highest down:

(i) social value in current use;

(ii) personal value in current use;

(iii) break-up value;

(iv) private value in current use.

(i) *Social value in current use* is the value to society of keeping an estate in its current use, including any beneficial effects on third parties, by comparison with the best alternative.

(ii) *Personal value in current use* is the satisfaction to the owner of keeping the estate in its current use (*satisfaction* in the sense of the economic term *utility*). It excludes third-party effects[19] except where they are reflected in satisfaction to the owner. Social value in current use can be *seen* to exceed personal value in current use whenever conservation bodies or others try to persuade an owner to carry on in his present position, or regret his unwillingness or inability to do so, or try but fail to find a successor. And social value in current use can be *expected* to exceed personal value in current use in more stable situations where this relationship cannot be demonstrated.

(iii) The *break-up value* is what the owner can realize by selling and pulling out of the area. Break-up can be partial or total. Since the owner is a free agent,[20] personal value in current use is by definition higher than break-up value. But it may be little higher, and it hovers uneasily above break-up value when the owner is losing heart, ceasing to care and on the verge of giving up.[21]

---

19 Effects on third parties are the *external effects* or *externalities* of economic jargon. The net result of third-party effects is assumed to be positive (positive effects outweigh negative). In other words, the public gains rather than loses, or gains more than it loses, from personal ownership of heritage estates.

20 It is significant that the hereditary owner is a free agent but not a volunteer, since he has never volunteered. A volunteer would be less likely to accept a large shortfall in the private value in current use below the personal value in current use.

21 This sentiment is vividly portrayed in the words that T.S. Eliot puts into the mouth of Lady Monchensey (*The Family Reunion*, Part II, Scene III):

(iv) *Private value in current use* is the value of the estate to the owner excluding all elements of vocation and service to the community. Since the owner is not on the breadline, it is not negligible and may even be substantial. But it may be far below the break-up value if the owner is making large personal sacrifices to soldier on. And it may be well below the wealth of someone in modest but comfortable circumstances with no responsibilities for heritage assets, especially when the owner is near the point where it is simply not possible, physically or financially, to carry on any longer.[22]

Vocational ownership may be defined as a situation in which *personal value in current use* exceeds *private value in current use*. It is a general concept and is not confined to heritage assets. The purchase of National Savings on financially unattractive terms in wartime, for example, is vocational saving, and their retention is vocational ownership. But *commitment* to heritage assets is the most striking and perhaps the most important example.

The tax system seeks in principle to levy capital taxes on or near the break-up value of heritage assets and thus to include the element of vocational ownership constituted by the excess of break-up value over private value in current use. The full rigour of this principle may be mitigated by reliefs. But the reliefs may do little to bridge the wide gap between break-up value and private value in current use, which latter is the true measure of taxable capacity. This has three unfortunate effects. First, it

---

I will let the walls crumble. Why should I worry
To keep the tiles on the roof, combat the endless weather,
Resist the wind? Fight with increasing taxes
And unpaid rents and tithes?

22 If an owner wishes to demolish, the ***break-up value*** in the economic sense is the break-up value in the contractor's sense and will be small or even negative if the value of the site does not cover the cost of demolition. The private value in current use is still smaller than the break-up value (or a larger negative). The social value in current use ought to be substantial if it is to justify a public authority in seeking to thwart the wishes of an owner by means of a conservation order, perhaps at the cost of a protracted legal wrangle. This example illustrates how the social value in current use can be far in excess (and a large multiple) of the break-up value and thus also of the personal value in current use (which may be little higher than the break-up value) and of the private value in current use (which may be much lower).

is unfair between taxpayers; assets with the higher break-up value may have the lower private value in current use, so that the heavier tax burden falls on the taxpayer with the smaller stock of assets for his private use. Secondly, tax on the excess of break-up value over private value in current use is a pure tax on vocation,[23] and this is undesirable in itself. Thirdly, the taxation of break-up value as though it were private value in current use gradually and systematically destroys the public interest in the personal ownership of heritage assets. In other words, taxing the committed owner on his commitment gradually and systematically destroys the public good represented by the excess of social value in current use over break-up value.[24]

---

23 A tax on vocation is a tax on altruism in earning, saving or owning. An example is the income tax levied on the sacrificial marginal earnings of a doctor who works during an epidemic until he is almost asleep on his feet. But for his sense of duty, he would prefer a good night's sleep to his marginal earnings even gross of tax, let alone net. Even gross of tax, he would prefer marginal leisure to marginal income. The levying of tax on the marginal income must *either* diminish his supply of services *or* constitute a pure tax on his altruism *or* combine both these effects in varying degrees. Any of these results is either unjust or inefficient or both. Similar arguments apply to vocation and commitment in saving and owning.

24 If the situation of the vocational owner is compared with that of the vocational doctor, the social value in current use includes all the third-party benefits in both cases. For the doctor working in an epidemic, the private value in current use represents the preferred position exclusive of altruism and the personal value in current use represents the preferred position inclusive of altruism. The tax on marginal earnings is a pure tax on altruism and reduces the personal value in current use towards the break-up value. If personal value in current use falls below the break-up value, the tax on marginal earnings is a total bar to altruistic endeavour and the doctor reverts to the egoistic position at which private value in current use increases to the break-up value. Similarly for the vocational owner. His commitment is the excess of personal over private value in current use. The heavier the tax burden, the smaller the excess of personal value in current use over the break-up value relatively to the excess of the break-up value over the private value in current use, and the stronger the incentive to economise on altruism by realising the excess of the break-up value over the private value in current use. The scales are finally tipped when taxation pushes the personal value in current use below the break-up value.

As I have argued elsewhere, the only taxes that are ultimately unavoidable (apart from poll taxes and taxes on necessaries) are those on vocation in earning, saving and ownership.[25] But taxes on vocation are unavoidable only as long as the vocation is not eroded financially or by loss of morale. The list of great houses and their collections destroyed and dispersed in recent years[26] gives some idea of the losses inflicted on society by the taxation of heritage assets at sums far in excess of their private value in current use. These social losses may from the beginning, and must in the end, far exceed the losses to the owners. The loss to society does not diminish over time.

3. Family Firms and Farms

Another distortion inflicted on the economy by inheritance tax is the burden it imposes on unquoted companies and other owner-managed family firms from which quoted companies are effectively exempt. In quoted companies death duties fall nominally and effectively on the shareholder; the shareholder can sell shares to defray the tax charge, and the company may be little affected, if at all. In unquoted companies death duties fall nominally on the shareholder but effectively on the company itself: the shareholder seldom has cash resources to meet a significant liability, and the liability has to be discharged either indirectly and expensively through the company (which weakens the company financially) or through sale to outsiders (which alters the company's character). It is quoted companies, not unquoted companies, that are open to criticisms of 'short-termism'; yet it is precisely the quality of owner-management (which gives unquoted companies and other unquoted businesses their long time-horizons) that attracts a discriminatory tax charge to which quoted companies are effectively immune. Once again, inheritance tax makes the economy more 'short-termist'. The ability of a company to pay for a takeover with its own shares also effectively discriminates against unquoted companies, perhaps unintentionally: capital gains tax is rolled over on payment in shares but charged at the time on payment in money, and the superior marketability of

---

25 See Barry BRACEWELL-MILNES (1979, p. 100).

26 A partial list up to 1974 is provided by John CORNFORTH (1974, pp. 5-11).

quoted shares enhances the purchasing power of quoted relatively to unquoted companies as predators.

The liability of unquoted companies to inheritance tax in the absence of entitlement to 100 per cent business property relief is particularly damaging given the dominant motivation of long-term family companies. "For all the family firms in the sample, the primary answer was unequivocal. They desire to maintain control, and to pass on a secure and sound business to the next generation."[27] In these circumstances, inheritance tax casts its shadow and distorts behaviour many years in advance of a taxable transfer and does damage out of proportion to its modest yield. The perception of the tax as an ever-present threat may be more important than the reality, especially as its real incidence depends on the lottery of death.

The argument is equally valid for family farms and for other family businesses in the unquoted sector that are not established in corporate form (partnerships, sole proprietorships).

4. The Relationships between the Discount Rates

Owner's surplus is the aggregate of perpetual saver's surplus and surplus value from personal assets; perpetual saver's surplus is the counterpart of a subjective rate of discount below the market rate.[28]

Suppose a man has a net-of-tax income of £100, of which he spends £90 and invests the remaining £10 in liquid assets with a net-of-tax yield of 10 per cent. His subjective rate of discount is less than the market rate and so his power to consume in the future is worth more to him now than £10 of immediate spending. In the second year, his income is £101; but saving is attractive to him for the same reason as before, and he spends £90 and saves £11. Similarly, in all subsequent years he spends £90 and saves the sum of the original £10 and the rising income from previous investment.

This is not an intertemporal shift in consumption. The man's consumption is lower in every year than it would be if he were saving nothing; there is no rate of discount, positive or negative, at which his

27 Donald A. HAY and Derek J. MORRIS (1984, p. 8).

28 The percentage rate of discount is $i/(1+i)$, where i is the percentage rate of interest. The relationship is the same as between gross and net rates of tax: 20 per cent gross is 25 per cent net and 50 per cent gross is 100 per cent net.

consumption is increased. The power to consume is preferred to its exercise. The preference is not irrational or perverse; it is a matter of individual choice.

Intertemporal shifts in consumption are conveniently thought of as shifts within a single human lifetime, whereas the preference for the power to consume over its exercise suggests a time-horizon extending beyond a single generation. These are the simplest and most typical cases, though they are not the only possibilities.

In the example just given, spending remains permanently at £90; the income elasticity of demand for consumption is zero. This logical extreme was assumed in order to simplify the argument. It can be relaxed without weakening the argument, though at the cost of making it more complex.

Suppose that new saving remains at £10 and that spending rises to absorb the increasing income from investments: £90, £91, £92 . . . etc. After 10 years the man's consumption attains the level at which it would have remained if he had saved nothing, and thereafter it exceeds this level. Eventually the missing consumption (£10 + £9 + ... + £2 +£1) appears to be made good and more than made good. But this is true only at a zero or low rate of interest. It is not true at or anywhere near an interest rate of 10 per cent, at which level the present discounted value of consumption in every year would be increased by saving less and spending more.

The subjective rate of discount, which makes saving attractive to the saver, is below the market rate.[29] The attraction of the power to consume also implies that the discount rate is positive; if the discount rate is negative, the motive for saving is not the power to consume but survival. It follows from the argument in the preceding paragraph that there is a break-even or watershed positive rate of discount below which consumption may be regarded as the purpose of saving and above which it cannot. Thus the four rates of discount are, in descending order:

(i) the market rate;
(ii) the saver's subjective rate;
(iii) the break-even rate;
(iv) zero.

At the two logical extremes, the saver's subjective rate may coincide with the market rate or with zero; if the subjective rate is zero, so is the break-

29 This saver's surplus or *economic rent* from saving is analogous to consumer's surplus from purchasing.

even rate. In the normal situation where the subjective rate is below the market rate but above zero, the break-even rate is below the subjective rate if the power to consume is the motive for saving. The three bands between the four rates of discount represent:

(I) from market rate to saver's subjective rate, saver's economic rent;
(II) from saver's subjective rate to break-even rate, power to consume;
(III) from break-even rate to zero, additional consumption.

The break-even rate is not a purely subjective rate, although it depends on the saver's preferences. If saving is mainly for consumption, the break-even rate is at or near the saver's subjective rate and total savings grow relatively slowly; if it is mainly for the power to consume, the break-even rate is little above zero and total savings grow relatively quickly; and if it is in perpetuity, the break-even rate is zero and the growth of total savings is maximised relatively to the amount saved each year. Over any finite period during which net saving is positive (that is, new saving exceeds spending out of old savings), the pattern of positive and negative saving from year to year determines the break-even rate of discount below which aggregate consumption is increased by saving and above which it is reduced. If net saving is nil over the period, the break-even rate and the saver's subjective rate coincide; as net saving increases, the break-even rate falls relatively to the saver's subjective rate. The longer the term of saving in any period, the larger the volume of net saving (since more saving is outstanding at the end of the period, even if it is intended for spending later). So, in any given period, there is a positive relationship between the term of saving and its motivation by the desire for spending power rather than actual spending. If the period is extended into the future without limit, the distinction between short- and long-term saving disappears and the only relevant distinction is between saving which is realised for consumption and saving which is not.

A preference for the power to consume over consumption is the characteristic mark of ownership and stewardship.

VII. Taxes on Spending and Taxes on Saving

So far the subject has been the process of wealth creation through saving in perpetuity, ownership, giving and inheritance. Section VIII shows how this process is affected by taxation. By way of preamble to Section VIII, the present Section analyses the tax system in terms of taxes on spending and taxes on saving.

1. Taxes on Spending and Taxes on Saving

All taxes except for capitation or poll taxes can be classified as taxes on consumption or on saving or on a mixture of the two.

Taxes on consumption (or spending) are the most straightforward. They are either proportional to the price (like value added tax) or specific (like the excise duties on alcohol, tobacco and petrol). If the goods or services subject to tax are used for business purposes and are not fully tax-relieved, the taxes concerned enter into production costs. Taxes other than value-added tax (VAT) are not relieved at all for business purposes, only deducted as an expense, and a wide range of business expenses is denied a deduction for input tax, even though this is contrary to the principles of VAT.

Taxes on labour earnings are a mixture of taxes on spending and taxes on saving, since all such earnings are eventually used for one or both of these two purposes. Taxes on business earnings fall partly on labour and partly on entrepreneurial investment. Taxes on production fall on consumers in so far as they are passed forward and on business earnings in so far as they are absorbed by the firm.

Taxes on saving include income tax (basic and higher rates), capital gains tax and inheritance tax. Income tax and inheritance tax are pure taxes on saving: they would be wholly avoided if the money funding the tax base had originally been spent instead of saved. Capital gains tax is a tax on consumption if savings are realised for spending; otherwise it is a tax on saving. The effect of the various taxes on saving is *cumulative*: the net-of-tax yield is reduced and may be obliterated or turned negative by the combined effect of income tax, capital gains tax and inheritance tax.

In the United Kingdom and most other countries, taxes on spending are calculated net of tax. If £100 worth of goods or services is subject to value added tax at 17.5 per cent and the tax is wholly passed on, the purchaser pays £117.5. If the tax is wholly absorbed by the seller, the purchaser pays £100 and the seller receives £85.1, since 117.5 per cent of 85.1 is 100. By contrast taxes on earnings and on saving (on income or capital) are calculated gross of tax. If £100 worth of labour income is taxed at 20 per cent and the tax is passed on to the purchaser (or employer), the cost of the labour rises to £125 and the tax on £125 at 20 per cent is £25, leaving the worker with £100, as before. If the tax is wholly absorbed by the seller, the employer pays £100, as before, and the seller receives £80. It is often assumed that taxes on spending are wholly passed on to the purchaser and taxes on earnings and saving are wholly absorbed by the seller; but these are unrealistic logical extremes[30], and the truth will generally lie somewhere between the two.

Financial turnover, or the amount spent by the purchaser, is an unambiguous concept and answers to the gross method of calculating tax rates. If national insurance contributions and any other parafiscal charges are ignored, the seller's turnover is what the shopkeeper is paid gross of tax by the consumer, the worker by the employer or client, the lender by the borrower.

Volume is also straightforward for goods. It is often easy to identify goods of a given quality, such as a case of whisky, and to work out how much the volume purchased has changed in response to a tax-induced change in price. This also holds good for services in so far as output can be measured and quality controlled. But most labour is not producing quality-controlled piecework; and the volume of (economically effective) labour input can mostly be measured only indirectly, through output sold in a free market and the profit it yields. Saving has its own difficulty. The volume of saving is not, properly speaking, the amount saved (which is turnover) but the amount of income purchased, just as the volume of whisky bought or sold is the number of bottles and not the amount paid or received. The amount of income purchased per £100 is the combined effect of the yield (or rate of interest) and the rate or rates of tax; and yield and tax rate vary independently of each other. Thus the common assumptions about changes in the volume of work and saving in response to changes in tax rates are doubly wrong: financial turnover is no more an accurate measure of volume than it is for whisky, and the assumption that gross-of-tax disbursements on saving and receipts from labour are unchanged by tax changes is an unrealistic logical extreme. This is the Government's own assumption.

Price is a net, not a gross, concept, since tax is a proportion or multiple of the net-of-tax price. If two-thirds of the cost of a bottle of whisky is tax,

30 See Barry BRACEWELL-MILNES (1994, note 34).

then the net-of-tax price is (by definition) 1 or 100 per cent, tax is 2 and the price is 3.

Taxes on *temporary* saving (for a holiday, for example, or a pension) are *anticipatory* taxes on consumption. They are open to the objections against all forms of *fiscal anticipation* (discussed below); they also increase the taxation of *postponed consumption* relatively to *immediate consumption*. Taxes on *saving in perpetuity* are by definition not taxes on spending at all; we consider below whether and in what sense saving in perpetuity offers a tax base and what are the costs of attempting to levy on that base.

The analysis of tax systems into taxes on spending and taxes on saving has the advantage that ultimately there are only two destinations for incoming funds: spending and perpetual saving. The analysis into taxes on consumption, on income and on capital obscures this truth, since income is a mixed category between spending and saving. The distinction between direct and indirect taxes compounds the confusion by contrasting a pure economic category (indirect taxes or taxes on spending) with a mixed category (direct taxes or taxes on income) and then adding a pure category (taxes on inheritance) to the mixed category as an optional extra.

2. Impact and Incidence of Taxes on Spending

The distinction between the impact and the incidence of taxes on spending has long been familiar, from the work of Seligman and others. The impact of value added tax is on the trader who must account for it to the government; but, in so far as the trader can pass the tax forward to the customer, the incidence of the tax is on the customer. Similarly for taxes on alcohol and tobacco. The impact of taxes on earned income is on the employer and the impact of taxes on investment income on the borrower, if the employer and borrower are obliged to account for the tax; but in so far as these taxes are passed backwards, the incidence is on the employee and the lender.

In a different sense of the distinction between impact and incidence, the impact of taxes on spending is on spending; but these taxes also have an incidence on saving: the value of saving is what it will buy, and this value is diminished by taxes on spending.

3. Two Concepts of Fiscal Neutrality

Since the ultimate destination of disbursements is spending or saving in perpetuity, there is a rate of exchange between the two, like the rate of exchange between the pound sterling and the dollar. In a tax-free world this rate of exchange is unity: each has an opportunity cost of 1 in terms of the other.

If taxes are levied, there are two concepts of fiscal neutrality between spending and saving, corresponding to the distinction between tax impact and incidence. Under impact-neutrality, the tax system is neutral between spending and saving if a tax of 25 per cent net on spending is matched by a tax of 25 per cent net (or 20 per cent gross) on the income from saving. Under incidence-neutrality, the tax system is neutral between spending and saving if the tax on saving is zero, since the value of saving is reduced by taxes on spending as much as the value of spending.

By the criterion of income taxation, fiscal neutrality between spending and saving is achieved when saving in all its forms is taxed as heavily as spending: this is sometimes called the 'low road' to fiscal neutrality. By the criterion of expenditure taxation, fiscal neutrality between spending and saving is achieved when saving is not taxed at all (the 'high road' to fiscal neutrality). Through the combination of the various taxes on investment income and capital, including inheritance tax, saving is taxed in much of the industrialised world even more heavily than under the impact-neutrality of income taxation. The removal of inheritance tax thus constitutes a move towards impact-neutrality and thence towards what this paper regards as the more logical and desirable regime of incidence-neutrality in which explicit taxes on saving are zero.

4. Two Concepts of Taxable Capacity

The traditional concept of taxable capacity is the taxpayer's ability to pay the tax. The trouble with this concept is that it is vacuous. It could be used to justify any tax, however high, on any capital, income or consumption, however low. It gives no indication of any logical stopping point short of this fiscal extortion or confiscation.

The concept of *economic taxable capacity* provides such a logical stopping point in the notion of *excess burden*, the damage done by taxation in addition to the amount of tax revenue. *Economic taxable capacity* is defined as the excess of the yield of a tax over the social loss it inflicts (exclusive of the yield).[31] It is wasteful to levy tax where there is no economic taxable capacity; we note below the implications of this argument for inheritance tax and other taxes on saving.

5. Two Concepts of Inequality

The inequalities of wealth, income and expenditure may move in different directions. For example, heavy taxes on saving and capital may reduce the inequality of wealth while increasing the inequality of spending.

Temporary saving is a producer activity. Just as a tax on earned income may induce a man to work harder if his aim is to attain a given standard of living, so and for similar reasons a tax on temporary saving may induce a man to save more (in the sense of putting more money into saving) if his aim is to secure a given income from capital, and thus a given standard of living. For saving this response is called the *Sargant effect* after the economist W.L. Sargant. For saving in perpetuity the Sargant effect is impossible, since the saver cannot by definition be saving to achieve a given standard of living or consumption.

I have shown elsewhere that, in the absence of the Sargant effect, all taxes on saving increase the inequality of spending.[32] The inequality of spending is increased more if the taxes on saving are graduated. Inheritance tax, like other taxes on saving, thus increases the inequality of spending; and this result is by egalitarian standards perverse.

6. Creative Accounting

All taxes on saving are by definition taxes either on temporary or on permanent saving. Permanent saving includes saving originally intended as temporary but in fact never drawn down.

By the criterion of expenditure taxation, all taxes on temporary saving are *anticipatory*: the tax on the temporary income reduces the eventual

31 See Barry BRACEWELL-MILNES (1994, Section 7).

32 See Barry BRACEWELL-MILNES (1981, Appendix III).

spending level and replaces the yield of consumption taxes on this lost additional consumption. The taxpayer loses; but the tax revenue need not gain. Taxes on temporary saving are what Adam Smith has called "(...) unthrifty taxes that increase the revenue of the sovereign, which seldom maintains any but unproductive labourers; at the expence of the capital of the people, which maintains none but productive."[33] This unthrifty anticipation of the income of future years is one of government's contributions to the art of creative accounting.

The situation is still worse if tax is levied on saving in perpetuity. The concept of saving in perpetuity implies that the saver prefers the immaterial satisfaction of ownership to the material satisfaction of consuming goods and services. This additional satisfaction, and indeed the whole satisfaction of ownership, exist only in the mind of the personal owner and cannot be appropriated in taxation. A tax on saving in perpetuity appropriates material wealth that was less valuable to the saver than the immaterial wealth of ownership, which was costless to society and which the tax has destroyed. Saving in perpetuity has negative economic taxable capacity.

The same argument may be expressed alternatively as follows. Suppose that in a tax-free world an individual receives a legacy which was 1000 on the day before receipt and increases to 1100 on the day of receipt as a result of an increase in stock-exchange prices. If he is a perpetual saver, most or all of this additional 100 may be saved in perpetuity. Since he gains more from saving than from consumption, he gains more than 100 of consumption. He may be assumed to prefer saving to consumption for each of the additional 100 units.

If the additional 100 worth of legacy is now charged to tax at 40 per cent, the situation is radically changed. If the saving is in perpetuity, he may prefer a legacy of 1000 with no tax charge to a gross legacy of 1100 (tax charge 40, net of tax 1060), either because he has no cash to pay the tax or because he is worse off in cash terms after paying the tax or because he gains nothing from an increase in the value of a personal asset which he is unwilling to sell or because he dislikes paying 40 in tax more than he likes an increase of 60 in the value of an unrealised asset. If he prefers a zero increase in the value of the legacy to a net-of-tax increase of 60, 40 of tax does more harm than 60 of saving does good; and 60 of costless saving is

33 See Adam SMITH (1976, Book V, Chapter II, Appendix to Articles I and II, p. 862).

worth in his eyes more than 60 of spending. This illustrates the negative economic taxable capacity of saving in perpetuity. The 'farmer's paradox' likewise identifies the paradoxical consequence of capital taxation that a rise in the value of an asset which apparently makes a taxpayer richer makes him in reality poorer if its value to him exceeds the new higher price.

Similarly for taxes on giving and inheritance. I have shown elsewhere[34]:

(i) that a tax on giving always causes a social loss, through the destruction of donor's countervalue and surplus;

(ii) that the social loss (or wealth destroyed) always at least equals the revenue yield;

(iii) that the social loss always exceeds the revenue yield if gross-of-tax giving decreases in response to the tax;

(iv) that the social loss exceeds the revenue yield even if gross-of-tax giving remains constant or rises, except in the limiting case.

Thus, except in the limiting case, giving and inheritance have negative economic taxable capacity.

Government's second contribution to creative accounting is to pretend or assume that saving in perpetuity, giving and inheritance have positive economic taxable capacity. In reality, the economic taxable capacity of these tax bases is never positive and is negative except in the limiting case. It follows that the abolition of these taxes not only benefits the taxpayer by the amount of tax remitted but also benefits the economy by an additional amount exceeding this tax remission.

VIII. The Taxation of Giving and Inheritance

The last Section showed how taxes on saving diminish or destroy the immaterial wealth obtainable through saving and ownership. Some people are natural savers, while others are natural spenders; taxes on saving distort the balance between the two and destroy wealth by levying on a base with no economic taxable capacity, which is the excess of the tax yield over the

34 The proofs of these propositions are given in Barry BRACEWELL-MILNES (1989, pp. 82-4). In the limiting case, the curve of donor's surplus is parallel to the 45° line of tax neutrality.

social loss the tax inflicts. Taxes on temporary saving *may have* negative economic taxable capacity, inasmuch as the taxpayer loses but the Treasury need not gain. Taxes on ownership and saving in perpetuity, including taxes on giving and inheritance, *have* negative economic taxable capacity, except in the limiting case where economic taxable capacity is zero: the tax yield never exceeds the social loss and falls short of it except in the limiting case.

The additional wealth created by personal giving[35] is personal to the donor: it cannot be captured by the government in taxation or transferred to anyone else. For the donor himself, the creation of additional wealth through donor's countervalue and surplus is in competition with its creation through owner's surplus or consumer's surplus: it is not rational for the gift to be made unless the satisfaction the owner obtains from giving exceeds the satisfaction he obtains from ownership or consumption. The *additional wealth created by personal giving,* although fully appropriated to personal use, is a *public good,* in the technical sense of a good or service the use or enjoyment of which by one person does not reduce the amount available for use or enjoyment by others; by contrast, *wealth is destroyed rather than created by government giving,* because the government has no funds of its own to give and has to raise the money coercively through taxation.

The present Section moves on from the *social losses* inflicted by taxes on saving to the related topics of *tax distortion* and *perverse pricing*.

1. Tax Distortion

The bias of policy against personal ownership and saving in perpetuity, whether intended or unintended, is expressed in a number of tax distortions, each of which causes a significant loss of economic wellbeing by altering taxpayers' behaviour (in addition to the losses due to the destruction of immaterial wealth subsisting in the mind of the taxpayer). Inheritance tax, in particular, does not destroy wealth in the material sense of iconoclasts desecrating churches or muslim fundamentalists smashing bottles of alcohol;

35 The argument holds good also for giving by companies, which are legal persons, in so far as the shareholders, who bear the cost, are aware of the donations and agree with their being made. Where this is not so, giving by companies creates no additional wealth in the form of donor's countervalue and surplus, although it may serve other useful functions such as improving the company's public image or fulfilling what are perceived as its social obligations.

but it distorts choices and annihilates immaterial wealth in the mind of the taxpayer, and the effect on economic wellbeing is no less damaging.

The simplest example of a tax distortion is the effect of inheritance tax on the choice between spending and saving. Marshall, as we have seen,[36] regarded a preference for saving in perpetuity over temporary saving as normal for the majority of families. This preference is distorted and frustrated by inheritance tax, since at a tax rate of 40 per cent (gross) the taxpayer expecting to pay the tax can have 100 of spending for each 60 of net-of-tax bequests; the effect is in principle the same whether he funds his own spending out of capital or purchases an annuity of which the capital element is tax-free. If the taxpayer prefers bequests of 80 to spending of 100, for example, but spending of 100 to bequests of 60, the loss of wellbeing to the testator is not less than 20 per 100 (= 100 - 80 - 100 + 60); and the maximum loss per 100 is 40, the rate of inheritance tax. It is also paradoxical that under a regime of inheritance tax at 40 per cent, the poor man's spending costs him 100 whereas the rich man's spending costs him only 60.

The loss of economic wellbeing through the frustration of giving and bequest is additional to the loss caused by the tax-driven diversion of saving into spending. I have shown elsewhere[37] that a tax on giving cannot be more than partially absorbed by the donor; the recipient therefore loses as well as the donor (or the recipients collectively lose), and the amount given is reduced by the distorting effect of the tax system.

The argument of the last two paragraphs would hold good even if the taxpayer's subjective rate of discount coincided with the market rate. If, as is normal, the subjective rate of discount is lower than the market rate, any form of tax on saving raises the subjective rate of discount by reducing saver's surplus; and inheritance tax reduces owner's surplus as well. An example of the loss of economic wellbeing caused by an increase in the subjective rate of discount is the owner who in the absence of inheritance tax is willing to contribute from his income year by year to the upkeep of a historic house of local importance. If inheritance tax is imposed and the house does not qualify for relief as national heritage property, it may be financially impossible to maintain the house from generation to generation; as saving in perpetuity becomes pointless, the taxpayer's subjective rate of

36 See Section III above.

37 See Barry BRACEWELL-MILNES (1989, pp. 82-4).

discount rises and saver's and owner's surplus are destroyed. The loss of economic wellbeing caused by an increase in the subjective rate of discount is additional to the losses explained in the last two paragraphs.

2. Perverse Pricing

Inheritance tax cheapens the rich man's spending. At a tax rate of 40 per cent, he can have 100 of spending for an opportunity cost of 60 of saving, the other 40 being paid for by the Treasury in lost inheritance tax. His spending is also cheapened relatively to the spending and saving of the poor man or non-inheritance-tax-payer. 100 of spending costs the poor man an opportunity cost of 100 of saving and 100 of saving costs him 100 of spending. The rich man has 167 (= 100/(0.6)) of spending for 100 of his own saving or for 100 of the poor man's spending or saving. Inheritance tax reduces the cost of the spending of the rich relatively to their own saving and to the spending and saving of the poor. The tax privilege enjoyed by the spending of the rich increases as the other taxes on saving are brought into the reckoning.

The social engineering or fiscal engineering of inheritance tax is thus in precise opposition to an earlier form of fiscal engineering: *sumptuary taxation*. There the idea was to impose additional taxation on items of expenditure that characterised the lifestyle of the rich: a coach and eight, for example, might attract a heavier tax than a coach and four on the argument that a man who could afford the extra four horses could afford the heavier taxation. The concept of sumptuary taxation lingers on in the value added tax, which commonly distinguishes between more and less necessary goods and services and taxes the more necessary less heavily or not at all. Although I am no enthusiast for sumptuary taxation (preferring a more neutral system), I recognise that it has the merit of a certain populist logic and popular appeal. I can find no merit, economic, social, moral, egalitarian or otherwise, in an anti-sumptuary tax like inheritance tax which grants tax privileges to the spending of the rich relatively to their own saving and to the saving and spending of the poor.

Spending and saving in perpetuity are jointly exhaustive and mutually exclusive logical categories for the financial dispositions of individuals. Everything that is not spent is saved and everything that is not saved is spent. There is no escape from the logical dilemma that rich people cannot at the same time be overtaxed relatively to poor people both on their spending and on their saving. If they are overtaxed on one, they are undertaxed on the other. Inheritance tax overtaxes the rich taxpayer's saving and thus undertaxes his spending. In a consistent system (thus one not subject to retrospective additional charges on savings accumulated under a more favourable or less hostile regime), the taxpayer's decision between spending and saving is respected; and this implies a zero rate of inheritance tax.

Inheritance tax not only cheapens the opportunity cost of spending by the rich. Its perverse pricing also leads to perverse redistributive results. That is the subject of the next Section.

IX. Equality of Opportunity

Equality of opportunity is regarded in some quarters as constituting an argument for inheritance tax. Equality of opportunity, the reasoning runs, is an ideal of social justice (or even economic efficiency). Without inheritance tax, opportunities will be unequal, since those who inherit significant sums will have an advantage over those who do not. Therefore there should be an inheritance tax.

The advantages and disadvantages of equality of opportunity and equality of outcome and the relationship between the two have been much discussed and I cannot do justice to the subject here. I merely make a few comments before turning to consider the consequences of pursuing equality of opportunity as an ideal.

(1) Equality of outcome is more important than equality of opportunity since it affects *behaviour* and *how people live*. Equality of opportunity merely concerns people's *positions at a particular time* (the start of their careers). If equality of opportunity were attained, it is not clear whether or how behaviour would be affected.

(2) There is little connection between equality of opportunity and equality of outcome. People who were equal at breakfast would in a competitive economy be unequal by teatime.

(3) The equality-of-opportunity argument for inheritance taxation is weak on its own terms, since most heirs do not inherit significant sums until many years after the start of their careers.

(4) Any serious attempt to achieve equality of opportunity would require a totalitarian control of education, in order to hold back the more intelligent students. The inheritance of ability and character is economically as important as the inheritance of wealth.

(5) Short of the totalitarian ideal of total equality, measures of equality vary and can point in different directions. In a free economy, the inequality of wealth normally exceeds the inequality of income, which exceeds the inequality of spending. There are many statistical measures of inequality, and distribution A may be more unequal than B by one measure but less unequal by another.[38] The effect of inheritance tax on this complex situation is obscure.

(6) The equality-of-opportunity argument is implicitly using *atomistic individualism* as its model of economic agency and underestimating the family. The importance of the family is shown, for example, by Marshall[39] and by the more recent work of Becker.[40]

(7) Equality of outcome has become less important as an ideal in recent years, being replaced by more manageable concepts such as acceptable rates of tax and an acceptable minimum standard of living.

(8) Similarly for equality of opportunity: what is important is not equality but a good start in life in the sense of an acceptable minimum or above. In any case, equality of opportunity includes the opportunity to make gifts or bequests.

(9) In a free economy, there is no problem of overconcentration that cannot be resolved by competition.

(10) Inheritance tax therefore receives no logical support from the ideal of equality of opportunity.

We now turn to the redistributive consequences of inheritance taxation if a heavy and inescapable tax is imposed either in the interest of equality of opportunity or for any other reason. How is the testator's behaviour affected by comparison with the no-tax situation?

38 See Barry BRACEWELL-MILNES (1971, Appendix I).

39 See Section III above.

40 See Gary S. BECKER (1991).

I have shown elsewhere[41] that a tax on giving cannot be more than partially absorbed by the donor: the recipient loses as well. Where the tax applies to the whole estate on death, the rational response of the testator is to shift resources from saving in perpetuity to spending. Saving is not a *Giffen good,* and there is no reason to believe that the amount saved will not fall in response to a rise in the price of saving. We saw in Section VIII how inheritance tax cheapens the rich man's spending: in a consistent or *going* tax system (one without changes or uncompleted effects of earlier changes), the effect of inheritance tax, certain in theory and likely in practice, is to increase the inequality of spending by increasing the spending of the rich relatively to that of the poor. This perverse distributive consequence is illustrated in Table 7.2, where the income elasticity of demand for saving in perpetuity is assumed to be greater than unity. The inequality of spending rises because there is a proportionately larger increase in the spending of the wealthier taxpayers.

Table 7.2
Anti-Sumptuary Taxation

	A	B	C
No tax on saving			
(i) Income	100	200	300
(ii) Saving in perpetuity	10	30	60
(iii) Spending	90	170	240
Prohibitive tax on saving			
(iv) Saving in perpetuity	-	-	-
(v) Income/spending	100	200	300
(vi) Increase in spending	10	30	60
(vii) Original spending	90	170	240

41 See Barry BRACEWELL-MILNES (1989, pp. 82-4).

Since lifetime giving is normally from richer to poorer, the frustration of this giving through taxation may also cause a rise in the inequality of wealth.

It is also possible that the introduction of inheritance taxation will cause a reduction in the inequality of wealth and an initial reduction but eventual increase in the inequality of spending. The inequality of spending initially falls as a result of the effect of inheritance tax on the stock of wealth at the time the tax is introduced and the income generated by this stock. As time goes by, new saving becomes more and more important relatively to the pre-tax stock of saving: there is an asymptomatic approach of total new savings to total savings, including the remnants of the stock of pre-tax savings. At this point the inequality of spending rises. This is illustrated in Table 7.3 which compares the pre-tax Situation 1 with the eventual post-tax Situation 2. The inequality of wealth falls, the richer taxpayer stops saving and the inequality of spending rises.

Table 7.3
The Effect of Inheritance Taxation on Equality

	Situation 1		**Situation 2**	
	A	**B**	**A**	**B**
Capital	1000	100	800	100
Income	50	5	40	5
Spending	30	5	40	5

The distributive results of inheritance tax are perverse because policy is overdetermined. I have argued elsewhere[42] that there are only three variables determining the political character of a tax system: its height; its intension (or degree of graduation or 'progressiveness'); and the relative taxation of saving and spending. 'Progressiveness' can be used or taken only once, not twice or more. Proportional and especially graduated taxes on saving have a regressive effect on spending.[43] That is why the most

42 See Barry BRACEWELL-MILNES (1971).

43 See Barry BRACEWELL-MILNES (1981, Appendix III).

important form of inequality, the inequality of spending, is increased by inheritance tax.[44]

X. Magnitudes

The total net wealth of the United Kingdom personal sector is given as £2550.9 billion at the end of 1994.[45] If £220 billion is added for consumer durable goods (for which the Blue Book no longer publishes a figure) and most of the £853.5 billion of assets in life assurance and pension funds is excluded as not available for giving or bequest, we reach a rounded figure of £2000 billion. If the transferable wealth of the personal sector is transferred by gift or bequest once every 30 years, this implies that the amount transferred in 1994-95 is of the order of £67 billion. This compares with the £43.3 billion yield of value added tax in 1994-95 and the £64.2 billion yield of income tax and is nearly 10 per cent of Gross Domestic Product (£678 billion).[46]

To put the same point differently, with personally held wealth amounting to over £2000 billion, a reduction of 1 per cent in the subjective rate of discount would yield over £20 billion a year, which is more than the yield of corporation tax in 1994-95 and some 3 per cent of Gross Domestic Product. Conversely, this is the amount that would be wasted if the subjective rate of discount rose by 1 per cent, as a result of taxation or otherwise. Any significant part of such a sum that could be captured by economic agents rather than wasted as at present would represent a significant increase in economic wellbeing.

It follows from the analysis of this paper that gifts and bequests of £67 billion create donor's countervalue of £67 billion in addition to the value of the transfer in the hands of the recipient. Donor's surplus may be anything from zero to twice the gift or its countervalue. If the real value of donor's

---

44 *Redistribution in reverse* is the title of Section 8 of Barry BRACEWELL-MILNES (1994).

45 *United Kingdom National Accounts 1995*, p. 106.

46 A more detailed account of the corresponding computation for end-1987 is given in Barry BRACEWELL-MILNES (1989, pp. 109-10).

surplus is the same as the countervalue (and thus intermediate between these extremes), the wealth that is created by giving and bequest is some £133 billion or more a year or about a fifth of Gross Domestic Product. Most of this wealth is beyond the reach of inheritance tax; but where giving or bequest is charged to tax, the wealth destroyed by the tax in the form of donor's countervalue and surplus is larger than the revenue yield (except in the limiting case) and may be much larger. This loss is additional to any loss that may be due to levying the gift tax or inheritance tax near or beyond the point of maximum revenue yield (the point beyond which attempts to increase the rate of tax inflict financial losses on the fisc itself and revenue is increased by rate reductions).

The yield of inheritance tax is forecast at £1.5 billion in 1995-96, which is 0.5 per cent of forecast general government receipts (£278.9 billion) and 0.2 per cent of forecast Gross Domestic Product (£720 billion). The destruction of wealth is larger than this: by a central estimate, twice as large at £3 billion. And this figure does not capture the losses and inefficiencies caused by tax distortion as the tax casts its shadow years in advance of being charged and taxpayers alter their behaviour in the interest of tax reduction. Nor does it capture the social losses and losses to third parties when family firms and landed estates go under.

I have argued elsewhere that the administrative and compliance costs of inheritance tax are exceptionally high[47]; that government costings exaggerate the effect on tax revenue of reductions in inheritance tax by ignoring second-round and supply-side effects[48]; and that if the government replaced its present unbusinesslike cash-flow method of accounting with accruals accounting, it might or would be found to be losing tax revenue year by year from inheritance tax, as the nominal yield fell short each year of the present discounted value of the reductions inflicted by inheritance tax on the yields of other taxes.[49]

In the present context, the purpose of these figures is only to show that the magnitudes are substantial both absolutely and relatively to other relevant sums such as total tax revenue and Gross Domestic Product. There is reason to believe that this conclusion holds good for other industrialised countries.

---

47 See Barry BRACEWELL-MILNES (1994, pp. 6-7).

48 *ibid.*, Section 3.

49 *ibid.*, Section 4 and Appendix C.

XI. Conclusion

Although some of the costs of inheritance taxation are plain for all to see, as when family firms or landed estates are destroyed by the tax, most of its costs are hidden. The start of Section II, above, mentions a number of hidden ways in which inheritance taxation destroys material wealth; they are discussed in *Will to Succeed*.

The subject of the present paper is the complementary and additional hidden costs imposed on the economy and society by inheritance taxation through its destruction of the immaterial wealth that can otherwise be created by means of low subjective discount rates, donor's countervalue and surplus and a gradual shift in the outlook of the owner towards that of steward. The pursuit of equality of opportunity likewise imposes hidden costs on the economy and society through tax distortion, by cheapening the spending of the rich and increasing the inequality of spending.

The more traditional arguments at the start of Section II concern the hidden costs of inheritance taxation imposed through tax distortion on the creation of wealth. The arguments of the present paper concern the costs of distorting the use of wealth, once created. Material wealth can create further immaterial wealth costlessly in a tax-free environment; or, through the distorting effects of inheritance taxation, this process of costless wealth creation can be frustrated by the substitution of spending for saving in perpetuity, with its consequence of a rise in the inequality of spending.

Two visions of society are in conflict here. Inheritance tax favours a one-generation society, short-termist, brash, materialistic, aggressively individualistic, high-spending at the top of the scale, competitive in outward lifestyles: in the eyes of its critics, vulgar. By contrast, a society free of inheritance tax favours a more traditional and stable way of life, more long-termist, more family-oriented, less materialistic, more attuned to spiritual and ethical values, cool or contemptuous towards competitive spending, sympathetic towards conservation and preservation, towards personal ownership and stewardship and towards the costless creation of wealth through personal ownership, saving in perpetuity and inheritance.

Although some may prefer the former vision, other supporters of inheritance tax may, through the law of unintended consequences and the overdetermination of the tax system, be helping to achieve the opposite of their wishes.

I believe that the social, moral and spiritual arguments against inheritance taxation are even stronger than the economic ones: at these levels, the hidden cost of inheritance tax is the corruption of society. But the economic arguments against the tax are themselves so strong and the damage it does is such a large multiple of its yield that even by economic criteria many would gain from the abolition of the tax and none need lose.

References

BAUER, LORD (1976): *Dissent on Development,* London (Weidenfeld and Nicolson).

BAUER, LORD (1994): *Development Aid: End It or Mend It,* San Francisco (International Center for Economic Growth) Occasional Papers 43.

BECKER, G.S. (1991): *A Treatise on the Family,* Cambridge (Harvard University Press).

BRACEWELL-MILNES, B. (1971): *The Measurement of Fiscal Policy: An Analysis of Tax Systems in Terms of the Political Distinction Between 'Right' and 'Left',* London (Confederation of British Industry).

BRACEWELL-MILNES, B. (1979): *Tax Avoidance and Evasion: The Individual and Society,* Upminster (Panopticum Press).

BRACEWELL-MILNES, B. (1981): *The Taxation of Industry: Fiscal Barriers to the Creation of Wealth,* London (Panopticum Press).

BRACEWELL-MILNES, B. (1982): *Land and Heritage: The Public Interest in Personal Ownership,* London (Institute of Economic Affairs), Hobart Paper 93.

BRACEWELL-MILNES, B. (1989): *The Wealth of Giving: Every One in His Inheritance,* London (Institute of Economic Affairs), Research Monograph 43.

BRACEWELL-MILNES, B. (1990): "The Economics and Theology of Giving", *Economic Affairs*, 10(5), pp. 30-1.

BRACEWELL-MILNES, B. (1991): "Earmarking in Britain: Theory and Practice" in: *The Case for Earmarked Taxes: Government Spending and Public Choice*, London (Institute of Economic Affairs), Research Monograph 46.

BRACEWELL-MILNES, B. (1994): *Will to Succeed: Inheritance Without Taxation*, London (Adam Smith Institute).

CORNFORTH, J. (1974): *Country Houses in Britain: Can They Survive?*, London (Country Life).

HAY, D.A. and MORRIS, D.J. (1984): *Unquoted Companies: Their Contribution to the United Kingdom Economy*, London (Macmillan).

MARSHALL, A. (1961): *Principles of Economics*, London (Macmillan for the Royal Economic Society).

MURRAY, C. (1984): *Losing Ground: American Social Policy 1960-1980*, New York (Basic Books).

ROTHBARD, M. (1970): *Power and Market: Government and the Economy*, Menlo Park, CA (Institute for Humane Studies).

SMITH, A. (1976): *An Inquiry into the Nature and Causes of the Wealth of Nations*, ed. by R.H. Campbell, A.S. Skinner and W.B. Todd, Oxford (Oxford University Press) (= The Glasgow Edition of the Works and Correspondence of Adam Smith, Vol. II).

WEST, M. (1908): *The Inheritance Tax*, New York (Columbia University Press).

United Kingdom National Accounts 1995, London (The Blue Book; Central Statistical Office, HMSO, 1995).

Chapter 8

Nothing Wrong With Unearned Wealth? A Comment on Haslett and Bracewell-Milnes[1]

PHILIPPE VAN PARIJS

Both David Haslett and Barry Bracewell-Milnes dare to stick their necks out and do so in an articulate, thoughtful way. I like that. Not because I love chopping heads off, but because I strongly believe that an active involvement in public policy debates is an essential part of a scholar's role in today's society. Moreover, I have great sympathy for Haslett's impatience with the great inequalities in life chances that result from a massively unequal access to external assets, while at the same time coming close to embracing Bracewell-Milnes's rejection of the "short-termist, brash, materialistic, aggressively individualistic" market rat race in favour of a "more traditional and stable way of life, more long-termist, more family-oriented, less materialistic, more attuned to spiritual and ethical values, cool or contemptuous towards competitive spending, sympathetic towards conservation and preservation" (Bracewell-Milnes, 1997, p. 199). And yet, I deeply disagree with both. Why?

By way of prelude, let me first note how ironical it is that authors who reach such opposite conclusions - one argues for the abolition of inheritance

1 This is a revised version of an oral comment on the papers presented in Antwerp on 8 November 1995 by David Haslett and Barry Bracewell-Milnes.

taxes, the other for the abolition of inheritance (beyond a strict quota) - should both appeal, at the most fundamental level, to utilitarian premises. Haslett explicitly states that maximizing 'overall well-being' or 'general welfare' is the ultimate aim. Bracewell-Milnes prefers to speak of 'wealth maximization', but it is clear from several of his examples - typically, a mutually beneficial trade that increases 'wealth' - that the relevant variable is aggregate utility. As our two authors claim to derive incompatible conclusions from the same fundamental normative principle, one of them is bound to be wrong. Obviously, they may also both be wrong. That this is indeed the case, I shall now endeavour to show.

I. To Each According to Her Productivity

Haslett's argument relies on a rule-utilitarian justification of the productivity criterion - "To each according to the productivity of his labour, or of the property acquired in return for the productivity of his labour" - as a prima facie criterion of distributive justice. The key premise is that, since people cannot be forced to be maximally productive, one must entice them to be so by paying them in proportion to their productivity, the latter being defined as what others would be willing to pay for their product on the basis of fully informed preferences. Since this productivity criterion is clearly at odds with the possibility of large private gifts and bequests, utilitarians must demand that these be subjected to a stiff (ideally 100%) taxation, at least beyond a threshold fixed at a sufficiently low level to be achievable by most beneficiaries.

His key premise holds fully, Haslett hastens to say, only if a number of conditions are satisfied. In particular, there must be no 'unnecessary' inequality of opportunities, i.e. no such inequality stemming from any source other than an unequal endowment in innate talents. There must also be no departure from Pareto-optimality as a result of externalities or other market imperfections. The problem is that, beyond these factors listed by Haslett, there are many more that mess up the connection between welfare maximization and the productivity criterion. For example, a utilitarian is bound to have to pay some attention to the welfare loss that would result from the starvation of the less talented - those who suffer from a 'necessary' inequality of opportunities -, or to the welfare loss that would result from overperformance in a 'tragedy of the commons' context, or from the failure to systematically overpay some economic agents (relative to their statically defined 'productivity') in order to foster alertness and innovation, or again from the suboptimal consumption of leisure by people whom idleness would make awfully happy.

With the key premise left in shambles, there are three ways in which Haslett might try to amend his argument. The first one consists in promoting the productivity principle from a (poor) utilitarian rule of thumb to a principle of justice in its own right. The problem, here, is that my productivity is powerfully affected, not just by what happened to be contained in one cell on a Summer night of 1950, but also by the smiles and patience I was surrounded by as a baby, by the good or bad luck I had with the choice of the teachers I was assigned to at school, by the luck I had when noticing the announcement of a scholarship, and by countless other undeserved contingencies. Hence, I must confess that I cannot even begin to make sense of an ideal of fairness that would consist in matching exactly people's incomes and their productivities, and therefore cannot blame Haslett for dismissing this first patching up strategy.

II. Direct Utilitarianism

A second possible strategy consists in discarding the productivity criterion as an unnecessary detour and arguing straight from utilitarian premises for the abolition of (quota-exceeding) inheritance. The most obvious link is provided by a highly plausible factual assumption: as the assets inherited by a person swell, their marginal contribution to that person's utility shrinks. If accepted, this assumption induces a strong utilitarian presumption in favour of an egalitarian distribution of assets. It must, however, be qualified in several ways.

Firstly, utility functions are not identical across people, and those who care more about riches, typically because they were brought up in luxury, should accordingly be allowed to inherit more.

Secondly, the extent to which inheritance is taxed may well have an overall negative effect on savings and the care taken of one's belongings, and this may also largely offset, in dynamic equilibrium, the aggregate welfare gain from a more egalitarian redistribution.

Thirdly - and this takes us to Bracewell-Milnes's (1982, 1997) most valuable insight -, a significant loss of welfare may arise from the break up or reappropriation of a piece of property, say a family estate, as a result of high taxation preventing parents from leaving it to their children. By no means does awareness of this sort of effect - the destruction of the 'owner's surplus' and the 'donor's surplus' - validate Bracewell-Milnes's (1997, p. 189) sweeping claim that "the social [welfare] loss [from any tax on giving] always exceeds [the contribution to overall welfare of] the revenue yield [...] except in the limiting case". At the very least, the net effect on overall welfare will crucially depend on the allocation of the tax revenues, and one needs more than a swift appeal to Adam Smith's critique of unthrifty taxes ("that increase the revenue of the sovereign, which seldom maintains any but unproductive labourers; at the expence of the capital of the people, which maintains none but productive", quoted *ibid.*, p. 188) to be persuaded that the net effect is bound to be negative.

The bottom line, for a utilitarian, can therefore neither be that all (quota-exceeding) inheritance should be abolished, nor that all inheritance taxation should. The welfare-maximizing gift and inheritance tax is most likely to be positive but fairly low - not just to preserve incentives but also to match the different preferences shaped by different family backgrounds. It will moreover be differentiated according to type of asset - family farm and family mansion, for example, would no doubt deserve a privileged status, relative to anonymous shares or rented real estate. And it may even be designed so as to encourage a better match between the age at which one needs the money and the age at which one inherits - for example, by involving a lower rate on bequests to one's grandchildren than to one's children.

Hence, this second strategy turns out to bring Haslett no more relief than the first one. Even assuming that there is nothing wrong with its premises, it has the great defect of yielding a conclusion that is admittedly a long way from what Bracewell-Milnes would like it to be, but is nonetheless very different from Haslett's bold view.

III. Equal Starts

There is, however, a third way of rearticulating the argument for stiff inheritance taxes that relies neither on a productivity conception of justice nor on the adoption of a utilitarian perspective. It provides an alternative to Haslett's argument, rather than a reconstruction of it, and appeals - unsurprisingly - to a conception of justice as equality of opportunities, a conception left unscathed by Bracewell-Milnes's (1997, Section IX) uncharacteristically sloppy treatment of it.[2] This conception, as repeatedly mentioned by Haslett, is not unrelated to his own productivity conception, while sufficiently differing from it to avoid its implausible implications. The central intuition of this alternative way of justifying inheritance taxation is simple enough. If you were born with a nice estate and a huge cheque waiting in your slippers, your opportunities are far greater, ceteris paribus, than those of the poor lad who was provided with barely enough to keep him fed through his childhood. It is hard to deny that this massive inequality is also a serious injustice, and the obvious way of redressing it is to share out the estate and the cheque by imposing stiff inheritance taxes.

On reflection, however, this 'equal starts' argument for inheritance taxation needs to be strongly qualified. To begin with, as aptly remarked by Bracewell-Milnes (1997, p. 194), "most heirs do not inherit significant sums until many years after the start of their careers". As the average heir is now over fifty years old, what is all this rhetoric, one may legitimately ask, about inheritance bringing unfairness to the 'starting gate'?

Secondly, as remarked long ago by Milton Friedman (1962, pp. 163-5), tough restrictions on the amount of material wealth parents can donate or bequeath to their children will lead them to spend even more - and by the same token even more unequally - on the education of their children. This need not directly bother Haslett, who boldly asserts: "For dependents, gifts that quickly depreciate in value, such as (ordinary) automobiles, or that take the form of education of any sort, are not to count toward the quota (...)." (Haslett, 1997, p. 148). This deep asymmetry may make sense if what one is after is reward according to productivity: "this exception for dependents will not, to any great extent, support idleness from people who otherwise would

2 The rationale and variants of opportunity-focused conceptions of justice are spelled out and discussed in Van Parijs (1997).

have been productive" (*ibid.*). But if one rejects the productivity conception of distributive justice in favour of a far more plausible equal-opportunity conception, this extraordinarily favourable treatment of endowments in human capital makes no sense at all. Those truly concerned with equalizing life chances 'at the start' should attach only secondary importance to the unequal bequests people increasingly receive, on average, at an age at which they are already contemplating retirement. They should worry far more about the immensely different opportunities children and young adults are given as a result of their parents spending very unequal sums on their education.

IV. Gifts Are Everywhere

This would seem to suggest that a consistent equal-opportunity reformulation of Haslett's anti-inheritance stance would involve extending to educational expenditure his lifetime inheritance quota scheme and giving this component of what a person receives particular weight because of the early age at which she receives it. Such an extension, it must be conceded, raises serious difficulties of at least two sorts. Firstly, think of someone whose quota has been exhausted, or even exceeded, by great expenditure on a training course that did not boost her earning power in any way, either because she failed the final exam and/or because the skills acquired through the course happened no longer to be in demand when the course was completed. Is it really fair to decree that the 'beneficiary' of this quota-busting training is not entitled to any other gift, or even has to pay some of it back in taxes (which is what exceeding the quota must mean)?

Secondly, think of someone of average innate talent whose earning power is high despite fairly low educational expenditure. It is just that her parents spent quite a lot of their time transmitting to her directly some useful knowledge, or perhaps not even that: their daily behaviour provided her unintentionally with the many cues she could easily draw on to build up her human capital. If this unwitting gift produces exactly the same effect on someone's earning power as some explicit cash payment for her education, surely the equalization of opportunities is not consistent with a quota scheme that takes full account of the latter while turning a blind eye to the former.

These two difficulties are serious. But they challenge neither the plausibility of the equal-opportunity conception as such, nor the idea that the opportunities afforded by one's endowment in human capital are no less relevant than those rooted in one's material endowment. They both find a smooth solution once it is realized that the economic life of our societies is packed full of (self-interested) gifts.[3] Compared to the massive heap of treats in the form of (unequally) scarce jobs, bequests are of miserable importance. Unequal access to jobs, whether rooted in differences in talents, in upbringing, in formal education and training, or in sheer queuing luck, is now the main form taken by inequalities in endowments. Hence the following paradoxical proposition. An appropriate taxation of the incomes derived from jobs, including self-employment, is therefore the most powerful tool for equalizing opportunities, including those deriving ultimately from inequalities in what we have been given nearly imperceptibly - and often undistinguishably - by our genes and our upbringing.[4]

If justice is to be interpreted along the lines of this broad opportunity-based conception, it is clear that Haslett is right in his attempt to keep in check the unequal opportunities brought about by inheritance. But he is wrong in focusing narrowly on one particular sort of gift, which is far from being the most significant one in the world we now live in, and in simply condoning thereby most of the massive inequalities in the endowments that underlie people's productivities. One needs to redress this unwarranted bias and distribute the proceeds in a fair, impartial way.[5] Doing so will have a by-product which Bracewell-Milnes should welcome. It will contribute as much as is justifiable to saving his society of stewardship and spiritual pursuits from an irrepressible decay into Haslett's world of maximum productivity and competitiveness.

---

3 Very roughly expressed, this is the central intuition behind my *Real Freedom for All* (Van Parijs, 1995).

4 It is of course important that this appropriate taxation should not seize more than the 'gift' component of job remuneration. This is guaranteed - at the expense of settling for maximin rather than strict equality - through subjecting the maximization of the tax yield to a ban on involuntary employment and the demand that taxation be predictable (see Van Parijs, 1995, pp. 113-9).

5 More concretely, this means opting for transfers of an unconditional type rather than in the form of an earned income tax credit, as advocated by Haslett (1994, Chapter 6).

In this light, and using the concept of wealth in an appropriately expanded sense, our ultimate disagreement can now be rephrased as follows. Bracewell-Milnes is right, against Haslett, in holding that there is nothing wrong with unearned wealth. Yet, Haslett is right in challenging the conservative position Bracewell-Milnes derives from this premise. To back this challenge, however, one must not deny the premise, as he does, but instead supplement it as follows: "There is nothing wrong with unearned wealth, except that not everyone has it".[6]

References

BRACEWELL-MILNES, B. (1982): *Land and Heritage: The Public Interest in Personal Ownership*, London (Institute of Economic Affairs), Hobart Paper 93.

BRACEWELL-MILNES, B. (1997): "The hidden costs of inheritance taxation", *this volume*.

BRITTAN, S. (1973): *Capitalism and the Permissive Society*, London (Macmillan).

FRIEDMAN, M. (1962): *Capitalism and Freedom*, Chicago (University of Chicago Press).

HASLETT, D.W. (1994): *Capitalism with Morality*, Oxford (Clarendon Press).

HASLETT, D.W. (1997): "Distributive justice and inheritance", *this volume*.

VAN PARIJS, PH. (1995): *Real Freedom for All. What (if Anything) Can Justify Capitalism?*, Oxford (Oxford University Press).

VAN PARIJS, PH. (1997): "Justice as the fair distribution of freedom: Fetishism or stoicism?", in: M. FLEURBAEY and J.F. LASLIER (Eds.): *The Ethics and Economics of Liberty*, London (Routledge), forthcoming.

---

6 I am here paraphrasing Samuel BRITTAN's (1973) lapidary justification of an unconditional basic income: "There is nothing wrong with unearned income, except that not everyone has it."

Chapter 9

A Reply to Bracewell-Milnes

D. W. HASLETT

Barry Bracewell-Milnes, in his powerful essay, 'The hidden costs of inheritance taxation'[1], argues against any restrictions upon inheritance at all, including any in the form of an inheritance quota such as I am defending here. His arguments are many; they are set out clearly, and they are set out with great skill. Nevertheless I think his arguments, in the end, fail. I shall, in this comment, attempt, in general outline, to show why. I shall not attempt to address all of his arguments and claims here, but only those that I think are most important.

1. Bracewell-Milnes is a conservative in the truest sense of the word. He is, first and foremost, concerned about saving, or preserving, family estates, family businesses, and family farms. He thinks that the preservation of these establishments intact is very much in the general welfare. His vision, which does have a certain appeal, is that of generation after generation of family members acting as 'stewards' for society by preserving these establishments 'in perpetuity', never consuming any of the assets for their own selfish purposes. But, he claims, if there are substantial inheritance taxes on these family estates, businesses and farms, then family members will inevitably have to break them up, selling them piecemeal, to pay these taxes. Or if, to pay the taxes, family members sell these establishments intact, the result will only be that fragmentation will then occur, sooner or later, at the hands of others. Either way, society as a whole will end up the losers. My reactions to these points are as follows.

Consider first family estates and farms. I grant that it may often be in the general welfare for them to be preserved intact. But let us face facts. The

---

1 See BRACEWELL-MILNES (1997).

days in which we could count upon children raised on farms or country estates following in the footsteps of their parents and themselves becoming farmers, or country squires, are, for better or worse, fast coming to an end. In today's modern industrialized countries, higher education and other forms of occupational training are readily available, people are far more mobile than ever before, and, typically, children choose not to follow in the exact footsteps of their parents anymore. As a consequence, in today's modern, industrialized countries, there is hardly any guarantee that country estates and farmlands will be preserved intact even if left, unrestricted, to family members. These days, family members who inherit a country estate or farmland will often break it up themselves, not for the sake of paying inheritance taxes, but for the sake of liquidizing the asset so that it can be divided up among themselves and the proceeds used as they prefer. So the preservation of estates and farmlands is not accomplished very well simply by having no restrictions on inheritance. The best way to preserve them intact is, I suggest, the most direct way. If it is in the general welfare to preserve them intact, then let us pass regulations preventing anyone from selling them, or giving them away, other than intact (except under certain extenuating circumstances which can be spelled out in these regulations).

Consider next family businesses. If the business's return on capital is higher than average, then it will probably be preserved intact even if sold to the highest, outside bidder rather than remaining in the family. And, incidentally, if, as should be the case, a 'worker-control format' and favourable credit terms are made available by law to workers, then the highest bidder may even be the current workers (i.e. employees) of the business, thereby transforming it into a worker-controlled enterprise. Such a transformation is, I have argued elsewhere, likely to be a very good thing.[2] If, on the other hand, the business's return on capital is lower than average, then breaking it up and using its assets for more efficient purposes is probably more in the general welfare than preserving it intact.

Do not misunderstand me. I grant that, for sentimental and other such reasons, the value that family estates or homesteads, family farms, and family businesses have for family members may well exceed their market value, in which case value clearly would be lost if they had to be sold to the highest, outside bidder rather than staying in the family. But, as I pointed out in Section II of my essay in this volume (Haslett, 1997), an inheritance

2 See Chapter 4 of HASLETT (1994).

quota, which can be used as a down payment, will enable small or medium-sized family homesteads, farms or businesses to be *purchased* by family members if they really do care enough, especially if this quota is combined, as it should be, with regulations that give first opportunity to purchase them to family members who have been designated by the decedent in his or her will, and that also give these same family members lenient, long-term credit terms. Moreover, the goal of purchasing these establishments someday will provide family members who care enough with the best of motives for saving their money, just like anyone else who hopes to make a major purchase must do. Of course *very large* family businesses will usually remain beyond the purchasing capacities of family members, even with the help of an inheritance quota. But for very large businesses to be run by those whose main qualifications may be merely that they are the decedent's son or daughter is of questionable social value anyway. In the interests of efficiency, very large businesses should be run instead by those who, through fair competition, have *earned* the right to do so, not merely have been given it as a gift.

Finally, I grant that no major, new restrictions, such as the inheritance quota defended here, should ever catch any children, with vested interests or expectations for future, by surprise. This means that such a quota should never be applicable to anyone born prior to the time that the quota becomes law (or, for the sake of fairness between brothers and sisters, to any of their siblings who may be born afterwards). Those born *after* the quota becomes law will not have expected, or counted on, inheriting a large homestead, farm or business in the first place, will already have planned for the future accordingly, and thus are not likely to suffer any great harm from the quota.[3]

2. Bracewell-Milnes' more specific argument against any restrictions upon inheritance or gifts proceeds as follows:

> "(...) far from contributing to a zero sum in which the gains of the gainers exactly match the losses of the losers, the act of giving at least doubles the value of the gift. If A gives £100 to B, the gift is worth £100 to B; but it is worth at least a countervalue of £100 to A, since otherwise he would not have preferred giving to the various other possible uses of his money." (Bracewell-Milnes, 1997, p. 168)

---

3 See BENTHAM (1952, pp. 290-2).

Bracewell-Milnes then concludes that there should, therefore, be no restrictions at all upon giving since the overall, total value, or utility, derivable from any such restrictions obviously could never come close in amount to that derivable from giving if left *un*restricted, since any giving, if left unrestricted, "at least doubles the value of the gift".

In real life, unfortunately, value, or utility, cannot be doubled quite as easily as Bracewell-Milnes apparently thinks. What leads him to think it can be is that he, like many economists, is implicitly assuming a false theory of value, or utility, one in which the utility of any given alternatives, *X* and *Y*, for any given person, *A*, is a matter solely of which alternative *A* prefers. So, according to this theory, if *A* preferred *X*, then, *ipso facto*, *X* would have more utility for *A*, whereas if *A* preferred *Y*, then, *ipso facto*, *Y* would have more utility for *A*, altogether regardless of what *X* and *Y*, in reality, happened to be. We may refer to this as the 'simple preference' theory of personal value. Any theory of personal value is, of course, supposed to delineate what is of value, or utility, for a person, what, in other words, is in the person's *own* best interests. Now, for certain technical purposes, the simple preference theory of value is useful for economists, and can yield interesting results. But one must be very careful not to apply this theory beyond these narrow, technical parameters, for the simple preference theory of value is, in general, false, as is easy to show.[4] One thing wrong with the simple preference theory is that it entails that a person can never be mistaken about what is in his best interests, whereas, obviously, people often are (as when they prefer to cross the street just as an unseen truck is fast approaching). Moreover, the simple preference theory entails that people can never, through weakness of will, fail to do what is in their best interests, whereas, once again, people obviously do. Just because John prefers to go to the movies, and thus does so, rather than study for his huge exam the next morning, it does not follow that going to the movies is therefore in John's best interests. It does not even follow that John *thinks* it is in his best interests. Another thing wrong with this theory is that, by interpreting everything one prefers to do as automatically being in one's own best interests, this theory, unjustifiably, destroys the distinction between, on the one hand, acting in one's own best interests and, on the other hand, acting

4 I attempt to show, in some detail, the faults of the simple preference theory, and try to set out a more satisfactory alternative theory in Sections 1.7-1.10 of HASLETT (1994).

altruistically - i.e. sacrificing one's own best interests for the sake of others. For example, the mother who, knowing that it will cost her life, nevertheless prefers above all else to run in front of a truck to save her child must, according to this theory, be acting in her own best interests (since that is what she prefers). In reality, however, she is almost surely not acting in her own best interests, but is instead performing an act of great self-sacrifice. We must be very careful not confuse what, all things considered, one *prefers* with what, all things considered, is in one's own best interests. Contrary to what the simple preference theory entails, they are not, in reality, always one and the same thing.

Having thus seen what is wrong with the simple preference theory of value, it is easy now to see where Bracewell-Milnes' argument, which presupposes this theory, goes wrong. Take any given parents. Just because, all things considered, they prefer to sacrifice consumption for themselves so as to give a large gift to their children, it does not follow, as Bracewell-Milnes assumes, that giving this gift was in their *own* best interests. It may have been. But the more likely interpretation is that, instead, they were sacrificing what was in their own best interests for the sake of their children. And whenever this more likely interpretation happens to be correct, then obviously giving the gift does not, as Bracewell-Milnes claims, automatically at least double the overall utility derivable from what was given. Instead, the parents will be sacrificing their own utility for the sake of that of their children, and thus the overall, total utility derivable from what was given will not double. Take another example. Say the government passes a law that requires all people to turn over all of their excess wealth - that is, whatever wealth they do not need for bare necessities - to the government (which, in turn, passes it on to the people in the form of benefits). People must then choose between the following three alternatives: (1) secretly spending their excess wealth on themselves; (2) secretly saving it; and (3) obeying the law and transferring it to the government. If it were as easy to double utility by transferring wealth as Bracewell-Milnes seems to think, then those who *preferred* the latter alternative would thus be doubling the overall, total utility of their excess wealth by transferring it to the government. I suspect Bracewell-Milnes would not be so happy with this consequence of the simple preference theory. He might reply that this case is different from the case of giving to one's children, since in this case people's preferences were *constrained* by the requirements of law. But then, in the case of giving to one's children, surely many people's preferences are similarly constrained by what they take to be the requirements of morality or good values. In short, one must not, as does Bracewell-Milnes, attempt to apply a false theory of personal value beyond the narrow parameters in which it was meant to be applied. Otherwise one will likely end up with the wrong conclusions. Finally, even if Bracewell-Milnes were right about giving doubling the value of gifts, he still would not be entitled to conclude that, therefore, no restrictions upon inheritance and other large gifts should exist, since he has not taken into account the negative externalities resulting from the practice of allowing unrestricted gifts, negative externalities in the form of the inequalities in opportunity, inequalities of wealth, and so on, that this practice perpetuates. These negative externalities are outlined in Section II of my essay in this volume.

3. Next, Bracewell-Milnes argues that giving should not be restricted because doing so has the perverse result of making it cheaper for the rich to spend money on themselves than it is for the poor. Take, he says, a restriction in the form of a 40 per cent tax on inheritance. With such a tax, he says, the rich man "can have 100 of spending for an opportunity cost of 60 of saving, the other 40 being paid for by the Treasury in lost inheritance tax" (Bracewell-Milnes, 1997, p. 192), whereas 100 of spending costs the poor man 100 in saving (since, being poor, he has no opportunity to leave an inheritance but will have to consume any savings instead, thereby avoiding the 40 per cent tax). Thus, he says, since this tax makes spending on themselves much cheaper for the rich than it otherwise would be, but does not cheapen it for the poor, the natural consequence will be more spending by the rich on themselves relative to that spent by the poor on themselves. But an even greater inequality between rich and poor in what they spend on themselves is perverse, just the result we do not want; therefore, he concludes, there should be no tax on inheritance.

I do not find this argument convincing. Even given the applicability of Bracewell- Milnes's argument to the current generation, one might wonder why it would apply to succeeding generations. That is, one might wonder why this alleged increase in the inequality of the amounts people spend on themselves would be any more than temporary. After all, if a high inheritance tax (without loopholes) of 40 per cent were, in fact, legislated, then it would appear that, whether by increased personal spending or by this tax, one way or the other great fortunes would tend to be broken up, thereby bringing about a more equal distribution of wealth in the *next* generation.

Assuming that the more equally wealth is distributed, the more equal personal spending is likely to be, it would seem to follow that, in the next generation, the generation in which wealth became more equally distributed, personal spending would likely be more equally distributed also. This is not, however, the reply to Bracewell-Milnes's argument that I wish to emphasize here; the reply I wish to emphasize denies the applicability of his argument even to the current generation.

Notice, first, that his argument is inapplicable to all those whose savings do not exceed the overall amount that the people to whom they want to give have left in unfulfilled quotas. As I pointed out in my essay in this volume, assuming, say, a quota of $100,000 in the United States, and assuming that most people will know at least five eligible people to whom they will want to leave their wealth, most people in the United States will then be able to bequeath at least $500,000 without any restrictions. Given the proliferation of grandchildren and great-grandchildren in many families, certainly some will know at least ten eligible people to whom they will want to leave their wealth. They will thus be able to bequeath at least $1,000,000 to loved ones. Since very few people today die with estates valued over $500,000, and even fewer with estates valued over $1,000,000, this means that, for almost all people, the quota proposal defended here will have virtually no effect upon their 'opportunity costs' or, therefore, upon the relative value to them of saving versus spending. This, incidentally, is one advantage of an inheritance *quota* over an inheritance *tax*. With an inheritance tax of any amount, Bracewell-Milnes's argument is applicable to everyone wealthy enough to bequeath anything, whereas, with a quota, his argument is applicable only to the most wealthy individuals throughout the country.

But, and this is my main point, although I admit that, with a quota, Bracewell-Milnes's argument is, in principle, applicable to the most wealthy, those in *this* particular group are the least likely to increase their spending upon themselves. Most people, after all, can spend only so much upon themselves before they become satiated. For people of ordinary means, this point of satiation is rarely ever reached, but, as I said, a quota is unlikely to have any affect upon the relative value of spending versus saving for these people anyway. The relatively few that actually will be affected by the quota can be divided into (1) the ultrarich, who have literally millions at their disposal, and (2) the moderately rich. The ultrarich are likely to be spending on themselves at a level of satiation even if there are no restrictions at all upon inheritance. Ultrarich people have the means to buy whatever they may want for themselves and still save as much as they may want for their children. If, therefore, they are already spending on themselves at a level of satiation, passing an inheritance quota, even if it does discourage saving, is unlikely to motivate them to spend still more on themselves - *provided*, that is, they have a reasonable alternative.

But do they have a reasonable alternative? Actually they do, and this is the crux of my argument. Their alternative is to spend for charitable purposes, spending which (we may assume) is completely exempted from the quota. I have in mind here charitable spending (gifts or bequests) such as contributing to medical research, helping people who are starving, founding an institute that is to be devoted to scholarly research, providing the funds for a university building, for a shelter for the homeless, for a much needed hospital, etc. As an added inducement, the institute, university building, shelter, hospital, or whatever, can be named after the donor, thereby becoming a permanent testimonial to his or her generosity, a kind of immortality no less. If an ultrarich person has any compassion at all for the suffering of others, has any ambitions at all for leaving the world a better place, then surely spending for some such charitable purpose will be preferred to spending still more on himself even though already at the level of satiation.

This argument is not quite as compelling with respect to those who are just moderately rich, since the moderately rich will not necessarily have already reached their point of satiation in spending on themselves. However, for any savings beyond what they may want to leave to individuals who have not yet reached their quota, spending it for charitable purposes provides, even for them, a major alternative to spending even more on themselves. For this reason, Bracewell-Milnes greatly overestimates the extent to which high inheritance taxes, and, in particular, an inheritance quota, is likely to cause people to spend more merely on themselves. In short, an inheritance quota, rather than encouraging the more base human sentiments of greed and materialism as Bracewell-Milnes thinks, is instead likely to encourage the more noble human sentiments of charity and compassion for others.

4. Bracewell-Milnes (1997, p. 194) claims that "The equality-of-opportunity argument for inheritance taxation is weak on its own terms,

since most heirs do not inherit significant sums until many years after the start of their careers."[5]

Even if restrictions on inheritance did not substantially increase equality of opportunity among those at the start of their careers, increasing equality of opportunity among those at other points in their careers is important also. But, contrary to what Bracewell-Milnes is suggesting, major restrictions on inheritance (and large gifts) do substantially increase equality of opportunity among those at the start of their careers; without such restrictions, the rich, even at the start of their careers, have vast opportunities unavailable to others. If your name is, say, Rockefeller, and it is therefore known that you are due to inherit a fortune someday, it is, even at the start of your career, bound to open up lines of credit and other opportunities for you not available to others. And with the safety net of this eventual inheritance to fall back upon, you will be able to take chances on certain careers - say, for example, a political career - that others can only dream about. Moreover, even though a child's main inheritance may not come until later, wealthy parents will almost always provide their children with whatever *large gifts* may be necessary for giving them opportunities that others do not have at the start of their careers. Finally, huge fortunes are often put in trust, not for children, but for grandchildren, with these funds then becoming available to the grandchildren upon their reaching age 21, thereby enabling them to get their inheritance at the start their careers after all. These generation-skipping trusts, especially common among rich Americans, are, typically, set up generation after generation. In short, the equality-of-opportunity argument for restrictions on inheritance remains strong.

5. The next claim by Bracewell-Milnes that I wish to consider, although it is stated without argument, nevertheless touches upon important matters. He claims that "a society free of inheritance tax favours (...) more family-oriented (...) values (...)". (*ibid.*, p. 199)

---

5 This is only one of nine brief pronouncements about equality of opportunity that BRACEWELL-MILNES sets out in Section IX of his paper. The others are, I think, less interesting and relevant than this one, and I shall not address them here. From his nine pronouncements, he concludes that "Inheritance tax therefore receives no logical support from the ideal of equality of opportunity." (*ibid.*, p. 194). I suggest that what lacks logical support is, instead, his conclusion, since, according to BRACEWELL-MILNES's own admission, his brief pronouncements do not "do justice to the subject" (*ibid.*, p. 193).

Now one hears much these days from conservatives about the importance of family values. It is not, however, always clear exactly what values they have in mind. I shall assume that the crux of family values is loyalty and devotion to family members, which, for parents, includes a willingness to do whatever necessary so that their children may have deeply satisfying lives of their own. Certainly if something like this is meant by family values, then it is not just conservatives who favour them, but decent people everywhere. But does not a quota on inheritance prevent parents from giving their children what they need, thereby serving to undermine family values, just as Bracewell-Milnes suggests? I do not think so. It is a rather perverse consequence of the institution of inheritance that many people seem to equate the most important thing that children need, the most important thing that parents can give them, with material wealth. Surely, however, there are far more important things that parents can give their children, such as their time and love.

I have heard rich, successful people say that probably the most deeply satisfying years of their lives were those exciting, challenging years in which they were struggling to make their own way in the world, rather than the opulent years after they had already succeeded. Satisfaction in life was found at least as much in the 'journey' as in the destination. If there is an inheritance quota, perhaps then parents will concentrate more on giving their children not mere wealth, but what is more important: the capacities, the values, the strength of character necessary for them to experience the deep satisfaction of succeeding on their own, rather than merely living off their parent's wealth. And, as a result, perhaps then children will be more inclined to appreciate their parents for their *own sakes*, not merely for the sake of their wealth. Bracewell-Milnes says that restrictions on inheritance reflect materialistic values (*ibid.*, p. 199). I say just the opposite. Restrictions on inheritance reflect the view that there are far more important ways - nonmaterial ways - in which parents can exemplify family values, can express their love for their children, than merely through material gifts and bequests.

6. Bracewell-Milnes concludes his essay by saying that, as between those who favour restrictions upon inheritance and those who do not, two visions of society are in conflict. Restrictions upon inheritance, he says, favour "(...) a one-generation society, short-termist, brash, materialistic, aggressively individualistic, high-spending at the top of the scale,

competitive in outward lifestyles: in the eyes of its critics, vulgar." (*ibid.*, p. 199) His unpleasant characterization of a society that restricts inheritance is premised largely on his claim that, in such a society, savings will necessarily be drastically curtained in favour of people spending far more upon themselves, a claim that I have already tried to show is false.[6] Thus I reject his characterization. I agree, however, that, as between those who favour restrictions upon inheritance and those who do not, two visions of society are in conflict. But, I suggest, the conflict is not as Bracewell-Milnes sees it. A restriction in the form of a lifetime quota is, I have tried to show, a step toward a society with freedom not just for the rich, but for all. It is a step toward a society in which people do not unjustly discriminate, but seek fair play and equal opportunity for everyone. And it is a step toward a society in which people have compassion not just for those close to them, but for all human beings. I suggest, therefore, that the two visions of society really at stake here are a society with little freedom for many people, with favouritism for the rich, and with narrowly focused compassion versus a society with freedom, fair play, and compassion for all.

References

BENTHAM, J. (1952): "Supply without Burthen, or Escheat vice Taxation," in: W. STARK (Ed.): *Jeremy Bentham's Economic Writings*, New York (Burt Franklin), Vol. I, pp. 281-367.

BRACEWELL-MILNES, B. (1997): "The hidden costs of inheritance taxation", *this volume*.

HASLETT, D.W. (1994): *Capitalism with Morality*, Oxford (Clarendon Press).

HASLETT, D.W. (1997): "Distributive justice and inheritance", *this volume*.

6 See Section 2 of HASLETT (1997) and point 3 above.

Chapter 10

Response to David Haslett

BARRY BRACEWELL-MILNES

This note responds in detail to Haslett's comment on my paper, in which I am mentioned by name, as well as more briefly to Sections I and II of his paper. The response starts with general comments and then addresses particular arguments. I cannot deal with all Haslett's arguments within a reasonable space and therefore restrict myself to the most important.

One problem all through Haslett's comments on my paper is an apparent confusion between the main thrust of my argument and minor qualifications and objections thereto. I was aware of most of these minor qualifications and objections when I wrote the paper and would have dealt with them in a full-length book. They remain minor qualifications, not refutations. They do not touch the main thrust of the argument.

Another main problem is Haslett's use of economic argument, which is sometimes correct but often simply eccentric and bizarre. Although economists differ profoundly among themselves, there are few, if any, who would buy the economic content of Haslett's paper; almost all would disagree strongly with much of what he says.

I. General Comments

I start by trying to identify areas of agreement and disagreement between Haslett and me.

The first area of agreement is that we are both interested in economic efficiency, although we interpret this concept very differently. Haslett defines efficiency in terms of (labour) productivity, which he seeks to increase through various forms of government intervention in the economy. I define efficiency in terms of wealth creation in a free economy, with maximum scope for costless wealth creation through giving and personal ownership.

Secondly, we are both interested in distributive justice, although here again we differ radically about what it means. Haslett's distributive justice is realised through a distribution based on an optimised or idealised labour productivity. My distributive justice is based on the economic or total productivity resulting from the free play of market forces, subject to a moral obligation on the more fortunate to help those who cannot help themselves. This latter concept of distributive justice is *wertfrei* in the sense of being independent of personal merit. The idea that material prosperity depends or should depend on personal merit is refuted by experience and common sense.

This may exhaust the areas of agreement between Haslett and me. The areas of disagreement are more numerous.

The most important area of disagreement is that Haslett is inspired by the old-fashioned and indeed romantic notion that democratic governments are Platonic guardians, able and willing to identify the public good and pursue it selflessly. His thinking is untouched by the argument of Gordon Tullock, (Nobel Prize winner) James Buchanan and others in the Virginia Public Choice school that politicians and bureaucrats are economic agents like anyone else, maximizing benefits and minimizing costs. Since the political market place is vastly more inefficient than the economic market place, many democratic governments are corrupt and most are incompetent. The idea that government intervention can make things better is a less usable model of reality than the opposite: there is no problem so dire, no situation so desperate, that government intervention cannot make it worse.

Of a piece with Haslett's sympathy for government intervention is his sympathy for regulation:

> "So the preservation of estates and farmlands is not accomplished very well simply by having no restrictions on inheritance. (...) If it is in the general welfare to preserve them intact, then let us pass regulations preventing anyone from selling them, or giving them away, other than intact (...)." (Haslett, 1997b, p. 211)

This enthusiasm for regulation runs right through Haslett's paper and is unlikely to appeal to anyone for whom the rising tide of government regulation is one of the most serious problems of our time.

Similarly, Haslett gives no weight to the agency principle, which states that in principal-agent relationships outside the immediate family the agent is never guided solely by the interests of his principal but always in some measure by his own. When the government acts as agent, the interests of the nominal beneficiaries are particularly likely to be neglected or forgotten through the workings of political calculation or red tape. The best counterweight to the agency principle is personal ownership with its corollary of inheritance.

Finally, Haslett wishes to impose drastic changes on present institutions in pursuit of a utopian ideal supported by speculative theoretical arguments. I reject utopian policies and all forms of social engineering and propose merely the preservation or reintroduction of a tax system free from inheritance tax, for which there are already trouble-free precedents in Australia and Canada and elsewhere. And, although Haslett might hesitate to consult anything so vulgar as public opinion, it is perhaps worth pointing out that in November 1995 the United Kingdom Government proposed the abolition of inheritance tax on all forms of business property: and this proposal has enjoyed all-Party Parliamentary support as well as being well received by the general public.

II. Comments on 'Theory'

Large gifts and bequests do not undermine productivity: they help to relieve the curse of Adam by substituting the productivity of capital for the productivity of labour. The capital of which gifts and bequests consist is built up by new saving. As long as the capital is maintained, it generates income, which is an element of capital productivity. Productivity is reduced only if the capital is spent, whether through taxation or otherwise. Haslett is mostly using a labour-only concept of productivity, whereas economists derive total productivity from the separate productivities of labour, land and capital which can at the margin be exchanged or traded for each other.

Haslett writes as though he has never met or had any dealings with family firms. Family firms are under the strongest compulsion to choose the best person for each job: if they do not, they may go under. By contrast, state concerns and quoted companies that fail may be saved through public subsidy.

III. Comments on 'Practice'

Will there ever be broad public support for a law abolishing inheritance? Recent evidence from Australia, Canada, the United Kingdom, France and elsewhere suggests that there will not; the reduction or abolition of inheritance tax is now a popular cause. There is much less public support for inheritance tax than for income tax.

Haslett argues that the abolition of inheritance will not significantly reduce people's incentives to be productive. This is labour productivity again, since there will be a fall in the amount of capital and its yield. As for labour productivity, among my own circle of acquaintances are the owner-managers of a number of family firms for whom death duties/inheritance tax have been the principal influence on their behaviour. When inheritance tax was high, they stopped their firms from growing because they could not afford the tax. As soon as the tax was abolished through the institution of 100 per cent business property relief, they resumed expansion. Other taxpayers, without the local commitment of family firms, emigrate to avoid the tax.

Haslett says that no one really knows for sure how, if at all, abolishing inheritance would affect savings and investment; and this seems a good reason for not abolishing inheritance. Combined with this argument, the argument that inheritance tax has no effect on labour productivity, amounts to saying that an increase from zero to 100 per cent in the taxation of inheritance funded by marginal earnings has little or no effect on behaviour. Although this may be true of particular people in particular situations, it is a rash assumption on which to base policy for a money economy. The complete removal of money incentives generally affects behaviour substantially or drastically. The main exception is patriotic work or saving in wartime, which is not relevant here.

Haslett believes that through the institution of investment subsidies investment efficiency may actually increase. Most economists believe the opposite, namely that investment subsidies lower the quality of investment by distorting investment decisions.

Haslett favours a lifetime inheritance quota. There are two things wrong with this concept: the fact that it is a *quota* and the fact that it is a *lifetime* quota.

A *quota* is substantially or even precisely equivalent to a tax structure that starts with an exempt tranche and suddenly rises to a marginal rate of 100 per cent gross. The precedent that springs to mind is food rationing in wartime, not a good pattern for the treatment of inheritance in peacetime. A tax structure of this kind is a discredited curiosity in the history of public-finance theory: it seeks to realise *minimum total sacrifice* if the *marginal utility of income diminishes*. This tax structure enjoyed a measure of academic favour earlier this century; but today it would rightly be regarded as bizarre, and few serious figures in the world of public finance, if any, would offer it any support.

A *lifetime* quota is worse than an annual quota for the same reason that a lifetime tax base is worse than an annual tax base. In Bracewell-Milnes (1979) I showed that the lifetime basis of charge for the capital transfer tax could and would violate both horizontal and vertical equity by charging the poorer taxpayer more heavily than the richer. This is because a lifetime tax structure is overdetermined in the precise sense of a set of equations with more equations than unknowns: such a set of equations produces inconsistent results. Over a lifetime there are large changes *inter alia* in prices, earnings and wealth and in their components and relativities. It is not possible to impose a lifetime charge without violating horizontal and vertical equity over the period of twelve months that is accepted as normal for other taxes. And under a lifetime system the reporting obligations would be very intrusive and oppressive.

Haslett believes that his lifetime inheritance quota will enable family heirlooms and all but the most expensive homesteads and small businesses to be purchased by family members. On the contrary, all but the smallest firms, farms and estates would be affected. It is entirely unrealistic to expect family members to club together to buy these things even if there are regulations (*regulations* again) that provide them with helpful credit terms. The admission that subsidised credit may be a necessary part of the scheme is a good illustration of how one form of government intervention in the economy requires another to offset the damage it does.

Taxpayers in general and the ultra-rich in particular are unlikely to stay around to pay Haslett's confiscatory tax at 100 per cent: they would emigrate. United Kingdom experience indicates that taxpayers are willing to go abroad temporarily or permanently in order to escape capital gains tax at 30 per cent. If Haslett's tax were to be enforceable, it would have to be accompanied by restrictions on emigration and by exchange controls, taxes or other restrictions on the export of personal capital.

Haslett mentions worker control capitalism only briefly. A major problem with any form of worker capitalism in which a large proportion of the worker's capital is invested in the firm for which he works is that he loses his savings as well as his job if the firm fails.

IV. A Reply to Haslett's Comments

My argument applies to assets in general as well as to family estates, family businesses and family farms in particular. Stewardship is an activity and an attitude of mind available to anyone. I do not argue that estates, firms and farms should always remain intact despite changes in circumstances but rather that the often considerable task of keeping them prosperous and in good order should not be aggravated or made impossible by taxation or other forms of government intervention. If a remote farm is no longer economically sustainable and reverts to scrub, the former value of the asset may simply disappear; but, apart from such extreme cases, there is a successor value on sale or change of use, and the concept of stewardship holds good for this successor value.

Haslett does not understand the distinction between family firms and quoted companies. They are different animals with different motivations and different patterns of behaviour. In particular, family businesses have much longer time-horizons than quoted companies and much more intense employee loyalty (second- and third-generation employees are virtually unknown in quoted companies, with the possible exception of particular industries like mining and the railways). Death duties (and Haslett's quota) are a burden on family businesses from which quoted companies are effectively exempt. Family firms and quoted companies are different forms of organisation and should (in the interest of economic efficiency and distributive justice) compete on fiscally neutral terms. This requires that inheritance tax on family firms be abolished, as has been done in the United Kingdom, and for just this reason, through the institution of 100 per cent business property relief (which Haslett would perhaps describe as an insidious loophole).

I have shown in Bracewell-Milnes (1982) that the value of family firms, farms and estates is economic as well as sentimental; indeed, the two cannot be separated.

Large family firms cannot afford to make an incompetent son or daughter an owner-manager. If there is no suitably qualified family member, they go outside the family.

In Bracewell-Milnes (1989, p. 37) I point out that the argument is not invalidated by examples of heroic or sacrificial giving: any apparent paradox lies in the situation that makes giving the preferable course of action for the giver. The giving of the parent who sacrifices his life for his child (not uncommon in the exceptional situations that give rise to this dilemma) is only an extreme form of the preference for bequeathing money to one's children rather than spending it on oneself. Haslett is on dangerous ground in making the distinction he does between one's own best interests and acting altruistically. This distinction is of little application to harmonious family life, although it is highly relevant to the distinction between an amicable (altruistic) and an acrimonious (own-best-interest) divorce. As long as family relationships are subject to no more than normal wear and tear, altruism within the family is *internalised* and *normal:* spouses help each other, parents help their children, children help their parents without recourse to the divorce-court distinction between one's own best interests and acting altruistically.

Haslett's distinction between one's own best interests and acting altruistically brings to mind Adam Smith's distinction between value in use and value in exchange. Why is water less valuable than diamonds when water is necessary for life and diamonds are not? Smith's problem was swept away by the marginal-utility value theory of Jevons, Menger and Walras in the 1870s and 1880s. I am trying to provide a similar service for Haslett.

Haslett's distinction between one's own best interests and acting altruistically falls foul of Occam's razor, the principle that *entia non multiplicanda praeter necessitatem*, entities should not be multiplied beyond what is necessary. In ordinary situations there is no conflict and need be no distinction: an element of altruism is internalised and thus *is* in the individual's own interest, while the element of altruism that is not internalised is ineffective and has no influence on behaviour. In exceptional and sacrificial situations the same argument holds good in more testing circumstances: giving your life for your child is the extreme, whereas giving your money to your child is normal. In the normal situation the pleasure from giving is more than the pleasure from not giving, whereas in the sacrificial situation the pain from self-sacrifice is less than the pain from remorse: the normal and the exceptional fall within the same logical framework and answer to the same motives.

I do not believe that a person can never be mistaken about what is in his best interests. I do believe that people are generally better off making their own mistakes than having other people's mistakes imposed on them through inheritance quotas and the like. Nor do I believe that people can never, through weakness of will, fail to do what is in their best interests; indeed, I have quoted to Haslett Ovid's *Video meliora proboque, deteriora sequor*, I recognise the better and approve it, but I follow the worse. (*Metamorphoses* VII 21). St. Paul puts the dilemma even more strongly: *For the good that I would I do not: but the evil which I would not, that I do.* (Romans VII.19). Here again, the individual is better off suffering from his own weakness of will than having it strengthened for him by the government or other outsiders.

In Bracewell-Milnes (1989) I distinguish sharply between voluntary transfers to charities or natural persons, on the one hand, and transfers to the government, constrained by taxation or otherwise, on the other: the latter create no countervalue or donor's surplus. I likewise distinguish sharply between legal constraints in the form of taxation or other obligations, and the requirements of morality or good values. The latter, if voluntarily accepted, are no constraints at all. As Cranmer says, God's *service is perfect freedom*. (1662 Morning Prayer, the second collect, for peace).

Haslett confuses two determinants of the inequality of spending: the inequality of wealth and the investment income it generates, on the one hand, and the relative taxation of spending and new saving, on the other. As I explain towards the end of Section IX of my paper, inheritance tax may temporarily reduce the inequality of spending under the first determinant as the existing stock of wealth is destroyed; but sooner or later this once-and-for-all effect is outweighed by the permanent increase in spending relatively to new saving at the top of the scale consequent on the change in price relativities caused by inheritance tax or quota. Sooner or later any temporary reduction in the inequality of spending is replaced by a permanent increase.

Personal spending is indeed subject to some kind of ceiling, at which every conceivable want is already satisfied: the stock of children's toys in many homes is already well above such a ceiling. But this is an argument *against* inheritance tax, which cheapens pointless and conspicuous spending on unnecessary goods and services at the top of the scale.

If additional spending at the top of the scale is unattractive or impracticable, this does nothing to increase the taxpayer's enthusiasm for paying inheritance tax at 100 per cent (which is the effect of a quota). As was noted above, the likely response of the taxpayer is emigration.

Charitable giving is possible and desirable both in a fiscally neutral situation, in which it enjoys no tax advantage, and also in a situation in which its advantage is significantly less than total. This is real charitable giving. By contrast, an inheritance quota implies that the opportunity cost of charitable giving is zero. This does nothing to encourage the more noble human sentiments of generosity and compassion for others, because the taxpayer's charitable giving is costing him nothing.

Gifts of money and money's worth are one way in which parents can show altruism by preferring transfers to their children to expenditure on themselves. They are not competitive with other expressions of affection, but complementary.

If the exciting, challenging early years of struggle are so deeply satisfying as Haslett believes, there is no need for parents to spoil their children's fun by giving them gifts or leaving them bequests: these are only options, not requirements or obligations. And all this jibes ill with Haslett's emphasis on equality of opportunity. It would seem that those with the worse initial opportunities should enjoy the excitement, challenge and deep satisfaction, whereas Haslett argues elsewhere that they are losers rather than gainers.

In sum, it is not possible to overtax the rich man's saving (wealth, capital, investment income) without at the same time (and correspondingly) undertaxing his spending. Saving is what the individual puts into the economy and society, spending is what he takes out. Spending is visible and even conspicuous, saving is inconspicuous and even invisible. If any form of inequality causes dissatisfaction and resentment, it is inequality of spending and lifestyles. Inheritance taxes and quotas cheapen first-generation high spending and make it difficult or impossible to exercise stewardship over the assets that fall subject to their charge. They shift resources out of productive and heritage assets into unnecessary and conspicuous consumption. At the top of the scale they can be avoided through emigration. They thus damage the economy and imperil the yield of the rest of the tax system; and, since they lower the cost of the rich man's spending relatively both to his own saving and to the poor man's saving and spending, their distributive consequences are not a beneficial offset to the economic damage they do, but even on their own terms perverse and counterproductive.

References

BRACEWELL-MILNES, B. (1979) "Lifetime cumulation of transfers", *British Tax Review*, 6, pp. 366-79.

BRACEWELL-MILNES, B. (1982): *Land and Heritage: The Public Interest in Personal Ownership,* London (Institute of Economic Affairs), Hobart Paper 93.

BRACEWELL-MILNES, B. (1989): *The Wealth of Giving: Every One in His Inheritance,* London (Institute of Economic Affairs), Research Monograph 43.

BRACEWELL-MILNES, B. (1997) "The hidden costs of inheritance taxation", *this volume*.

HASLETT, D.W. (1997a), "Distributive justice and inheritance", *this volume*.

HASLETT, D.W. (1997b), "A comment on Bracewell-Milnes", *this volume*.

INDEX OF NAMES

(Page numbers in bold type refer to a chapter written by the person indicated.)

—A—

—B—

—C—

INDEX OF NAMES

List of Authors

LUC ARRONDEL, DELTA-CNRS, 48 Boulevard Jourdan, 75014 Paris, France

BARRY BRACEWELL-MILNES, 26 Lancaster Road, Banstead, Surrey SM7 1RR, United Kingdom

GUIDO ERREYGERS, Studiecentrum voor Economisch en Sociaal Onderzoek (SESO), UFSIA, Universiteit Antwerpen, Prinsstraat 13, 2000 Antwerpen 1, Belgium

D.W. HASLETT, Department of Philosophy, University of Delaware, Newark, Delaware 19716-2567, USA

ANDRÉ MASSON, DELTA-CNRS, 48 Boulevard Jourdan, 75014 Paris, France

PIERRE PESTIEAU, CREPP, Département d'Economie, Université de Liège, Boulevard du Rectorat 7 (B31), 4000 Sart Tilman/Liège 1, Belgium

ERIK SCHOKKAERT, Centrum voor Economie en Ethiek, K.U.Leuven, Naamsestraat 69, 3000 Leuven, Belgium

PHILIPPE VAN PARIJS, Chaire Hoover d'Ethique Economique et Sociale, Université Catholique de Louvain, Place Montesquieu 3, 1348 Louvain-la-Neuve, Belgium

TOON VANDEVELDE, Centrum voor Economie en Ethiek, K.U.Leuven, Naamsestraat 69, 3000 Leuven, Belgium

Printing: Weihert-Druck GmbH, Darmstadt
Binding: Buchbinderei Schäffer, Grünstadt

GPSR Compliance

The European Union's (EU) General Product Safety Regulation (GPSR) is a set of rules that requires consumer products to be safe and our obligations to ensure this.

If you have any concerns about our products, you can contact us on ProductSafety@springernature.com

In case Publisher is established outside the EU, the EU authorized representative is:

Springer Nature Customer Service Center GmbH
Europaplatz 3
69115 Heidelberg, Germany

Batch number: 10755292

Printed by Printforce, the Netherlands